THE POLICING OF TERROI

MW00389428

This book offers an analysis of the policing of terrorism in a variety of national and international contexts. Centered on developments since the events of September 11, 2001, the study devotes its empirical attention to important police aspects of counterterrorism in the United States and additionally extends its range comparatively to other nations, including Israel and Iraq, and to the global level of international police organizations such as Interpol and Europol. Situated in the criminology of terrorism and counterterrorism, this book offers a fascinating look into the contemporary organization of law enforcement against terrorism, which will significantly influence the conditions of global security in the foreseeable future.

Mathieu Deflem is Associate Professor in the Department of Sociology at the University of South Carolina. His research and teaching specialties include terrorism and counterterrorism, policing, law, and theory. He is the author of *Sociology of Law* (2008) and *Policing World Society* (2002). He maintains a website at www.mathieudeflem.net and a companion site for this book at www.polterror.net.

Criminology and Justice Studies Series

Edited by **Chester Britt**, *Northeastern University*, **Shaun L. Gabbidon**, *Penn State Harrisburg*, and **Nancy Rodriguez**, *Arizona State University*

Criminology and Justice Studies offers works that make both intellectual and stylistic innovations in the study of crime and criminal justice. The goal of the series is to publish works that model the best scholarship and thinking in the criminology and criminal justice field today, but in a style that connects that scholarship to a wider audience including advanced undergraduates, graduate students, and the general public. The works in this series help fill the gap between academic monographs and encyclopedic textbooks by making innovative scholarship accessible to a large audience without the superficiality of many texts.

Books in the Series
Published:
Biosocial Criminology: New Directions in Theory and Research edited by Anthony Walsh and Kevin M. Beaver
Community Policing in America by Jeremy M. Wilson
Criminal Justice Theory: Explaining the Nature and Behavior of Criminal Justice edited by David E. Duffee and Edward R. Maguire
Lifers: Seeking Redemption in Prison by John Irwin
Race, Law and American Society: 1607 to Present by Gloria J. Browne-Marshall
Today's White Collar Crime by Hank J. Brightman
White Collar Crime: An Opportunity Perspective by Michael Benson and Sally Simpson
The New Criminal Justice: American Communities and the Changing World of Crime Control edited by John Klofas, Natalie Hipple, and Edmund McGarrell

Forthcoming:
Crime and the Lifecourse by Michael Benson and Alex Piquero
Criminological Perspectives on Race and Crime, Second Edition by Shaun L. Gabbidon

Also of Interest from Routledge:
City Life from Jakarta to Dakar: Movements at the Crossroads by AbdouMaliq Simone
Military Legacies: A World Made by War by James A. Tyner
Racist America: Roots, Current Realities, and Future Reparations, Second Edition by Joe R. Feagin
GIS and Spatial Analysis for the Social Sciences by Robert Nash Parker and Emily K. Asencio
Regression Analysis for the Social Sciences by Rachel A. Gordon
Operation Gatekeeper and Beyond: The War On Illegals and the Remaking of the U.S.–Mexico Boundary by Joseph Nevins

THE POLICING OF TERRORISM

ORGANIZATIONAL AND GLOBAL PERSPECTIVES

Mathieu Deflem

Routledge
Taylor & Francis Group

NEW YORK AND LONDON

First published 2010
by Routledge
270 Madison Ave, New York, NY 10016

Simultaneously published in the UK
by Routledge
2 Park Square, Milton Park, Abingdon, Oxon OX14 4RN

Routledge is an imprint of the Taylor & Francis Group, an informa business

© 2010 Taylor & Francis

Typeset in Caslon by HWA Text and Data Management, London
Printed and bound in the United States of America on acid-free paper by
Edwards Brothers, Inc.

Library of Congress Cataloging in Publication Data
Deflem, Mathieu.
    The policing of terrorism : organizational and global perspectives / Mathieu Deflem.
    – 1st ed.
        p. cm. – (Criminology and justice studies series)
    Includes bibliographical references and index.
    1. Terrorism—Prevention. 2. Terrorism—Prevention—International cooperation.
    3. Terrorism—Government policy. I. Title.
    HV6431.D4354 2010
    363.325´16–dc22   2009029802

ISBN10: 0-415-87539-0 (hbk)
ISBN10: 0-415-87540-4 (pbk)
ISBN10: 0-203-86038-1 (ebk)

ISBN13: 978-0-415-87539-4 (hbk)
ISBN13: 978-0-415-87540-0 (pbk)
ISBN13: 978-0-203-86038-0 (ebk)

Contents

Figures

Series Foreword

Criminology and Justice Studies offers works that make both intellectual and stylistic innovations in the study of crime and criminal justice. The goal of the series is to publish works that model the best scholarship and thinking in the criminology and criminal justice field today, but in a style that connects that scholarship to a wider audience including advanced undergraduates, graduate students, and the general public. The works in this series help fill the gap between academic monographs and encyclopedic textbooks by making innovative scholarship accessible to a large audience without the superficiality of many texts.

In *The Policing of Terrorism: Organizational and Global Perspectives*, Mathieu Deflem explains how counterterrorism – the prevention of and the response to terrorism – may be viewed as an issue of crime control for a wide range of police institutions. After describing the criminalization of terrorism, Deflem carefully explains the bureaucratization theory of policing, which emphasizes the relative autonomy of police institutions and the development of professional standards for investigating criminal activities and how these standards can in turn be used for counter terrorism. *The Policing of Terrorism* provides a systematic application of the bureaucratization theory of policing to counter terrorism in the United States (at all levels of policing – federal, state, and municipal) and in other nations, with specific attention given to the International

Criminal Police Organization (Interpol), the European Police Office (Europol), and Israel. Deflem's work is a thoughtful and compelling application of organizational theory to one of the most important challenges currently facing police institutions across the globe.

Chester Britt
Nancy Rodriguez
Shaun Gabbidon

Acknowledgments

In the course of preparing this book, I have been able to rely on the generous help and critical feedback from a great many fine people, including fellow scholars and students and professionals in the police and counterterrorism community. For their generous help at various stages of my research and for useful comments on selected chapters of this book, I thank Jay Albanese, Amit and Vered Almor, Ersel Aydinli, Gregg Barak, Michael Bayer, Bonnie Berry, Donald Black, Boaz Ganor, Chester Britt, Carl Dahlman, Kelly Damphousse, Dilip Das, Willem de Lint, Laura Dugan, Huseyin Durmaz, Jonathan Fighel, James Fyfe, Nadia Gerspacher, Joshua Gleis, Sergio Herzog, Jennifer Hunt, Aaron Kappeler, Victor Kappeler, Aytül Kasapoğlu, Richard Kilroy, Joanne Klein, Charles Kurzman, Gary LaFree, Paul Leighton, Joe Lockard, Otwin Marenin, Gus Martin, Gustavo Díaz Matey, William McDonald, J. Mitchell Miller, Terry Mills, John Nomikos, Brian Nussbaum, Vincent N. Parrillo, Ami Pedahzur, William Rosenau, Richard Rosenfeld, Jacqueline Ross, Richard Schwartz, Yaron Schwartz, John Shutt, Brent Smith, Lynne Snowden, Gal Soltz, Kevin Strom, Michael Thomas, Holly Ventura Miller, and Margaret Zahn.

In my professional home of the Sociology Department at the University of South Carolina, I am grateful to Lucy Dai, April Dove, Lisa Dilks, Lynn Frederick, Brook Hansen, Samantha Hauptman,

Mitch Helms, Brian Hudak, Kyle Irwin, Peter Lawrence, Shannon McDonough, Jonathan Miner, Darwin Ramsey, John Shutt, Christine Sixta, and Suzanne Sutphin, who as graduate students or research assistants worked with me on various studies related to my work or theirs. At the undergraduate level, I am most thankful to the many students it was my pleasure to teach from my work on counterterrorism in my course on Sociology of Social Control, which I have been organizing every year since 2002, and in the proseminar on Policing International Terrorism, which I taught in the Honors College in the fall of 2003.

Some of my earlier article-length studies on the policing of terrorism have been reworked into the present study, although great care has been taken to ensure that this book stands alone as one coherent work. Previously published materials have been revised accordingly and updated where necessary. An article that appeared in *The American Sociologist* (Deflem 2004a) inspired much of Chapter 2, whereas papers published in *The Annals of the American Academy of Political and Social Science* (Deflem 2006a) and *Justice Quarterly* (Deflem 2006b) served as a basis for Chapters 7 and 8, respectively. Sections of Chapter 1 and 2 incorporate ideas presented in essays that appeared in the *Encyclopedia of Social Problems* (Deflem 2008) and the handbook on *21st Century Criminology* (Deflem 2009). The parts of Chapter 10 that deal with the police situation in Iraq are revised and updated from an article, co-authored with Suzanne Sutphin, that was published in *Sociological Focus* (Deflem and Sutphin 2006). I am grateful to the editors, reviewers, and collaborators who assisted with these publications.

Various ideas in this book also benefited from oral presentations given at meetings organized by the American Sociological Association in Montréal, 2006, Atlanta, 2003, and Chicago, 2002; the American Society of Criminology in Toronto, Canada, 2005, Nashville, 2004, and Denver, 2003; the World Congress of Criminology in Pennsylvania, 2005; the Academy of Criminal Justice Sciences in Las Vegas, 2004; the Social Science History Association in Baltimore, 2003; and the Eastern Sociological Society in Philadelphia, 2003.

Additional feedback was provided by the organizers and attendants of invited presentations and lectures I was in the fortunate position to deliver at the Université de Québec à Montréal, Canada, 2009; the University of Coimbra, Portugal, 2008; the Université de Montréal,

Canada, 2008; Bilkent University, Ankara, Turkey, 2007; Carleton University, Ottawa, Canada, 2006; the workshop on Social Dynamics of Global Terrorism in Ankara, Turkey, 2006; the International University Bremen, Germany, 2005; Syracuse University, 2005; Brandeis University, 2005; the University of Illinois Law School, Urbana-Champaign, 2005; the College of Charleston, South Carolina, 2005; the Professional Society of International Studies at the University of South Carolina, 2004; the Shepherd Center, Columbia, SC, 2004; Queen's University, Kingston, Canada, 2004; the Palmetto Forum, Columbia, SC, 2004; the conference on Transportation and Critical Infrastructure Homeland Security in Alexandria, Virginia, 2003; and the Faculty Research Seminar, Walker Institute of International Studies, Columbia, SC, 2003.

Among the agencies that provided funding to support research for this book, I am most grateful to the Richard L. Walker Institute of International and Area Studies at the University of South Carolina; the Foundation for the Defense of Democracies; the College of Arts and Sciences in the University of South Carolina; and the NATO Programme Security Through Science.

I am grateful to Peggy Binette, Indy Jones, and Margaret Lamb at the University of South Carolina Office of Media Relations for providing access to various media outlets, both at home and abroad, which greatly helped me to sharpen my ideas. The many helpful suggestions by Stephen Rutter, able editor at Routledge, were likewise useful to make me aim my work at a wider audience beyond the world of academia. If this book reaches its target audience, it is largely owing to Steve's keen insights. I thank him and Leah Babb-Rosenfeld and the other good folks at Routledge for seeing this book through production.

I am grateful to the many public agencies that have provided the photographs that have been used in this book.

Finally, I also thank the many professionals from public and private agencies, government departments, and other institutions involved with counterterrorism who have been so generous in helping me with my work, typically in the form of granting interviews and providing access to various pieces of information. It is unquestionable to me that their hearts are always in the right place when they do their valuable jobs. Although we may differ in our approaches, I am hopeful that they will also find something useful in my work, even if it is only a small fraction of what there is to learn from their experiences.

    May we live to see the dawn.

Abbreviations

ACLU	American Civil Liberties Union
ANP	Afghan National Police
CBP	U.S. Customs and Border Protection
CIA	Central Intelligence Agency
CSI	Container Security Initiative
CSIS	Canadian Security Intelligence Service
CTG	Counter Terrorism Group
DEA	Drug Enforcement Administration
DHS	Department of Homeland Security
DS	Bureau of Diplomatic Security
DSS	Diplomatic Security Service
DST	Directorate of Territorial Surveillance (France)
EU	European Union
FBI	Federal Bureau of Investigation
FEMA	Federal Emergency Management Agency
FISA	Foreign Intelligence Surveillance Act
FSB	Federal Security Service (Russia)
ICE	U.S. Immigration and Customs Enforcement
ICITAP	International Criminal Investigative Training Assistance Program
INS	Immigration and Naturalization Service

IPS	Iraqi Police Service
JRIC	Joint Regional Intelligence Center
JTTF	Joint Terrorism Task Force
LAPD	Los Angeles Police Department
NCB	National Central Bureau
NSA	National Security Agency
NSL	National Security Letter
NYPD	New York Police Department
PCTF	Police Chiefs Task Force
PKK	Kurdistan Workers' Party
RCMP	Royal Canadian Mounted Police
TREVI	Terrorism, Radicalism, Extremism, and International Violence
TSA	Transportation Security Administration
USCIS	U.S. Citizenship and Immigration Services

PREVIEW

Why There Is No War on Terror

This War on Terror is not just a simple law enforcement matter.

George W. Bush, 2008.[1]

There is no war on terror.

Sir Ken Macdonald, 2007.[2]

This book analyzes the central organizational and global dimensions of the policing of terrorism from a criminological viewpoint. For reasons that are too obvious to mention, terrorism has in recent years moved to the center of public attention and has become an important subject matter across a wide range of social institutions, including politics, law, the military and police and criminal justice. As a result of the significance of terrorism in contemporary society, various aspects of terrorism and counterterrorism have become central topics of scholarly research. However, there are still aspects in the field of terrorism studies that have as yet not received due attention. Among them, the policing of terrorism presents an as-yet relatively unexplored and often not properly understood topic of research. To fill this gap in the literature on terrorism, this book develops an analysis of the most important characteristics and dimensions of the policing of terrorism in a variety of national and international settings.

Example Cases in the Policing of Terrorism

Providing an introduction to the theme of this book, a few concrete examples in the policing of terrorism may clarify the value of the criminological perspective that is applied throughout this work.

Case 1: September 11 and the Federal Bureau of Investigation

On September 11, 2001, members of al-Qaeda crashed hijacked airplanes into the World Trade Center towers in New York City and the Pentagon building in Washington, DC, while a fourth hijacked plane crashed into a field in Pennsylvania. Soon after the attacks, the law enforcement (and intelligence) communities in the United States were severely criticized for not having been sufficiently vigilant to the threat coming from al-Qaeda. In actuality, however, political representatives along with much of the media had remained mostly inattentive and unresponsive to the warnings from law enforcement officials against the dangers facing the United States from international terrorist groups. As early as January 1998, then director of the Federal Bureau of Investigation (FBI) Louis Freeh had already characterized "loosely affiliated extremists," such as Ramzi Yousef, as posing "the most urgent threat to the United States at this time."[3] On September 3, 1998, a few weeks after the bombings of the U.S. embassies in Tanzania and Kenya, Freeh explicitly added to this group "international terrorist financier Usama bin Ladin."[4]

By February 1999, FBI Director Freeh pronounced that "loosely affiliated extremists, characterized by rogue terrorists such as Ramzi Ahmed Yousef and international terrorist financier Usama bin Laden... may pose the most urgent threat to the United States,"[5] a warning that Freeh repeated every time he thereafter appeared before Congress. In June 1999, bin Laden was placed on the FBI's most wanted fugitives list, and a Radical Fundamentalist Unit and an Usama bin Laden Unit were established at FBI headquarters. When the *USS Cole* Navy ship was bombed in October 2000, the FBI was assigned to investigate the case and attributed the attack to the al-Qaeda network. In May 2001, Director Freeh (who would be replaced by Robert Mueller on September 4, 2001) again warned against the dangers coming from jihadist extremist groups, more specifically "Sunni Islamic extremists, such as Usama bin Laden and individuals affiliated with his Al-Qaeda organization."[6] As the lead agency in the investigations of the September 11, 2001, terrorist attacks, the FBI identified, within just a few days of the attacks, all of the 19 hijackers.[7] On October 10, a new Most Wanted Terrorists List that was announced had the name of Osama bin Laden at the top.

Case 2: March 11, July 7, and International Police Cooperation

On March 11, 2004, jihadist extremists inspired by the al-Qaeda movement exploded a series of bombs on the railway system of Madrid, the capital of Spain, thereby killing almost 200 people and wounding more than 1,800. Immediately after the events, the Council of the European Union (EU), the leading political decision-making body of the international union, swiftly moved to condemn the attacks and proposed a series of counterterrorism measures.[8] Yet, many of the measures suggested by the Council were subsequently not implemented at the national level of the EU member states, where political-ideological squabbling prevented the passing of appropriate legislation.[9] Separate from the meetings of the EU politicians, however, several gatherings of police and intelligence officials were also held, with many more-concrete results.[10] Within days of the Madrid bombings, the European Chiefs of Police Task Force, an international police organization that represents all EU states held a 2-day conference in Dublin, Ireland, with dozens of representatives from the international police organizations Europol and Interpol and police officials from the EU states, Norway, and Iceland. Coinciding with the police meeting was an additional meeting of intelligence chiefs of five European nations (Spain, Britain, France, Germany, and Italy) in Madrid. At both meetings, information was exchanged to help the investigations of the bombings, and additional agreements were reached to enhance further collaboration.

On July 7, 2005, a small group of jihadist extremists set off bombs on three London underground trains and a city bus, thereby killing 52 passengers and injuring some 700. A few days after the bombings, a confidential meeting of police, intelligence officials, and forensic experts was held at Scotland Yard.[11] Among the attendants were officials from about 30 countries, including the United States, Israel, Australia, Japan, and all European Union states and representatives from Interpol and Europol. The meeting attendants agreed upon a number of methods to improve information exchange and assist with counterterrorism investigations.

Figure 0.1 World Trade Center building 6 following the attacks of 9/11 in New York City, September 2001. Destroyed by the collapse of the two main World Trade Center towers, building 6 was the U.S. Customs House in which various federal agencies, such as the Bureau of Alcohol, Tobacco, and Firearms, were stationed. (Photo by James Tourtellotte, courtesy of U.S. Customs and Border Protection.)

Studying the Policing of Terrorism

The foregoing cases show that police organizations are heavily involved with counterterrorism activities by investigating specific cases to track down the suspected perpetrators and, additionally, by organizing cooperation among agencies across national borders. These policing activities take place even when political leaders and legislators are unable to implement concrete counterterrorism measures and fail to reach international agreements, as the governments of the world are at times very divided over terrorism on ideological grounds. Such political frictions in the world community are especially pronounced when counterterrorism involves military operations whereby the world's nations are divided into allies and opponents in a "war on terror." From the police point of view, however, as the preceding cases show, terrorism is approached differently, from a viewpoint that involves criminal investigations that, additionally, can offer a basis for wide international cooperation.

In studying the policing of terrorism, then, questions must be asked about the role of police institutions in the fight against terrorism to reveal the counterterrorism strategies of police and the reasons why, as British counterterrorism official Ken Macdonald argued, there is from the police point of view no war on terror. These questions are all the more important when police organizations can be observed to be heavily involved in counterterrorism activities, yet when it is also claimed, such as by former U.S. President George W. Bush, that the war on terror is not "just"a matter of law enforcement.

Important questions beg for a useful approach to arrive at appropriate answers. With this book, I seek to argue that a criminological perspective based on the sociology of crime and social control is illuminating in analyzing the policing of terrorism. Such an approach can elucidate what is important and peculiar about police work against terrorism relative to other efforts in the wider constellation of counterterrorism. All too often, sweeping statements can be heard about counterterrorism that are based on interpretations of very specific aspects of certain responses to terrorism, without clarifying which institutions and agents play a part in these practices and how they might differ from other efforts. The criminological model used in this book precisely seeks to show that there is something unique about the policing of terrorism, which makes it stand out relative to other counterterrorism efforts, such as those that are of political, legal, and military nature.

In this book, special attention goes to the organizational and global developments in the policing of terrorism. The focus on the organization of counterterrorism policing implies an analysis of the strategies and objectives police pursue in the fight against terrorism. The criminal investigations that are conducted by police in specific terrorist incidents are not a primary focus of this work, although such efforts are used to illustrate the relevance of key aspects of the organization of counterterrorism policing. The global orientation of this book includes both a focus on the cross-border dimensions of terrorism-related activities by police agencies in different parts of the world and an orientation toward the dynamics of counterterrorism at the level of international police organizations.

The perspective of this book is guided by the bureaucratization theory of policing (Deflem 2000, 2002). As further clarified in Part I, this perspective holds that counterterrorism—from the police point of view—is not a matter of war oriented at enemies but a matter of crime control oriented at criminal suspects approached on the basis of professional standards of policing. *Police* is hereby defined as the institution that is formally charged by states to lawfully execute the monopoly over the means of internal coercion (Deflem 2002:11). As such, this study conceives of police (in the singular) as an institution of social control, not —or at least not primarily— the police (in the plural) as the body of people who professionally inhabit this institution.

Methodologically, the research for this book relies on a large number of primary and secondary sources and interviews with counterterrorism officials. The analyzed printed documents were retrieved from archives, libraries, police agency Web sites, and government departments and private and public agencies involved in various aspects of counterterrorism. Additionally relied upon were national and international media sources retrieved through the electronic database Lexis-Nexis or via Internet search engines. News reports from print sources and all online materials are cited in the chapter endnotes, whereas all academic writings quoted in the text are listed in the Bibliography.[12] The interview data that were used in this book rely on semi-structured interviews with personnel at various police organizations, civilian and military counterterrorism agencies, and private and public security groups, which were conducted in 2003, 2004, and 2007. No identifying data of the interviews are revealed to guarantee anonymity of the respondents.

A Look Ahead at the Chapters

The specific aim of this book is to unravel the policing of terrorism in selected contexts around the world, especially since the events of 9/11. Although this book is not about terrorism but about the policing thereof, it would be careless to not position the police aspects of counterterrorism in relation to broader terrorism concerns. The first part of this book, therefore, clarifies the theme and the approach of this work. Chapter 1 traces key elements in the history of terrorism and counterterrorism and their analysis from a criminological perspective. Within this background, Chapter 2 outlines a model of the policing of terrorism on the basis of the bureaucratization theory of policing. The

Figure 0.2 President George W. Bush praising U.S. Customs employees, Washington D.C., August 8, 2002. Although counterterrorism efforts are all too often understood in exclusively political terms, specifically in relation to the presidentially directed war on terror, it is important to recognize the relative autonomy of policing and other security activities from the political environment. Counterterrorism essentially involves multiple components. (Photo by James R. Tourtellotte, courtesy of U.S. Customs and Border Protection.)

chapter thereby explains, in general terms, the approach that is applied in the book's subsequent chapters.

Turning to the empirical analyses, each chapter focuses on the counterterrorism police strategies as they are developed among a particular national or international agency. These strategies are first described in terms of their relevant characteristics and subsequently discussed, on the basis of the stated bureaucratization perspective, in a section on the dynamics of counterterrorism policing. A first group of empirical chapters deals with the policing of terrorism in the United States. Chapter 3 first provides an overview of the policy and legal responses to terrorism in the United States, specifically the creation of the Department of Homeland Security, the passage of the USA PATRIOT Act, and the launch of the so-called war on terror, including the implementation of domestic surveillance programs. Chapter 4 then charts the most important dimensions of counterterrorism policing in the United States at the federal level, including the activities of the FBI in the Department of Justice, U.S. Immigration and Customs

Enforcement, and U.S. Customs and Border Protection in the Department of Homeland Security, and the Bureau of Diplomatic Service in the Department of State. Chapter 5 next focuses on the role of local law enforcement, especially at the state and municipal levels.

The chapters that make up Part III of this book broaden the scope of analysis to the international arena. Chapter 6 is devoted to uncovering aspects of the policing of terrorism in different nations across the world. The analyses in Chapters 7 and 8 uncover the dynamics of the policing of terrorism by two important international police organizations: the International Criminal Police Organization (Interpol) and the European Police Office (Europol).

The final part of this book is devoted to the analysis of some of the most remarkable cases of counterterrorism policing in distinct national settings. In Chapter 9, attention is devoted to the policing of terrorism in the state of Israel. Specifically scrutinized are the undercover counterterrorism efforts that Israeli police agencies employ in Jerusalem and in the administered territories of Gaza and the West Bank. Chapter 10, finally, examines how the increase in terrorist violence and civil unrest in Iraq and Afghanistan has affected the development of new civilian police forces since the invasions of these two countries.

In the concluding section of this book, some important reflections are discussed on the basis of the findings from the prior empirical chapters. Most importantly, I argue that the many components that exist in ongoing counterterrorism efforts at the levels of politics, law, military, and police cannot be assumed to neatly harmonize. Instead, the world of counterterrorism involves many differences and potential clashes among the manifold strategies against terrorism as they are defined in the variable terms of national security, legality, warfare, and crime control. As such, this book hopes to clarify the central characteristics of the policing of terrorism to contribute to drawing an accurate comprehensive picture of the counterterrorism efforts that shape our world today and in the near future.

PART I
PERSPECTIVE OF THE BOOK

1

THE CRIMINOLOGY OF TERRORISM AND COUNTERTERRORISM

To usefully situate the policing of terrorism, this chapter reviews the themes of terrorism and counterterrorism and their study from a criminological perspective. The field of terrorism studies broadly encompasses both terrorism, as a particular activity involving the infliction of harm for specified purposes, and counterterrorism, involving practices and institutions concerned with defining and responding to terrorism. It is the special province of a criminological viewpoint to focus on terrorism as a form of crime or deviance and on counterterrorism as social control.

Terrorism: Concept and Development

Terrorism refers to the use of illegitimate means for political-ideological purposes.[1] With respect to its means, terrorism typically involves violent tactics aimed at civilians on a relatively massive scale, much like in the case of war. Yet, terrorism is different from warfare in that it exists outside, and purposely operates against, the principles of war as they are regulated in the international community of nations. Acts of terrorism are politically oriented and ideologically motivated, ranging from specific goals formulated in terms of the might of political nation-states to more general aims related to the plight of certain peoples and groups. Because of the political-ideological objectives of terrorism, the underlying ideas of terrorism are important to consider as the motivating forces that fuel terrorist groups and individuals. Strategically, the instilling of fear is an important immediate objective of terrorism.

Forms of terrorism can be distinguished on the basis of its means and aims. From a historical viewpoint, for example, the distinction between revolutionary, nationalist, and religious terrorism can usefully bring out important shifts in terrorist activity over the ages. Revolutionary terrorism is associated with attempts to violently seize political power in the context of nation states. Nationalist terrorism involves the violent quest by certain groups, who define themselves mostly on the basis of ethnicity as a nation, to gain autonomy and establish a new state. Religious terrorism is ideologically rooted in strands of various religious traditions that typically oppose secularization processes in society.

Historically, terrorism has been mostly associated with revolutionary movements involved with seeking to overthrow political regimes. The term *terrorism* originated during the aftermath of the French Revolution, when the French National Assembly in 1793 decreed a mass mobilization (*"levée en masse"*) of all able-bodied men to secure the republic and thwart off both internal and external enemies of the revolution. During the resulting "Reign of Terror," several tens of thousands of people, most of them ordinary workers and peasants, were massacred as purported enemies of the people. Since then, as the establishment of national states took on a more permanent hold, nationalist terrorism increased to secure the rights of specific ethnically defined minority groups, such as the Irish in the United Kingdom, the Basques in Spain, and Zionists in the former British Mandate of Palestine. In most recent times, religious terrorism has gained prominence, especially on an international level. The most conspicuous example is the al-Qaeda movement, which is held responsible for the attacks of September 11, 2001.

Whereas the invention of dynamite, the favorite tool of the nineteenth-century bomb-throwing anarchist, has been argued to signal the beginning of terrorism from a technical point of view, today the means employed by terrorist organizations and individuals are more varied than ever. Contemporary terrorism is also highly sophisticated in technological respects and organized across national borders. The methods of personnel recruitment, training, and intelligence gathering have likewise modernized. Modern-day terrorism is also feared to involve the use, or at least the deliberate pursuit, of lethal means of unprecedented proportion (such as weapons of mass destruction) and has occasionally taken on a more widely organized character, involving

Figure 1.1 The Mercaz HaRav religious school in Jerusalem, Israel, March 6, 2008. In some societies, terrorism is a relatively rare phenomenon, but in others, such as in Israel, it is a part of daily life.
In March 2008, the Mercaz HaRav school in Jerusalem was attacked by a lone Palestinian gunman
who killed 8 students and wounded 11 more. (Photo by Avi Ohayon, courtesy of the Israel Project,
www.theisraelproject.org.)

globally organized terrorist networks. The contemporary world of
terrorism is also more complex, involving multiple domestic and
international forms and a growing number of causes, as varied as the
environment, white supremacy, and abortion. Terrorism today, also, can
be perpetrated or sponsored by states in addition to a host of non-state
actors.

Dimensions of Counterterrorism

A wide range of counterterrorism strategies have been developed to
deal with the causes and consequences of terrorist activities.[2] Politically,
counterterrorism involves measures taken by the governments of
national states and by international governing bodies. Such (inter)
governmental responses to terrorism are historically most developed,
dating back to at least the second half of the nineteenth century, when
governments in Europe sought to disrupt political activities aimed
at overthrowing established regimes (Deflem 2002). In 1937, a first
intergovernmental treaty specifically dealing with terrorism was drafted

by the League of Nations (the precursor of the United Nations) in the form of an international convention on the Prevention and Punishment of Terrorism. Yet, although the convention was signed by 24 nations, it was ratified only by India.

During the twentieth century, intergovernmental counterterrorism measures would develop in a piecemeal fashion to focus not on terrorism as such but on selected issues commonly associated with terrorist activity, such as hijackings and bombings (Guiora 2007). For example, the United Nations drafted the International Convention against the Taking of Hostages in 1979 and the International Convention for the Suppression of Terrorist Bombings in 1997.[3] Other international governing bodies, such as the Organization of American States and the Council of Europe, have likewise developed international protocols to prevent and punish terrorist activity.

International agreements against terrorism have been complemented by legislative efforts at the national level. Various nations in Europe, for instance, drafted counterterrorist legislation throughout the 1970s, when extremist political organizations threatened to destabilize the political order. In the United States, the Act to Combat International Terrorism and the Omnibus Anti-Terrorism Act were passed during the administration of President Ronald Reagan in the 1980s. Subsequently, the terrorist incidents that hit the United States in the 1990s, specifically the World Trade Center bombing on February 26, 1993, and the bombing of the Alfred P. Murrah Federal Building in Oklahoma City on April 19, 1995, led to passage of the Antiterrorism and Effective Death Penalty Act during the Bill Clinton presidency.

No historical event has had as much of an impact on the course of counterterrorism policies as the terrorist attacks of September 11, 2001. In the United States, a comprehensive USA PATRIOT Act (the Uniting and Strengthening America by Providing Appropriate Tools Required to Intercept and Obstruct Terrorism Act) was passed to intensify surveillance against terrorist activity (see Chapter 3). A new Department of Homeland Security was created, and exceptional measures to detain and try terrorist suspects in military tribunals were instituted.

Policies against terrorism extended on a global level to military operations when the governments of the United States and other NATO

Figure 1.2 The Alfred P. Murrah Federal Building in Oklahoma City, April 26, 1995. The Oklahoma City Bombing on April 19, 1995, not only brought terrorism to the heartland of the United States, it led the way to a comprehensive legal response against terrorism by the U.S. government. (FEMA News Photo, courtesy of the Federal Emergency Management Agency.)

countries decided to undertake armed operations against the Taliban government in Afghanistan. The global impact of the events of 9/11 took hold on the legal front as well, for many nations across the world have since 2001 strengthened their legislative efforts against terrorism (see Chapter 6). A host of intergovernmental treaties have additionally been developed to foster cooperation among states in the fight against (international) terrorism. At the global level, the United Nations has adopted a Global Counterterrorism Strategy to appeal to the nations of the world to unify their counterterrorism efforts. Similar initiatives have also been developed by other international organizations, such as the Organization of American States, the Commonwealth of Independent States, and the League of Arab States.

Terrorism and Counterterrorism: A Criminological Perspective

From a criminological viewpoint, terrorism and counterterrorism can be conceptually approached as crime or deviance and social control, respectively. This approach is rooted in the sociology of crime or deviance, as forms of norm-violating behavior, and the practices and institutions of social control, broadly defined as the definition of and response to crime or deviance.

First, terrorism can be conceived as a form of violence, the causes of which can be analyzed at the micro- and macro-level (Black 2004; Rosenfeld 2004). From the micro-viewpoint that focuses on the characteristics of terrorist perpetrators, research can concentrate on the people who are more likely to become terrorists or to join, or to be recruited by, a terrorist organization. At the macro-level, criminological analyses of terrorism concentrate on the fluctuations of terrorism in function of other societal developments, such as periods of political strife, economic conditions, and cultural-ideological conflicts.

To understand terrorist actions, criminological research can focus on terrorism as a form of deviance (Arena and Arrigo 2006). Deviance theorists will be particularly interested in the motives of terrorist conduct and the development of a terrorist identity. Additionally, the societal context in which such acts of deviance are formally labeled or criminalized as terrorism can be studied (Altheide 2006). This criminalization involves the definition of certain acts as terrorism, typically by means of legislation, and its subsequent enforcement.

Second, counterterrorism can be criminologically analyzed as a matter of social control, including various mechanisms and institutions that define and respond to terrorism (Deflem 2004a, b; Costanza, Kilburn, and Helms 2009). The most formal component of social control is represented by the criminal justice system, including its agents and organizations, such as the police.

In the realm of social control and criminal justice, the counterterrorism activities of police have been of growing importance. Most available studies on the policing of terrorism, however, are policy-oriented and highly normative, arguing for or against aspects of counterterrorism policing, instead of analyzing them, or they are of a technical nature, written from the viewpoint of the police professional (e.g., Brandl 2003; Das and Kratcoski 2003; Henry 2005; Müller-Wille 2008; Oliver 2007). The available scholarly work on the policing of terrorism has typically treated counterterrorist policing as one element in a broader study or focused on specific police institutions (e.g., Jiao and Rhea 2007; Kappeler and Miller-Potter 2004; Marenin 2005; Pickering, McCulloch, and Wright-Neville 2008). As explained

Figure 1.2 A fugitive illegal alien apprehended by U.S. federal officers as part of the so-called Return to Sender program, San Diego, April 3, 2007. Besides analyzing terrorism as an act of crime or deviance, criminologists also study counterterrorism as a matter of social control or criminal justice. They thereby observe the wide range of operations that are conducted, including both terrorism-related activities and criminal enforcement tasks such as the rendition of fugitives. (Photo courtesy of U.S. Immigration and Custom Enforcement.)

in Chapter 2, the bureaucratization theory of policing in this book is applied to offer a broad and scholarly grounded perspective of the policing of terrorism.

Conclusion

Terrorism and counterterrorism have historically evolved in various ways. Terrorism has increasingly diversified in terms of the objectives that are pursued and the means that are used. Counterterrorism efforts have likewise proliferated across a range of institutions. Criminologists contribute to the study of terrorism and terrorism-related phenomena by focusing on terrorism as crime or deviance and counterterrorism as social control. Studying counterterrorism as a form of social control, criminological research can reveal important elements of counterterrorism that are not of a military, legal, or political character.

Much of the contemporary public discourse typically focuses on counterterrorism in the world of politics and in relation to military interventions and war. Yet, every dimension of counterterrorism has to be researched carefully before any general pronouncements can be made. The present study is, therefore, situated in the sociology of social control to focus on the manner in which police institutions conceive of and respond to terrorism. In Chapter 2, I outline the bureaucratization theory of policing that is empirically explored in the remainder of this book.

2

A THEORY OF COUNTERTERRORISM POLICING

Situated in the sociology of social control, this book's empirical investigations of the policing of terrorism are based on the theory of bureaucratization. Following the work of Max Weber (1922), the bureaucratization theory holds that modern counterterrorist police efforts are autonomously conducted on the basis of professional standards regarding the means and objectives of counterterrorism (Deflem 2000, 2002, 2004a). The bureaucratization perspective recognizes that high-profile terrorist incidents, such as the events of 9/11, can lead to attempts by governments to redirect police efforts against terrorism in function of political objectives. Yet, because the bureaucratization of modern police institutions is at an unprecedented high level, police agencies can better resist such (re-)politicization attempts to continue counterterrorism activities on the basis of an understanding of terrorism based on professional expertise. Relatedly, the theory holds that national and, more generally, regional persistence marks counterterrorism policing efforts, even when those efforts explicitly involve cooperation among police of different nations and regions. This chapter clarifies the theory more fully.

The Bureaucratization of Policing

The bureaucratization theory maintains that police institutions have historically gained a position of relative independence because the execution of their duties has become guided by criteria of efficiency and an impersonal calculation of means. The reliance on technologically sophisticated means of criminal investigation is the most concrete expression of this development among police. From a position of autonomy, police agencies can develop professional systems of knowledge that delineate police work in function of crime control and order maintenance. Bureaucratization then leads police institutions to become independent to determine the means and a specification of the objectives of their tasks.

Historically, it can be observed that police bureaucratization has been successfully accomplished across many nations that have achieved a modicum of peace and that, typically, are industrialized and democratically organized. Of course, pacification is a historically relative condition inasmuch as no nation-state, past or present, has ever attained complete peace (Bittner 1990:104–107). Periods of war and other moments of extreme political upheaval will draw police again closer to the political center of the state. Under such conditions of politicization, police institutions may again take up politically defined tasks related to national security. Yet, such politicization efforts occur progressively at times when police institutions have solidified a position of autonomy that enables them to better resist attempts at political control.

The theory of police bureaucratization accounts for the development of policing at both the (intra)national and international level. Specifically, the theory holds that international police activities are, under conditions of bureaucratization, characterized by a persistence of nationality in at least three ways (Deflem 2002:215–219). First, police institutions prefer to engage in unilaterally enacted transnational activities, most typically through a system of international liaisons stationed in foreign countries. Second, international cooperation among police typically takes place in a bilateral form, between the police of two nations, and will be maintained only on a temporary basis rather than permanently structured. Third, in the case of international police organizations with multilateral membership, such as Interpol and Europol, national persistence is revealed in the fact that such cooperation is of a collaborative nature and does not involve the formation of a supranational police force. These features of regional persistence apply not only to international police work but can be observed with respect to the activities of police institutions at other levels of jurisdiction (municipal, state, federal, and international) and thus affect multiple levels of inter-agency cooperation.

Figure 2.1 FBI fingerprint files during World War II. The orderly keeping of files is, according to sociologist Max Weber, one of the central characteristics of modern bureaucracies. In charge of the nation's fingerprint records, the FBI dramatically raised its profile as an efficient federal law enforcement organization. Though the Bureau oversaw some 13 million fingerprint files in 1940, by the end of World War II it had collected the fingerprints of no fewer than 92 million people. (Photo courtesy of the Federal Bureau of Investigation.)

The Policing of Terrorism: A Model of Inquiry

It is appropriate to assume that the function and organization of police in the United States and in other nations across the world will have changed considerably in response to the terrorist events of 9/11. Political pressures can be expected to be among the most important contextual determinants of counterterrorist policing. Expanded and intensified means of formal policy and legislation intended to control the conduct of police in matters of terrorism will most concretely articulate such political efforts. However, on the basis of the bureaucratization theory, it can also be expected that police institutions can resist political influences to continue to conduct their activities in a manner that is congruent with professional police standards. Moreover, in terms of cooperation in counterterrorist policing, it can be predicted that national and, more generally, regional persistence characterizes counterterrorist police work. An application of the bureaucratization theory to the policing of terrorism, then, implies investigation of the four dimensions that follow.

The Historical Context

With respect to the conception of terrorism as a crime, it is important to note that terrorism has instigated police activities for many years. Terrorism was from the late 1960s onward generally more of a concern to police in Europe, Israel, and the Middle East than in the United States. However, with the growing internationalization of terrorist groups during the 1980s, terrorism began to have distinctly global effects. International terrorist incidents, such as the 1988 bombing of Pan Am flight 103 over Lockerbie, Scotland, propelled the expansion of counterterrorist police powers. The 1990s brought about a particular increase in the police attention to terrorism because of the high-profile terrorist incidents in that decade. These developments accelerated in an unprecedented manner in the wake of the attacks of September 11.

As the cases examined in this book show, the September 11 attacks had ripple effects that could be felt across the world and that led to major reorganizations of counterterrorist police in many countries. In view of the magnitude of the concern over terrorism, it can even be postulated that police institutions in nations and regions that have only a limited experience with terrorist activities will nonetheless engage in counterterrorism reorganizations to be able to cooperate on the basis of shared concerns and be accepted in the professional police culture. Continued concerns over the spread of terrorism, driven by events such as the bombings in Madrid in March 2004 and in London in July 2005 and the Glasgow International Airport attack in 2007 and the failed plots in Germany in July 2006 and in the United Kingdom in August 2006, will further intensify these developments.

The Political Context

Political responses to terrorism, including government policies and related legislative initiatives, developed in a piecemeal fashion until the events of September 11. Since then, however, more resolute efforts have been taken to respond to the terrorist threat in the form of news policies and laws. The passage of the Patriot Act and the creation of the Department of Homeland Security in the United States are prototypical in this respect. Yet, similar developments have also taken place in many other nations around the world (see Chapters 3 and 6).

The political treatment of terrorism as an issue of national security puts pressure on police institutions to align their efforts to government policy but also enables an expansion of police powers in matters of counterterrorism. As the coming chapters illustrate, the momentous events of September 11, in particular, have brought about a considerable increase of police duties in function of the terrorism threat. Police forces have been given new and exceptional means of enforcement, such as technologically advanced tools of surveillance, additional personnel, and an augmented budget. Police institutions have thereby also been realigned with military forces and intelligence agencies. Such reorganizations of policing may lead to structural adjustments that will last until long after the more immediate repercussions of 9/11 have faded.

Figure 2.2 Iraqi police outside a polling station, Iraq, December 15, 2005. Though meant to provide security during the legislative elections of 2005, Iraqi police sometimes also voice their political allegiance as demonstrated (in the photo shown here) by the sticker on the windshield of the police vehicle, which shows an image of the popular but controversial cleric Muqtada al-Sadr. The independence of police from politics is an important challenge in societies with an autocratic past such as Iraq's. (Photo by Jim Garamone, courtesy of the U.S. Department of Defense.)

The Institutional Context

On the basis of the bureaucratization theory, it can be suggested that the events of September 11 have implied only in circumscribed ways a return to a politicized policing. In most important respects, bureaucratic persistence and resistance against political attempts to redirect police institutions will have prevented counterterrorist police efforts from being politicized to instead remain subject to professional standards in matters of means of objectives.

With respect to the means of counterterrorist policing, technological developments and concerns of efficiency are among the primary considerations in establishing police arrangements against terrorism. Counterterrorist police work employs sophisticated technological methods of surveillance and investigation. Relatedly, counterterrorist police work will be especially concerned with bio-terrorism, the use of computers and special investigative techniques, and the financial assets of terrorist groupings. Such efficiency considerations will on an organizational level be revealed in a functional division of police work in terms of investigative matters and management issues. Additionally, the efficiency of means that is emphasized in counterterrorist policing will be reflected in (international) police cooperation and information exchange methods that are accomplished through direct communication among police. Such direct forms of cooperation are often precisely meant to avoid the hurdles of government policies and legal arrangements.

With respect to the objectives of counterterrorist policing, the bureaucratization of police work involves a de-politicization of the target of police activities and a focus on the distinctly criminal aspects of terrorist activities. From the police point of view, domestic and international crimes, such as terrorism, form the basis of professional systems of knowledge that can be shared among police of different jurisdictions. To accomplish such a criminalization, terrorism is defined as a crime to become a basis for counterterrorism police work. An additional strategy in the criminalization of terrorism is to disentangle terrorist activities into its various constituent parts, only the criminal elements of which are the target of police work (e.g., hijackings, assassinations, and bombings). Thus, the target of terrorism is defined in a professional language that can be shared among police institutions across the world. As a political, legal, or moral issue, terrorism cannot function as a basis for policing activities. It is precisely for this reason that the so-called war on terror is, from the viewpoint of policing, not a war at all.

The Global Context

The historical trend toward a global police culture has not prevented that national and, more broadly, regional police objectives remain of paramount concern. The preference among police agencies to work unilaterally applies both to national or federal police organizations whose jurisdiction extends to other countries and to local (municipal or state) agencies whose jurisdictional spaces are less extensive. In the context of a nation, therefore, terrorism will be perceived differently by police in parts of the country where domestic terrorist groups are more prevalent than in larger metropolitan centers and border regions or points of entry with large ports or airports where international terrorism will be of more concern. At the international level, similar principles are at work in shaping international counterterrorism policing to be, as suggested earlier, primarily unilateral, limited in function or scope, or collaborative in the case of international police organizations.

Knowledge systems on terrorism can be shared among the police of national states to the extent that a common understanding has developed about the nature and occurrence of (international) terrorism. As noted, such a shared notion is accomplished by conceiving of terrorism in general terms as a crime and by disentangling criminal components in terrorist incidents. Cooperation in a fragile global order, however, may not always be very effective, because major police powers will not only have less need for an international organization but not trust many of its members. Therefore, more limited regional police cooperation efforts will also emerge.

Conclusion

The theoretical model introduced in this chapter suggests that police institutions that have gained a high degree of professional autonomy are confronted with renewed attempts by the political centers of national states to gain control over policing activities. The key question of

Figure 2.3 Members of the FBI and FEMA at the Pentagon, Arlington, VA, September 12, 2001. In counterterrorism operations, special attention goes to inter-agency cooperation among law enforcement forces and between law enforcement and other first-responders. In the image shown here, members of the Federal Emergency Management Agency (FEMA) and the Federal Bureau of Investigation (FBI) coordinate their respective tasks at the Pentagon crash site the day after the 9/11 attacks. (Photo by Jocelyn Augustino/FEMA News Photo, courtesy of the Federal Emergency Management Agency.)

9/11 concerns the course and outcome of this clash between attempts to politicize police institutions on the one hand and the bureaucratic resistance those institutions can offer on the other. As the coming chapters show, a politicization of counterterrorist policing may not be easily accomplished. Instead, police institutions may continue to claim and gain autonomy in the control of terrorism. In the coming chapters, these theoretical ideas are applied to examine a variety of cases of counterterrorism policing across the globe. Given the centrality of the events of September 11 for the contemporary policing of terrorism, the analysis begins with developments in the United States and from there extends to other national and institutional settings.

PART II
THE UNITED STATES

3

COUNTERTERRORISM POLICY AND LAW

Terrorism is responded to in various ways by multiple institutions. This chapter reviews recent developments in counterterrorism policy and law in the United States. Specifically addressed are the establishment of the Department of Homeland Security, the passage of the USA PATRIOT Act, and related intelligence activities. In popular discourse and the media, these policy and legal components of the U.S. counterterrorism approach have aroused much discussion and debate. Though the value of such normative contemplations cannot be denied, the scholarly approach adopted in this book chooses a different route, which is geared strictly toward an examination of empirical developments as they have in recent years taken place. It is hoped that this approach can also restore some realism and logic to the debate over the ideal course of relevant policy and law.

The Road to 9/11

The legal framework on terrorism that was swiftly adopted in the United States in the weeks after September 11 did not come out of nowhere but, instead, was the culmination of a series of initiatives that had been taken since the 1980s and that continued during the 1990s. It is, therefore, important to note the extraordinary impact of 9/11, not as a singularly unique event but as an occurrence of special significance that took place within a longer historical process.

As in other nations of the world, counterterrorism law in the United States progressed in a piecemeal fashion, evolving from legislation on activities typically associated with terrorism to a more comprehensive approach.[1] During the 1970s, antiterrorism laws were passed on such matters as air transportation security and the hijacking of airplanes. In the 1980s, during the presidency of Ronald Reagan, terrorism was approached in a more inclusive fashion but primarily as a foreign menace, directed at or taking place in nations other than the United States. Abroad, however, terrorism on occasion also involved American targets and victims. Establishing and enhancing cooperation with foreign authorities or, conversely, engaging in limited military interventions were the primary U.S. strategies to deal with terrorist issues. The 1984 Act to Combat International Terrorism instituted a program to provide for rewards to anyone who would furnish information useful to solving a terrorist act against the United States or U.S. property. Confirming the view of terrorism as a foreign problem, the 1986 Omnibus Diplomatic Security and Antiterrorism Act made terrorist attacks against Americans abroad a federal crime.

The administration of President George H. W. Bush treated terrorism predominantly as a matter of international relations to be dealt with in the political (diplomatic and military) arena of world affairs. The prototypical case in this instance was the response to the bombing of Pan American Flight 103 (scheduled from London to New York) that occurred over Lockerbie, Scotland in December 1988. Investigations into that incident pointed toward evidence that Libyan officials were involved, leading the Bush administration to see the attack as a retaliation for the 1986 U.S. bombing of Tripoli, the capital city of Libya. The latter military strike, in turn, had been ordered by President Reagan after the U.S. administration had blamed the Libyan government for the bombing of a discotheque in Berlin, Germany, that was often frequented by U.S. soldiers.

The relatively isolated terrorist events of the 1980s would make way for a more concerted legislative response in the wake of an apparent escalation of terrorism during the 1990s. The World Trade Center bombing on February 26, 1993, and, particularly, the Oklahoma City Bombing on April 19, 1995, influenced passage of the Antiterrorism and Effective Death Penalty Act in 1996 during the administration of President Bill Clinton.[2] The Act expanded U.S. authority to sue foreign governments that supported terrorism. Other enacted measures focused on the financing of terrorist groups and the treatment of suspected foreign terrorists as enemy aliens. From a criminal justice viewpoint, the Act made terrorism subject to federal criminal law. Federal law enforcement authorities were authorized to investigate terrorism cases and were accordingly provided with supplementary funding.

The Antiterrorism and Effective Death Penalty Act paved the way for the post–9/11 legal climate by focusing on the international dimensions of terrorism and, in particular, by emphasizing the need for coordination in counterterrorism. During the Clinton presidency, three commissions were set up to establish a properly coordinated approach in the U.S. fight against terrorism (Shutt and Deflem 2005).

First, the Advisory Panel to Assess Domestic Response Capabilities for Terrorism Involving Weapons of Mass Destruction (chaired by Virginia governor James Gilmore) was authorized by U.S. Congress in 1999.[3] Noting many inadequacies in the existing U.S. counterterrorism approach, the Commission called for a unified national counterterrorism strategy and the creation of a "National Office to Combat Terrorism" to be located in the President's office.

Second, the United States Commission on National Security/21st Century (co-chaired by senators Gary Hart of Colorado and Warren Rudman of New Hampshire) was chartered by the Department of Defense in 1998.[4] In a January 2001 report, the commission recommended the establishment of a "National Homeland Security Agency" in the White House to coordinate the United States terrorism response. Such a specialized agency was needed, according to the commission, because a "direct attack against American citizens on American soil is likely over the next quarter century."[5]

Third, the congressionally mandated National Commission on Terrorism (chaired by ambassador Paul Bremer) in June, 2001, issued a report that did not propose a new agency but recommended that the U.S. intelligence and law enforcement communities should be equipped to adequately function in their respective counterterrorism activities.

Thus, when George W. Bush assumed the office of the U.S. Presidency in January, 2001, there were three recent counterterrorism policy proposals available, two of which called for the creation of a new national homeland security office, either as a separate government agency or as an office in the executive branch. Yet, in the initial months of the Bush presidency, terrorism was not at the forefront of U.S. policy considerations. The events of September 11 would drastically alter this situation.

The Department of Homeland Security

Less than a month after 9/11, on October 8, 2001, President G. W. Bush issued an executive order to create an Office of Homeland Security in the White House, along with a new cabinet position in the executive branch, the Director of Homeland Security, to which Bush appointed former governor of Pennsylvania Tom Ridge (Shutt and Deflem 2005). A year later, the Office was turned into a full-fledged department in the federal government. After initial debates in January 2002, the U.S. Congress passed the Homeland Security Act on November 25, 2002, to create the Department of Homeland Security.[6] The Department formally commenced operations in January 2003 when Tom Ridge was sworn in as the nation's first Homeland Security Secretary. Ridge stayed in office until February 15, 2005, when former federal prosecutor Michael Chertoff became the Department's second Secretary. On January 21, 2009, Janet Napolitano became the third Secretary of Homeland Security as part of the new administration of President Barack Obama.

As specified in the Homeland Security Act, the primary missions of the Department of Homeland Security (DHS) include "preventing terrorist attacks within the United States, reducing the vulnerability of the United States to terrorism at home, and minimizing the damage and assisting in the recovery from any attacks that may occur."[7] To achieve these goals, the DHS provides a unified network of agencies and institutions involved in various efforts aimed at securing the United States from terrorist attacks. The unification of U.S. counterterrorism agencies into one overarching structure is the central mechanism through which the goals of the DHS are to be accomplished.

Some of the agencies in the DHS have been newly created, whereas others have been transferred from other federal departments. Among them, U.S. Citizenship and Immigration Services, U.S. Customs and Border Protection, and U.S. Immigration and Customs Enforcement (ICE) have been newly created out of the U.S. Customs Service, which used to be part of the Department of the Treasury, and the Immigration and Naturalization Service in the Department of Justice.

Figure 3.1 A U.S. Customs and Border Protection officer processes an airline passenger entering the United States. The agencies of the Department of Homeland, including Customs and Border Protection (CBP) and Immigration and Customs Enforcement (ICE), have as their central mission the protection of the United States from terrorist attacks. The screening of all persons entering the United States is, thereby, a central objective, often relying on advanced technologies, such as electronic fingerprinting and digital imaging. (Photo by James Tourtellotte, courtesy of U.S. Customs and Border Protection.)

In view of the fact that airline security was among the most striking lapses in the terrorist attacks of September 11, the Transportation Security Administration (TSA) was created to oversee security at U.S. airports. Initially part of the Department of Transportation until its transfer to the DHS in 2003, the TSA is well known among the public at large because of its screening functions of airline passengers. The TSA also oversees the Federal Air Marshal Service, but it has no other law enforcement responsibilities. Despite the fact that the TSA is not a police force, it was announced in June, 2008 that its 45,000 screeners would receive a new uniform, including a police-style blue shirt and copper and zinc badge, to convey an image of authority. The move was quickly met with criticisms from regular airport police officers because they feared that passengers might confuse TSA personnel with law enforcement officials with arrest powers.[8]

Other important DHS agencies include the Federal Emergency Management Agency (transferred from the federal cabinet), which is in charge of the national response to disasters; the U.S. Coast Guard (from the Department of Transportation), which is responsible for security matters in maritime regions (and which during times of war is placed under the Department of the Navy); and the U.S. Secret Service (from the Treasury), best known for its duties to provide security for the U.S. President.

The DHS presently oversees some 180,000 employees in about two dozen agencies, directorates, and offices that are variously aligned into one overall structure. Initially, the organizational structure of the DHS consisted of five functionally specialized directorates (Border and Transportation Security; Emergency Preparedness and Response; Science and Technology; Information Analysis and Infrastructure Protection; and Management). In July, 2005, however, the five-directorate structure was abolished to increase the Department's preparedness to respond to disasters, improve security, and enhance information-sharing capacity. Among the adaptations, the directorates dealing with security, emergencies, and information were abolished, whereas other directorates (such as the Office of Intelligence and Analysis and the Directorate for Preparedness) were newly created. Among the DHS agencies with law enforcement objectives, ICE and Customs and Border Protection stand out (see Chapter 4).

The Patriot Act

Whereas the formation of the DHS constitutes the most important change in U.S. counterterrorism at the policy level, the passage of the USA PATRIOT ACT has been the most significant legal development after 9/11. The Patriot Act was initially drafted by the Department of Justice as the "Anti-Terrorism Act of 2001." It was introduced to the U.S. House as the "Provide Appropriate Tools Required to Intercept and Obstruct Terrorism (PATRIOT) Act of 2001" and was, upon congressional approval, signed by President Bush on October 26, 2001, as the "Uniting and Strengthening America by Providing Appropriate Tools Required to Intercept and Obstruct Terrorism (USA PATRIOT ACT) Act of 2001."[9] Because several of the Act's provisions were to expire by the end of the year 2005, a revised Patriot Act was signed into law by President Bush in March, 2006 as the "2005 USA Patriot Improvement and Reauthorization Act," along with amendments specified in the "USA PATRIOT Act Additional Reauthorizing Amendments Act" of 2006.

The Patriot Act consists of 10 titles that detail various provisions to deter and prosecute terrorist acts, strengthen law enforcement efforts against terrorism, and pass a number of related measures. Among its key components, the Act includes several provisions to enable specific counterterrorism investigative measures. To enhance domestic security against terrorism, funding for the Federal Bureau of Investigation was increased. Military assistance in domestic law enforcement can be provided in certain emergencies. Various surveillance procedures were also expanded, including the authority to intercept communications related to terrorism and computer fraud, to share information resulting from criminal investigations, and to allow for so-called roving surveillance authority under the Foreign Intelligence Surveillance Act (FISA). The FISA was passed in 1978 to allow for electronic surveillance within the United States on foreign agents and international terrorists on the condition that a judge in a specialized court issues a warrant. Such surveillance is roving when it is not restricted to a physical locale or device (such as a phone in a home) but can be used on any phone lines, mobile phones, and Internet connections that are potentially used by a suspect.

Additional titles of the Patriot Act deal with enhanced border controls and a tightening of U.S. immigration policies. The Act further expands the authority to issue National Security Letters by the FBI and other government agencies. Through such letters, information about somebody is requested from a third party without requiring probable cause or judicial oversight and additionally containing a gag order whereby the recipient of the national security letter is not allowed to reveal that the letter was ever issued. Additional titles of the Patriot Act expand the counterterrorism capacities of the intelligence community, responsibilities for which are placed with the director of the Central Intelligence Agency (CIA), and seek to coordinate the law enforcement response to terrorism at the federal, state, and local levels. Among the most important aspects of the reauthorization of the revised Patriot Act in 2006, various measures, such as those concerning seaport security and the financing of terrorism, were strengthened. Most of the provisions of Title II that would have expired in 2005 were reauthorized to expire at the end of 2009.

The Patriot Act has been the subject of considerable discussion among civil liberties advocates (Shulman 2003; Wong 2006). It has been suggested that the Act was passed too quickly and with little or no congressional debate because it was seen in the light of the immediate impact of September 11 when the general mood was favorable to any, even sweeping measures against terrorism. Famously, in Michael Moore's film *Fahrenheit 9/11*, a representative in U.S. Congress remarked that no legislator had even read the complete bill. Civil libertarian groups, such as the American Civil Liberties Union (ACLU), have expressed concerns on various provisions of the Act that are seen as intrusive of people's rights. According to data provided by the ACLU, more than 400 resolutions have been passed against various aspects of the Patriot Act, and an additional 274 efforts were being prepared by June of 2009.[10]

The War on Terror

The DHS and the Patriot Act constitute important elements in a broader range of policy and legal changes in U.S. counterterrorism developed since 9/11 that U.S. authorities refer to as the war on terror (Abrams 2006). The expression *war on terror* arouses strong feelings among both proponents and opponents of recent U.S. counterterrorism measures. George W. Bush first used the expression on September 20, 2001, during his special address at a joint session of the U.S. House and Senate, referring to the events of September 11 as "an act of war against our country" that had to be responded to by a "war on terror" that "begins with al Qaeda" and extends globally to other terrorist groups.[11] Important is that the expression was from the start meant to have strategic import as well, specifically by relating counterterrorism operations to military interventions. The accompanying use of the term *global war on terror* (or GWOT) additionally brings out the international dimensions of contemporary counterterrorism strategies, both in forging multilateral coalitions to conduct relevant strategies and in identifying the "axis of evil" nations that are their targets. Though newly elected President Obama was reported to have ordered an end to using the term in March, 2009, his administration has to date largely stayed on course in terms of the use of military means against terrorism.[12]

Though U.S. intelligence and security experts almost immediately attributed the September 11 attacks to the al-Qaeda movement connected with Osama bin Laden, the war rhetoric that was introduced by the Bush administration also had more than metaphoric meaning in linking 9/11 to nations suspected of aiding terrorism, thus opening up the possibility of actual warfare. The connection with al-Qaeda was a logical one in view of the prior targeting of the United States by the jihadist movement, particularly the World Trade Center bombing in 1993, of which number the perpetrator, Ramzi Yousef, had been training with members of al-Qaeda, and, even more clearly, the bombings of the U.S. embassies in Dar Es Salaam, Tanzania, and Nairobi, Kenya, on August 7, 1998, which killed more than 200 people, and the suicide bombing attack against the *USS Cole* on October 12, 2000, which killed 17 U.S. sailors, both of which attacks were organized by bin Laden. The al-Qaeda connection to 9/11 led to the military intervention in Afghanistan, which started on October 7, 2001. The military action against the Taliban government in Afghanistan could readily be justified in terms of the regime's intimate connections with al-Qaeda. The measure was also in line with, though enacted on a much more massive scale than, the cruise missile strikes that the Clinton administration had authorized against terrorist bases in Afghanistan (and Sudan) on August 20, 1998, after the U.S. embassy bombings in Africa that year.

Additionally brought into relation with the events of 9/11 was the U.S.–led invasion of Iraq, which commenced on March 20, 2003. Although also finding a precedent in a military campaign of the Clinton presidency, when in December 1998 strikes were launched against Iraq for the Ba'athist government's failure to comply with United Nations Security Council resolutions and for interference with the work of weapons inspectors, it was the specter of the 1990–1991 Gulf War, initiated during the presidency of George H. W. Bush, and the climate created during the preceding decades of the Cold War that provided justification for why Iraq was brought into the picture, politically and militarily, in response to the events of September 11. Many of the leading figures in the Bush presidency, such as Vice President Richard Cheney, Secretary of State Colin Powell, and Secretary of Defense Donald Rumsfeld, had politically come of age during the decades of the Cold War and were accustomed to thinking of security issues, especially those

Figure 3.2 U.S. military personnel of the Fleet Anti-Terrorism Security Team Pacific during a drill in the Pacific Ocean, June 12, 2009. The war on terror is not always a metaphor, as counterterrorism operations are also undertaken by military units. (Photo by Bryan Reckard, courtesy of the U.S. Department of Defense.)

exhibiting strong international dimensions, in terms of relations among nations rather than among nations and criminal groups or other non-state actors.[13] From the start, the so-called war on terrorism launched by the Bush cabinet could indeed include an actual war. Within hours of the 9/11 attacks, key figures in the Bush administration raised the option of retaliatory military measures against the regimes of nations that were suspected of aiding al-Qaeda, including the Ba'athist government of Saddam Hussein in Iraq.

Labeling the fight against terrorism a war allowed the U.S. government to introduce a series of emergency measures on the basis of the status of President Bush as commander in chief. A week after 9/11, the U.S. House and Senate jointly passed a resolution on the "Authorization for Use of Military Force" to allow the President to use "all necessary and appropriate force against those nations, organizations, or persons he determines planned, authorized, committed, or aided the terrorist attacks that occurred on September 11, 2001, or harbored such organizations or persons."[14] Once these powers had been granted, many of the counterterrorism measures initiated by the executive branch could lack further congressional oversight and were often not even known to exist until they were revealed some time after implementation. Decisions could be reached from "the dark side... in the shadows of the intelligence world," to use the words of Vice President Dick Cheney.[15]

Most notorious among the many wartime counterterrorism measures that were instituted by U.S. authorities after 9/11 are to be mentioned the use of coercive interrogation techniques in the case of captured terrorist suspects, especially the prisoners that were transferred to the U.S. detention facilities in Guantanamo Bay, Cuba; the torture and abuse of prisoners in the Abu Ghraib prison in Iraq, which were discovered in 2004; the suspension by the Bush administration of the Geneva Convention for captured terrorists; the use of military tribunals to prosecute non–U.S. terrorists (including Khalid Sheikh Mohammed, the alleged mastermind of the 9/11 attacks, and four other defendants whose trial on charges of war crimes and multiple murder counts began on June 5, 2008)[16] without all due process protections such as are guaranteed to U.S. citizens in a civilian court; and programs of intensified and sweeping surveillance directed at U.S. citizens. Among the latter, the Terrorist Surveillance Program conducted by the National Security Agency (NSA) deserves special consideration.

Domestic Spying: The National Security Agency Terrorist Surveillance Program[17]

Among the special presidentially authorized counterterrorism measures, the secret domestic surveillance program conducted by the NSA in the wake of 9/11 has led to much debate after the program was first reported in the *New York Times* in December 2005.[18] Established in 1952, the NSA is responsible for designing high-tech cipher systems that will protect the integrity of U.S. information systems and for searching for weaknesses in the systems and codes that are used by adversaries of the United States. The domestic surveillance program that was discovered in 2005 had been initiated in early 2002 upon the secret authorization of President Bush. Referred to as the "Terrorist Surveillance Program," the program has allowed the NSA to intercept, without a court-approved warrant, communications that involve one overseas and one domestic party when at least one party is suspected of holding ties to al-Qaeda or an affiliated terrorist group.

The reaction to the revelation that President Bush had secretly ordered the NSA domestic spying program was intense.[19] In January 2006, the ACLU and the Center for Constitutional Rights filed lawsuits arguing that the NSA eavesdropping program violated Americans' civil rights. That same month, the Electronic Frontier Foundation filed a class-action lawsuit against the telephone company AT&T, accusing it of providing the NSA with free access to customer phone calls and internet communications in violation of the Fourth Amendment and federal wiretap and communication laws. In May 2006, an additional revelation about contemporary domestic surveillance was made when the newspaper *USA Today* reported that the NSA had kept logs of billions of domestic calls, a program that had begun, without court approval, soon after 9/11.

When President Bush in a televised address admitted that he had authorized domestic warrant-less monitoring of calls involving an overseas party, he defended his actions as crucial to national security.[20] Yet opponents argued that the President's expansion of executive power violated constitutional rules of judicial and congressional oversight and Fourth Amendment protections against illegal search and seizure.

After a federal judge in August 2006 ruled the NSA surveillance program to be unconstitutional,[21] U.S. Congress the following year passed the "Protect America Act of 2007" that removed the warrant requirement for the surveillance of foreign targets that are "reasonably believed" to be outside of the United States.[22] The bill was enacted but expired in February 2008 because of a so-called sunset clause (allowing for a limited period for a law to be in effect to evaluate its impact). In November, 2007, the U.S. House passed the "Responsible Electronic Surveillance That is Overseen, Reviewed, and Effective Act" (RESTORE Act), which revised the FISA while offering protections of the constitutional rights of Americans whose communications might be involved.[23] It was followed by the "FISA Amendments Act of 2008," which was enacted in July 2008.[24] The law was supported by then-Senator Barack Obama, whose presidency since has not fundamentally altered the legal situation of U.S. counter terrorism.[25]

The Debate on Counterterrorism: Coordination and Security

The present state of counterterrorism in the United States in regard to matters of policy and law is extremely complex. Besides the mentioned components of the DHS and the NSA, U.S. counter terrorism (excluding law enforcement) further involves many other longstanding policy programs and institutions. Most important from the intelligence viewpoint abroad, for instance, are the activities of the CIA, which collects, analyzes, and disseminates intelligence on foreign terrorist groups and persons.[26] In the U.S. Department of State, a specialized Office of the Coordinator for Counterterrorism provides policy oversight and guidance for the United States' international counterterrorism activities.[27] Among its activities, the Office maintains the Foreign Terrorist Organizations list designated by the Secretary of State. In the Treasury Department, the Office of Terrorism and Financial Intelligence seeks to protect the financial system of the United States from terrorism and combat-related national security threats.[28] Besides overseeing the FBI, the Department of Justice also administers the National Security Division, created in 2006 with the reauthorization of the Patriot Act, to coordinate counterterrorism activities across several departments.[29]

In view of the complexity of the U.S. counterterrorism infrastructure, an important recent development has been the creation of the cabinet-level Office of the Director of National Intelligence. The office was established in 2004 through the Intelligence Reform and Terrorism Prevention Act, which amended the National Security Act of 1947 (which created the CIA).[30] The Office seeks to streamline and coordinate the various components of intelligence-related efforts in U.S. counterterrorism.[31] The accompanying position of Director of National Intelligence oversees all U.S. intelligence work, replacing the previous position of Director of Central Intelligence (the head of the CIA), who is now referred to as the Director of the Central Intelligence Agency.

Given the multifarious nature of U.S. counterterrorism, a primary focus in policy changes since 9/11 has consisted of enhancing coordination and harmonization. In this respect, the efforts of the DHS stand out as the most comprehensive and ambitious effort to coordinate U.S. counterterrorism. The main principle of the Department is to establish coordination through a unified structure.

Figure 3.3 A member of the Coast Guard stands watch in the Gulf of Mexico as part of a counterterrorism exercise. Critics have voiced concerns over the war on terror because of the invasive nature of some counterterrorism operations and the militarization of security measures within and at the borders of the United States. (Photo by Adam Eggers, courtesy of the U.S. Department of Defense.)

Because of the policy-driven rather than institution-based nature of the homeland security structure, the coordination of agencies in the DHS also implies an attempt to centralize and politically supervise counterterrorism functions into a vertical structure between (federal) security agencies and the executive branch of U.S. government. Relatedly, the Homeland Security Advisory System, a series of warnings specifying different risk levels of the terrorist threat to the nation (or regions thereof), was created in direct response to a Presidential directive.[32] The creation of the new position of Director of National Intelligence also fits in these Presidentially directed coordination plans.

Conclusion

Given the continued anxieties over the terrorist threat and the sensitivity over civil rights in American culture, the normative debate on counterterrorism is likely to stay in the public consciousness for some time in the foreseeable future. Yet, in this popular discourse, hardly any attention goes to the impact and mechanisms of the surveillance and security measures that are in place at the institutional level. Further not recognized is how various components within the broad field of U.S. counterterrorism may clash or harmonize in terms of scope and manner of operations. The often-heard populist expression that "the government" is in charge of U.S. counterterrorism fails to recognize the complexity of counterterrorism operations and institutions and cannot be helpful to their analysis and understanding.

The emphasis that is placed on coordination in the DHS is of a specific kind. Unification in the DHS is accomplished through a (top-down-determined) network structure of various, functionally specialized and, at times, overlapping organizations, without much attention to the (bottom-up-developed) mechanisms of cooperation between them. Among the implications, the officials working in the various DHS agencies may know where they stand and how they are positioned in relation to one another but will not necessarily know how to interact with one another absent a specification of procedures of cooperation. It is more than tragic in this respect to note that the 2005 reorganization of the DHS directorate structure, which among other reasons was conducted, as Secretary Chertoff stated, to "increase preparedness with particular focus on catastrophic events,"[33] came just a little more than a month before Hurricane Katrina hit the U.S. Gulf Coast region and revealed extreme shortcomings in the Department's emergency response system.

Though the unification of counterterrorism functions in the DHS also implies an attempt at centralization of authority under presidential control, it should not simply be assumed that relevant institutions have readily subjected to these new conditions and might not be able to continue to operate on the basis of achieved standards of professional expertise. Immediately striking from the security viewpoint, for instance, the nation's two most important counterterrorism agencies, the CIA in the intelligence community and the FBI in federal law enforcement, are not part of the DHS network. The structure and mechanisms of counterterrorism activities by law enforcement institutions within and outside the DHS structure and their relation to developments in law and policy are addressed in Chapters 4 and 5.

4

HOMELAND SECURITY

The Role of Federal Law Enforcement

Chapter 3 has shown that coordination is a central concern in U.S. counterterrorism policy. An examination of the most important policing components of counterterrorism may reveal the extent and manner in which such coordination efforts have practically been realized since September 11. In this chapter, I first offer an overview of the long-standing involvement in counterterrorism by the Federal Bureau of Investigation (FBI), the lead investigative agency in the U.S. Department of Justice. Next, I examine the major organizational and functional aspects of counterterrorism operations by selected security organizations in the Department of Homeland Security (DHS) structure, specifically U.S. Immigration and Customs Enforcement (ICE) and U.S. Customs and Border Protection (CBP). Also discussed is the counterterrorism role of the Bureau of Diplomatic Security (DS), the main security and law enforcement branch of the U.S. Department of State.

The Federal Bureau of Investigation

The primary investigative arm of the U.S. Department of Justice, the Federal Bureau of Investigation (FBI) is organized on the basis of a decentralized model, with a central headquarters in Washington, DC, 56 field offices in major cities throughout the United States, and more than 400 resident agencies in smaller U.S. cities and towns.[1] In addition, some 165 FBI agents (of a total force of 12,590) are stationed permanently in oversees offices, in all continents of the world, through a system of so-called legal attachés (or legats).

The mission to investigate terrorism in the United States is at the heart of the post–World War II expansion of the FBI. Federal acts on air transportation and hijacking that were passed in the 1970s indirectly influenced Bureau counterterrorism work by addressing crimes intimately connected to terrorism in those years. During the 1980s, the FBI expanded its counterterrorism operations after the increasing number of federal regulations on terrorism that were passed in that decade. Most important, on April 10, 1982, President Ronald Reagan signed National Security Directive 30, which for the first time gave lead-agency counterterrorism authority to the FBI. In response, the Bureau then began to maintain a specialized Terrorism Section within its Criminal Investigative Division.

The focus of the FBI's counterterrorism efforts are concerned with both international and domestic terrorism. As conceived by the FBI, international terrorism transcends national boundaries in terms of the means of attack or the persons or locale involved, whereas domestic terrorism is carried out in the United States without such international dimensions. Historically, the activities of the FBI have always, though in a fluctuating manner, involved both domestic and international forms of terrorism. During the 1960s and 1970s, the main focus was on domestic reactionary groups, such as the Ku Klux Klan, and antiwar extremist organizations, such as the Weather Underground. After the criticisms that erupted against the FBI in the wake of the COINTELPRO program in the late 1970s, the Bureau shifted attention away from domestic subversive groups to organized crime. Yet, by the mid-1980s, terrorism had again become a concern for the FBI, mainly because of the increasing number of American victims in terrorist attacks abroad.

The 1990s experienced a sharp increase in the FBI's counterterrorism missions, both domestically (propelled by various domestic terrorism incidents on U.S. soil, such as the high-profile bombings that occurred in Oklahoma City in 1995 and at the Centennial Olympic Park in Atlanta, Georgia in 1996) and abroad (under influence of such international incidents as the World Trade Center bombing in 1993 and the bombings of two U.S. embassies in Africa in 1998). In 1994, a separate Counterterrorism Division was set up within the Bureau, while the Justice Department's National Security Division retained foreign counterintelligence responsibilities. On June 21, 1995, President Bill

Clinton issued Presidential Directive 39, which affirmed the FBI as the lead investigative agency for acts of terrorism committed against Americans in both the United States and overseas.[2] The 1996 passage of the Anti-Terrorism and Effective Death Penalty Act expanded the FBI's authority to include investigations of international acts of terrorism and the activities of international terrorist groups that take place in the United States.

By the late 1990s, counterterrorism had become one of the FBI's central missions. Yet since the events of 9/11, the Bureau has undergone several additional changes that manifest the growing centrality of counterterrorism. Chief among these adaptations is the fact that counterterrorism is now no longer just one among other enforcement tasks but has formally become the Bureau's primary mission. Following the guidelines that were promulgated by then Attorney General John Ashcroft on May 2002, it is presently the "FBI's central mission of

Figure 4.1 Members of the FBI at the World Trade Center, New York City, September 18, 2001. Although the FBI is primarily responsible for criminal investigations to track down the perpetrators of terrorist attacks, the Bureau also maintains many other relevant functions. After the attacks of 9/11, FBI chaplains provided moral and religious support to rescue workers. (Photo by Andrea Booher/FEMA News Photo, courtesy of the Federal Emergency Management Agency.)

preventing the commission of terrorist acts against the United States and its people."[3]

The FBI's shift of attention to terrorism since 9/11 has also brought about important changes. Bureau agents have been relocated from other criminal programs (mainly in the area of drug enforcement) to counterterrorism, whereas the number of intelligence analysts has doubled and the number of linguists has tripled. The FBI has also raised its intelligence capabilities, particularly through the use of National Security Letters and increased surveillance operations. Besides the Counterterrorism Division, several other specialized programs have been set up, such as the FBI Terrorism Financing Operations Section, a Weapons of Mass Destruction (WMD) Directorate, and the Terrorist Screening Center to maintain the U.S. Government's Consolidated Terrorist Watchlist. To promote inter-agency cooperation, a Foreign Terrorist Tracking Task Force has been set up in which the FBI partners with other federal agencies, including the CIA and ICE, and the Department of Defense, while an inter-agency National Counterterrorism Center, set up in August 2004, integrates intelligence related to terrorism.[4]

Perhaps the most important counterterrorism tool developed by the FBI is the Joint Terrorism Task Force (JTTF). These Task Forces are overseen by the FBI but are composed of agents from various law enforcement agencies, including other federal agencies, state and local law enforcement, and other first-responder organizations. JTTFs act as the primary investigative counterterrorism forces in the FBI, involved with following up on leads, gathering evidence, collecting intelligence, and making arrests and providing security for special events and conducting training. At present, there are about 100 such local JTTFs across the United States, some 65 of which were created after 9/11. The local JTTFs coordinate their efforts through an inter-agency National Joint Terrorism Task Force in Washington, DC.

Immigration and Border Security: U.S. Immigration and Customs Enforcement and U.S. Customs and Border Protection

The formation of the DHS was meant not only to coordinate various components of counterterrorism but to specify the functions involved therein and to have specialized agencies for every identified function. Thus, the immigration duties that were traditionally taken care of by one agency, the former Immigration and Naturalization Service (INS), are now split into administrative and enforcement functions: The U.S. Citizenship and Immigration Services is in charge of all administrative aspects of immigration, whereas two new agencies are responsible for immigration enforcement: ICE specializes in the interior investigative and enforcement functions of immigration, and CBP is in charge of border-related security tasks. Though not yet well known, these two agencies have since the events of 9/11 steadily expanded, organizationally and operationally, to gain an ever-more-important role in U.S. counterterrorism .

Immigration and Customs Enforcement

It was not altogether without reason that immigration became a key security concern after 9/11. The 19 hijackers involved with the September 11 attacks had all legally entered the country (Shutt and Deflem 2005). However, finding would-be terrorists among the many people entering the United States every day also meant that legitimate immigrants and visitors should still be allowed to enter the country. To properly oversee the enforcement components of immigration, the new agency—ICE— was established as the primary investigative branch of the DHS.[5] Initially called the Bureau of Immigration and Customs Enforcement, ICE is responsible for enforcing federal immigration and customs laws.[6]

Touted as the largest Homeland Security investigative force, ICE comprises several specialized divisions, such as an Office of Intelligence, an Office of Investigations, an Office of Detention and Removal Operations, and an Office of International Affairs. Headquartered in Washington, DC, ICE additionally maintains 27 field offices across the United States and some 50 international offices in 39 nations around the world.[7] ICE offices abroad work on the basis of the legat model and are involved in establishing partnerships with, and organizing training of, local counterparts. Bringing together some 17,000 employees in its various Divisions to oversee hundreds of special operations, ICE has become one of the most important U.S. federal law enforcement agencies with counterterrorism duties.

Although not yet widely known, ICE has since its formation in 2003 been involved in a plethora of enforcement activities, both in matters involving migration and terrorism and in other crime areas. During the first 8 days of June 2008 alone, for example, ICE reported 17 successful cases, including the arrest of 149 gang members, indictments in 10 alien smuggling cases, the removal of 83 individuals to Nigeria and Albania, several child pornography cases, and the arrests of 491 fugitives and immigration violators in a month-long operation in the New Jersey–New York area. Immigration issues are handled by ICE as part of the Student and Exchange Visitor Information System that was instituted in August 2003 on the basis of the Enhanced Border Security and Visa Reform Act of 2002 (Salter 2004). ICE secures such monitoring in part through cooperation with educational institutions, which are to comply with the program if they seek to accept foreign students.

Given the concerns over several forms of cross-border criminal activity, ICE has established a partnership with other law enforcement agencies to create the Border Enforcement Security Task Force. This effort consists of a series of multi-agency task forces that share information among participating agencies to target criminal organizations that pose significant threats to border security. Also providing cooperation among law enforcement under the direction of ICE is the Law Enforcement Support Center, a national enforcement operations facility that acts as the single national point of contact in the DHS to provide immigration status and identity information to local, state, and federal law enforcement agencies on aliens suspected of, arrested for, or convicted of crimes. With private industry, moreover, the ICE has established cooperation through Project Shield America. The project is developed to prevent the export of sensitive U.S. munitions and strategic technology to terrorists, criminal organizations, and foreign adversaries.

Customs and Border Protection

Along with the formation of ICE as the specialized enforcement agency in immigration matters, CBP was newly created out of the U.S. Customs Service, U.S. Border Patrol, the INS, and the enforcement divisions of the Department of Agriculture.[8] The primary mission of

CBP is the protection of the borders of the United States, with a special focus on protection from terrorists and their weapons, while at the same time also securing legitimate trade and travel. Much like the control of immigration, safeguarding the U.S. borders presents a daunting task (Shutt and Deflem 2005). Every year, more than 500 million people enter the United States, most of whom are non-citizens.

CBP consists of several functionally divided divisions, such as the Office of Field Operations, the Office of Border Patrol, and the Office of Alien Smuggling. The agency has developed a number of special programs to facilitate its law enforcement missions. Under the Secure Border Initiative, CBP seeks to control the U.S. borders, strengthen interior enforcement, and promote a temporary worker program. The most famous component of infrastructure is the fence that is being built along the U.S.–Mexican border on the basis of the Secure Fence Act of 2006.[9] In matters of border control, the traditional practice of "catch and release," whereby non-Mexican illegal aliens who were arrested at the border were granted routine parole pending immigration hearings, has been abolished in favor of temporary detention. Special emphasis in border controls is placed on potential terrorist and criminal organizations involved in the illegal cross-border transportation of goods and humans. The strengthening of interior enforcement and compliance is aimed at investigating and penalizing the employment of illegal aliens, whereas a temporary worker program is promoted to lessen illegal immigration and gain effective control of the border.

A few months after the attacks of 9/11, the Container Security Initiative (CSI) was established to ensure that all containers that pose a potential risk for terrorism can be identified and inspected at foreign ports before they enter the United States (Shutt and Deflem 2005). The basic principle of this initiative is to begin with terrorism detection at foreign ports. CBP has, therefore, stationed teams of U.S. officers from both CBP and ICE to work together with foreign agents in the host countries. CSI partnerships have been established at 58 foreign ports covering about 86% of all maritime containers heading to the United States. Moreover, CBP has implemented joint initiatives with Canadian and Mexican border forces. Among them, Integrated Border Enforcement Teams have been set up with state and local law enforcement from Canada and the United States to target smuggling

Figure 4.2 Agents from the Border Enforcement Security Task Force (BEST), Los Angeles, December 4, 2008. Demonstrating the importance accorded to inter-agency cooperation, the Los Angeles BEST task force includes officers from no fewer than nine federal and local agencies, including ICE, CBP, the U.S. Coast Guard, the U.S. Secret Service, the Bureau of Alcohol, Tobacco, Firearms and Explosives (ATF), the Federal Air Marshal Service, the Los Angeles County Sheriff's Department, the Los Angeles Port Police, and the California Highway Patrol. (Photo courtesy of U.S. Immigration and Customs Enforcement.)

and cross-border terrorist movements between the two countries. Pushing the border outward, CBP also partners with the private sector via the Customs-Trade Partnership Against Terrorism, in which presently 6,500 companies are involved. Additional partnerships have been established with the departments of State and Defense and with ICE. Finally, CBP is also the executive agency for the Department of State's Export Control and Related Border Security program that is focused on the prevention of the international distribution of nuclear, chemical, and biological weapons.

The Bureau of Diplomatic Security

In the U.S. Department of State, the Bureau of Diplomatic Security (DS) represents the main security and law enforcement arm. The Bureau conducts investigations in matters of passport and visa fraud, international security technology, including Internet security, the protection of U.S. persons, property, and information abroad, and international terrorism.[10] In charge of the protection of the Secretary of State and foreign dignitaries below the level of head of state who are visiting or residing in the United States, the Bureau is also involved in protecting U.S. embassies and personnel overseas and conducting a variety of other security and counterterrorism operations.

DS was created as a direct result of mounting concerns over terrorist attacks against Americans. In view of the gradually increasing terrorist threat against U.S. missions and citizens abroad during the 1970s, the Office of Security, which had been created in the State Department in 1916, responded by ascertaining the threat-level against U.S. people and facilities and providing advice to U.S. personnel stationed overseas. As the number of terrorist attacks against Americans increased during the 1980s, DS and its subdivision of the Diplomatic Security Service were officially established on November 4, 1985. Since then, the DS has continually expanded its security missions, especially overseas. The role of DS in the rendition of fugitives from justice from foreign nations to the United States is also by far the largest of any U.S. law enforcement agency.

DS first acquired a mandate to focus on security measures against terrorism with the enactment of the 1986 Omnibus Diplomatic Security and Antiterrorism Act. Since 1992, the Rewards for Justice Program (established in 1984 to provide for financial rewards to anyone who would furnish information useful to solving a terrorist act against the United States or U.S. property) has also been maintained by the Bureau. Since the 9/11 attacks, DS has stepped up its counterterrorism role and currently maintains a number of programs specifically related to counterterrorism, such as an Antiterrorism Assistance Program to train security personnel from foreign nations and an Office of Investigations and Counterintelligence to fight the efforts of foreign intelligence services targeting Department of State missions abroad.

Several recent high-profile counterterrorism investigations in which DS served a critical role have helped to increase the notoriety of the Bureau. For instance, information received through the Rewards for Justice Program administered by DS resulted in the apprehension of Ramzi Yousef, the mastermind of the World Trade Center bombing in 1993. After the events of 9/11, DS received accolades for its investigation of the kidnapping and murder of *Wall Street Journal* correspondent Daniel Pearl in Pakistan in 2002. The investigation got special attention because the Hollywood movie *A Mighty Heart*, starring Angelina Jolie, recounted the actions of DS special agent Randall Bennett, the lead investigator in the case.[11]

More problematic for the public image of DS was the resignation of its head, Richard Griffin, in October 2007, the day after Secretary of State Condoleezza Rice had ordered new measures to strengthen government oversight of private security contractors in Iraq.[12] Giving more control to military forces over private security firms operating in a war zone, the ruling came after employees of Blackwater USA had been accused of killing 17 Iraqi civilians. DS had initially taken on the investigations into the killings, but the FBI took over when it was discovered that statements by Blackwater guards made during the investigations could not be used in court because DS agents had given the private guards a waiver that granted them limited immunity, including the barring of statements in a criminal case. Since then, stricter rules have been imposed on Blackwater security activities in Iraq, including the mandatory presence of DS agents in all contractor security convoys.[13]

The Dynamics of U.S. Counterterrorism Policing

This review of the major federal law enforcement dimensions of counterterrorism in the United States readily demonstrates that the world of counterterrorism policing is expansive and highly complex, involving several organizations and strategies. Also apparent from a mere review of the major agencies involved is that the events of September 11 had a tremendous effect that greatly impacted the current state and future course of law enforcement measures against terrorism. The following discussion concentrates on some of the major issues that are involved in these developments.

The Extra-legality of Counterterrorism Policing

The majority of the discussions on terrorism and counterterrorism are normative in nature, contemplating the morally, politically, and legally appropriate and, mostly, inappropriate components of counterterrorism measures. This debate has also, albeit in a less pronounced fashion, contemplated aspects of the police and security dimensions of counterterrorism. The brunt of these (largely negative) comments has gone to organizations in the intelligence community rather than in the world of law enforcement. Typical for this debate was the consternation that was felt when the domestic surveillance program of the NSA was discovered. Likewise telling were the criticisms that were leveled at the CIA for not having been able to prevent the attacks of 9/11 and, later, for having been wrong about the weapons of mass destruction assumed to have been developed by the Ba'athist government of Saddam Hussein, eventually leading to the resignation of then-director of the CIA George Tenet (Graham and Nussbaum 2004; Miller and Stone 2002). The fact that the intelligence world is by definition highly secretive no doubt contributes to such reactions.

It is already telling of the relative lack of attention that is devoted to the policing of terrorism that the role of law enforcement in counterterrorism has generally been much less subject to popular criticisms. Among the normative concerns that have been raised against counterterrorism policing, the FBI's use of National Security Letters (NSLs) and its authority to collect materials useful for terrorism probably stand out. The use of NSLs has been especially criticized because the measure would have been improperly implemented, enabled by the fact that an NSL is not subject to court review.[14] Additionally, the FBI authority to search terrorism-related materials (such as library books) has been argued to be unconstitutional because such materials are held by third parties whose rights are violated.[15]

Problematic about the normative concerns raised against counterterrorism surveillance is not so much that the FBI has denied the misuse of its investigative tools[16] but the fact that these practices are long-standing means that had already been devised and implemented beyond any legal context. The NSL measure, for instance, dates back to the late 1970s as a method to circumvent restrictions on financial searches in the course of terrorism and espionage investigations. Though the Patriot Act broadened the use of NSLs, it was the practice as implemented by federal law enforcement that drove its expanded use, not its legal framing. The ideologically driven normative debate on counterterrorism so misses the mark by focusing on the legal and policy context rather than the actual organizational dimensions and practices of law enforcement, such as they can be revealed by adopting a scholarly approach on which a normative perspective might be grounded or on the basis of which at least it should proceed.

In line with the lack of foundation in the reality of policing that is characteristic of the normative debate on counterterrorism, the terrorism-related activities of the FBI have been much less discussed than those of the new agencies established in the DHS, especially ICE and CBP. In fact, judging from the general lack of attention given to these new agencies in the media and in the scholarly literature, it is safe to assume that the organization and practices of these agencies are not even known, let alone subject to analysis or critique. Existing academic discussions on migration and border security have generally focused on legal and policy developments, often fused with strongly normative contentions, to the exclusion of an analysis of the enforcement dimension, which poses a peculiar void given the rather enormous expansion of law enforcement operations in these areas (Dow 2007; Welch 2003, 2004, 2006).

Because of an over-concentration on law and policy, other normative concerns that have been raised against counterterrorism police practices typically relate to the purported expansions of power that would have been granted to DHS agencies, the FBI, and other law enforcement organizations (and intelligence and military forces) as a result of the passage of new legal provisions, especially the Patriot Act, under the comprehensive banner of the war on terror. Such an understanding of law enforcement is not only legalistic (to view policing as residual to law and policy); it requires no independent analysis of the organization and dynamics of counterterrorism policing. It is more than a mere sarcastic wink at *Fahrenheit 9/11* to ask the question who among the critics of the Patriot Act has actually read it and examined its actual impact on law enforcement.

It is noteworthy also that popular concerns against counterterrorism policing are especially pronounced when federal-level agencies are involved. This peculiar but often overlooked fact in the normative debate on counterterrorism is due to the relatively strong concerns in the United States over the sovereignty of states and other local communities. More

Figure 4.3 A U.S. Customs and Border Protection helicopter flying over Raymond James Stadium, Tampa, January 29, 2009. Though explicitly set up for security functions related to the protection of the borders, CBP activities extend to other domains as well. For instance, CBP also provided security for Super Bowl XLIII, which was held on February 1, 2009. (Photo by Gerald Nino, courtesy of U.S. Customs and Border Protection.)

broadly, the sensitivities that exist in U.S. culture about government power and its potential to intrude into people's private world and violate their civil rights will further, and independently, impact these developments. Recent research on the assumed misuse of NSLs by the FBI and other counterterrorism measures (such as the NSA Terrorist Surveillance Program) finds that the number of civil rights violations since 9/11 is very small as compared to the alleged threat they would pose to civil liberties (McDonough and Deflem 2008). Especially in the United States, the assumption that surveillance is powerful and harmful to rights and liberties drives allegations of civil liberties violations independently from the actual occurrence thereof. Thus, a fear of counterterrorism results from a culture in which civil liberties protections are accorded centrality.

Change and Continuity

As noted with respect to the NSL measure used by the FBI, there is continuity and change to be observed in the evolution of counterterrorism policing. In general terms, it is to be noted that terrorism has been among a task of police institutions since well before September 11. The historical roots of the FBI's counterterrorism mission, by example, can be traced back to the authority that was invested in the Bureau to investigate intelligence matters with the advent of, and during, World War II. Thereafter, the FBI steadily expanded its counterterrorism capabilities, especially from the 1970s onward and during the 1990s. Of course, the events of 9/11 brought about an expansion of relevant security activities, even leading to the creation of new federal agencies.

The expansion of U.S. police powers after 9/11 also brought about a refocusing of police functions toward counterterrorism and a realignment of federal, state, and local police agencies as all levels of police now more than ever focus on terrorism. These developments are revealed across the board as all police agencies in the United States have amplified their counterterrorism role, even at the local level (as discussed in Chapter 5). The centrality given to the coordination of these activities is observed from the transfer of existing agencies into a single DHS, the creation of new security-oriented federal enforcement agencies in the DHS, and the formation of inter-agency partnerships, such as the FBI-managed JTTFs, which include officials from federal, local, and state agencies.

Historically, many of the reorganizations that have taken place in counterterrorism policing since 9/11 are in continuity with developments that had been set in well before. For example, the first JTTF was set up in New York City in 1980 in response to domestic terrorism issues posed by ethnic-nationalist groups. The NSL methodology dates back to the 1970s, and other measures were likewise influenced by the shifting climate in the perceived terrorist threat. The FBI, for instance, steadily increased its counterterrorism personnel, especially in the wake of the concerns over domestic terrorism in the 1970s and 1980s, the World Trade Center bombing in 1993, and the bombings of the U.S. embassies in 1998 (Reeve 1999).

In the immediate period after September 11, the FBI reassigned some 4,000 of its then 11,500 special agents to counterterrorism. At some point, no fewer than 6,000 FBI agents (about half of the force) were working on half-a-million investigative leads in the 9/11–related operation code-named "PENTTBOM." Since then, al-Qaeda terrorism has continued to be a special concern at the FBI as jihadist groups have remained active since September 11.[17] Among the successful outcomes of the FBI's counterterrorism operations are several dozen indictments and convictions, including the guilty verdicts of Richard Reid (who was arrested in December 2001 for planning to detonate a shoe bomb aboard an airplane); John Walker Lindh (a young U.S. citizen who lived with and assisted the Taliban); and other individuals trialed on charges of providing material support to al-Qaeda and other terrorist groups.

Although the formation of ICE and CBP as specialized security agencies separate from the administratively oriented CIS presents an important development, it is to be noted that issues of migration and border security were not invented in the post–9/11 era but, on the contrary, have very deep historical roots (Deflem 2004c; Nadelmann 1993). As early as 1845, after the U.S. annexation of Texas, agents from the U.S. Customs Service were sent to the southwestern border territory to detect smugglers. Later, the U.S. Immigration Service and, after 1924, a specialized Immigration Border Patrol took on such security functions. Typically depending on the political conditions between the United States and Mexico (and, to a much lesser extent, Canada), changes that took place in the border security issues received primary attention. Irrespective of the nature of these changes, however, relevant policing activities were also based on prior experiences and practices. Even in the present era of concerns toward foreign terrorists and illegal aliens, there remains a continuation of concerns toward the illegal entry of goods and people, whether they be drugs or weapons, illegal workers, or terrorist suspects.

Reviewing the changes in counterterrorism policing since 9/11, it is to be noted that the greatly expanded attention that has gone to terrorism among police agencies since 9/11 has brought about that other crimes besides terrorism have received relatively less scrutiny from police and, therefore, may have been on the rise. In the cities of New York and Washington, DC, the events of September 11 had a negative impact on the crime rate in the period immediately after 9/11, but other major cities, such as Los Angeles, Chicago, Houston, and Boston, had more violent deaths over the course of 2001, reversing the trend from years prior, because of an increase in the period after the terrorist attacks.[18] Loosened controls, with many police deployed to assist in counterterrorism efforts, have been blamed for the rise.[19] After the overall crime index in the United States had been continually in decline since the early 1990s, it went up again after 2001 and did not get back down to pre-2001 levels until 2005.[20]

At the organizational level of policing, the reorganization of federal law enforcement in view of the threat of terrorism has also shifted security responsibilities among federal law enforcement agencies. Most notably, the FBI has been reaffirmed and strengthened as the nation's lead investigative agency for counterterrorism. However, the FBI has not been transferred into the DHS, although the coordination of U.S. counterterrorism functions is the Department's primary mission. Instead, within the DHS, law enforcement agencies have been absorbed, and new agencies have been established with counterterrorism and terrorism-related functions. The ICE has thereby arguably become to be the security organization that is now in a factual competitive position with the FBI in terms of functional scope and organizational strength. However, it is too early to tell whether the two agencies will also be competing for budget and authority and engage in the "turf wars" that have long marked other inter-agency relations (such as between the FBI and the CIA).

The Relative Irrelevance of Policy and Law

As the theory defended in this book suggests, the politicization of police work is a distinct possibility, especially under conditions of societal upheaval. At the same time, no assumptions should be made that the functions and consequences of law and policy will overlap. The creation of the DHS and the passage of the Patriot Act may be seen as the clearest attempts to direct counterterrorism policing and bring the law enforcement community in line with political goals to fight terrorism as a matter of national security. However, contemporary police institutions have attained a level of bureaucratic autonomy and professional expertise that is unprecedented in scale and can, therefore, resist external pressures. In that sense, at least two important observations must be made.

First, the Patriot Act and related policy measures have not taken away counterterrorism functions from law enforcement (to be transferred to the military or the intelligence community) but have, on the contrary, reaffirmed the role of law enforcement in counterterrorism. The FBI has retained its status as lead-agency in counterterrorism, whereas the ICE, CBP, and DS have expanded their related law enforcement roles. It is accurate to claim that counterterrorism is not only a matter of law enforcement, but it is always that too, and the organization and dynamics, thereof, are surely not simple.

Second, the specification of the law enforcement role in counterterrorism as it is outlined in the Patriot Act and related legal measures is entirely congruent with prior achievements in counterterrorism policing. The Patriot Act betrays a conspicuous emphasis on the means to combat terrorism, rather than a concern to define terrorism. The Act focuses on efficient methods to track down terrorists, on measures to ensure inter-agency cooperation, and on the technological challenges posed for police (and intelligence) agencies because of advances in communications technology. Among the special surveillance tools mentioned in the Act are secret searches and seizures, the tapping of telephones, and the use of detention without charges for seven days. All these measures are in line with achieved standards of police technique and favor the bureaucratic development of counterterrorism police procedures (much as did the 1996 Anti-Terrorism and Effective Death Penalty Act, which greatly enhanced funding for law enforcement). A closer reading of the legal and policy dimensions of counterterrorism in the light of the bureaucratic dynamics of counterterrorism policing is, therefore, in order.

The Professionalism of Counterterrorism Policing

It is not because political and legal efforts have been made to plan and coordinate security organizations involved with counterterrorism that these efforts can be assumed to have effectively guided the organization and implementation of counterterrorism strategies at the level of law enforcement. For the degree to which the bureaucratization of police institutions and the professionalization of their activities has developed in the decades prior to the time when such political and legal plans were enacted, especially in the aftermath of 9/11, will not be inconsequential to counterterrorism policing thereafter. Examining the characteristics of counterterrorism policing at the level of U.S. federal law enforcement reveals dimensions of bureaucratic autonomy with respect to the means and goals of counterterrorism policing.

Considering the means of counterterrorism policing, professional standards of efficiency and the role of technology played therein are revealed in various strategies. The FBI is arguably best developed in this respect because of the Bureau's long history of instituting advanced techniques of criminal investigation, such as fingerprinting and scientific crime analysis (Deflem 2002). Given the centrality the FBI currently accords to the prevention of terrorism, the organization has separated its counterterrorism function more clearly in terms of intelligence and investigation tasks. The shift toward intelligence (in which the FBI also has a long history) is thereby especially telling because intelligence work, unlike investigation and prosecution, is meant to proactively prevent terrorism by casting a wide net of surveillance practices. The liberal use of NSLs and advanced snooping techniques of computer and Internet activities exemplifies the primacy of a broad, open-ended quest to acquire information, the actionability of which can later on be decided upon (Ventura, Miller, and Deflem 2005). Precisely these methods that are subject to much criticisms in the public debate are the strongest manifestations of the bureaucratic drift toward efficiency.

With respect to the means of counterterrorism, the law enforcement agencies in the DHS likewise place a premium on advanced technologies, such as special scanning devices for biological and nuclear weapons or explosives and transportation security technologies relating to such issues as terminal security, vessel tracking, and cargo integrity (Ackleson 2005). ICE and CBP have, like the FBI, also developed more clearly an intelligence component next to security functions within its overall mission. Both DHS agencies seek to monitor all people and goods entering the United States by collecting information and identifying all that moves. CBP relies on specialized techniques of surveillance such as through its Secure Border Initiative, whereas ICE oversees special screening systems such as the Student and Exchange Visitor Information System. Although DS is more confined in its scope of operations to political dignitaries and U.S. personnel abroad, it too has taken on intelligence and investigative roles in counterterrorism and relies heavily on technology and advanced systems of communication such as the Internet.

Organizationally, counterterrorism policing is seen to be guided by efficiency considerations inasmuch as relevant organizations are functionally divided into specialized offices that are specifically focused on certain, often technical aspects of police work. In the FBI, for instance, the Terrorism Financing Operations Section and the WMD Directorate are involved with investigations of particular aspects of terrorism. Likewise, ICE and CBP activities are functionally divided over specialized sections for intelligence, detention and removal, border patrol, and alien smuggling, among others. Of peculiar interest in this functional division of labor are the many inter-agency partnerships that have been set up. From the viewpoint of professional policing, such partnerships bring about many advantages. They function as so-called force multipliers to effectively expand the number of agents involved in counterterrorism missions without imposing additional strains on agency budget.

The JTTFs are prototypical as cost-efficient cooperation structures, because they allow the FBI to recruit agents from other federal and local and state agencies to work on counterterrorism matters under the Bureau's control. Other partnerships, such as the Foreign Terrorist Tracking Task Force (which includes the FBI, ICE, the CIA, and others), the Border Enforcement Security Task Force (including ICE, CBP, the FBI, and others), and the Integrated Border Enforcement Teams managed by CBP and Canadian and Mexican counterparts likewise respond to the need for efficient communication exchange and integrated enforcement. Important is that these partnerships are practical arrangements, independently set up by participating law enforcement agencies, outside the context of legal arrangements or political considerations.

The emphasis placed on efficiency in counterterrorism police work might be understood to offer justification of the criticisms from civil liberties advocates against the broad "snooping" powers of the FBI and other law enforcement and intelligence agencies. However, more thoroughly developed criticisms have actually focused on the limitations of the FBI's intelligence activities. When the bipartisan National Commission on Terrorist Attacks Upon the United States (also known as The 9/11 Commission) released its findings in *The 911 Commission Report* in July 2004, it was stated that the FBI had not adequately diverted resources to counterterrorism in the years leading up to 9/11, even though terrorism matters had by then become a major focus in the Bureau (National Commission 2004:74–80, 423–427). The agency was further urged to continue to strengthen its terrorism-related intelligence functions in the post–9/11 era. In 2008, a report of an inquiry by the Senate Intelligence Committee still called on the FBI to better develop its intelligence role.[21]

It is important to note that efficiency in police work does not necessarily equate with effectiveness. The number of arrests by federal law enforcement in recent cases involving suspected terrorist groups or individuals has been relatively small. Although claims are made that more than a dozen terrorist incidents in the United States have been prevented since 9/11 because of law enforcement actions (at home and abroad), there is not always convincing evidence that they involved serious security threats.[22] Some people have been arrested in the United States on charges that they provided support to al-Qaeda or planned to conduct al-Qaeda inspired attacks. Among them, "shoe bomber" Richard Reid was sentenced to life imprisonment on terrorism charges in 2003. Jose Padilla, who had been arrested in May 2002 as an illegal enemy combatant charged with planning to detonate a radioactive bomb in the United States, was sentenced on conspiracy charges, in January 2008, to serve 208 months in prison. Possibly the best-known (and most-publicized) case began when the FBI arrested seven people in Miami in June, 2006 on accusations of planning to blow up the Sears Tower in Chicago and the FBI building in Miami.[23] Of the seven, one was acquitted in a jury trial in October 2007, with the jury deadlocking on the other six. In April, 2008, a third trial was planned after a second mistrial had been declared.[24] A year later, a jury convicted five of the six men charged.[25] Related arrests in the United States involved foiled plots to blow up a fuel system at John F. Kennedy International Airport in New York in 2007 and alleged plans to bomb a Jewish temple and attack a U.S. military base in 2009 in the state of New York.[26]

As to the objectives of counterterrorist policing, the bureaucratization theory holds that counterterrorism policing involves a de-politicization of terrorism in favor of a professional conception of terrorism as crime.

Figure 4.4 A representative of the U.S. Department of State congratulates and hands over payment to an informant, Republic of the Philippines, June 7, 2007. In the State Department, the Bureau of Diplomatic Security is responsible for the Rewards for Justice Program through which informants are paid for providing information in terrorism investigations. In the case shown here, financial rewards were handed out for information that led to the neutralization of two leaders of an Islamic fundamentalist group operating in the Philippines. (Photo by Troy Latham, courtesy of the U.S. Department of Defense.)

This criminal understanding of terrorism is a common theme among all federal law enforcement organizations. "In accordance with U.S. counterterrorism policy," a recent official FBI document states, "the FBI considers terrorists to be criminals."[27] The document goes on to differentiate between domestic and international terrorism in terms of the definition of terrorism, based on the United States Code, as "the unlawful use of force and violence against persons or property to intimidate or coerce a government, the civilian population, or any segment thereof, in furtherance of political or social objectives."[28] Though this definition contains references to the motives and goals of terrorism, it is only the quality of the means ("unlawful use") that justifies a law enforcement response. Those means are legally not further specified, for which reason the definition is precisely useful to law enforcement. Questions on the motives or objectives of terrorism are abandoned in favor of a criminal-justice focus that enables a police response. The Patriot Act likewise enables this police conception of terrorism because it does not define terrorism at all, instead referring to Section 213 of the Immigration and Nationality Act on terrorist organizations. That Act, however, does not offer a definition of terrorism but provides a list of certain criminal activities, such as hijackings, assassinations, and bombings, that are commonly associated with terrorism but would otherwise also be criminal.

Based on a depoliticized understanding of terrorism as a crime, the term *war on terror* is mostly avoided by law enforcement officials. It appears nowhere in any of the documents posted on the ICE Web site and is only sparingly used by law enforcement leaders. FBI Director Robert Mueller, for instance, has occasionally spoken of the "war on terrorism," and the expression also appears elsewhere in official FBI communications.[29] Yet, these references are meant to serve public relations functions in showing the value of law enforcement within a broader counterterrorism response wherein the "war on terror" metaphor has become standard usage.

In line with the criminal understanding of terrorism, the law enforcement community devotes attention to both domestic and international terrorism. The FBI is focused in its operations on al-Qaeda and other foreign extremist groups, but the Bureau is also attentive to the continued threat posed by domestic terrorist groups. In fact, though FBI officials recognize that "much of the national attention is focused on the substantial threat posed by international terrorists," they emphasize that the Bureau "must also contend with an ongoing threat posed by domestic terrorists based and operating strictly within the United States."[30] Among such domestic groups, the FBI includes white-supremacist organizations, the militia movement, U.S.-based black separatist groups, and animal rights extremists and eco-terrorists.

Both in the FBI and among other federal agencies, such as ICE, CBP, and DS, the criminal focus in policing is further revealed from the fact that a very broad range of criminal violations is included among relevant policing tasks. Moreover, ordinary criminal problems are redefined in terms that fit with the general focus on terrorism. The obvious examples are immigration and border control, but the war on drugs also is connected to the fight against terrorism, specifically through a focus on so-called narcoterrorism (Andreas and Nadelmann 2006:197–198). Thus, although the DEA remains specifically involved with drug control, the agency not only cooperates with other federal law enforcement agencies with terrorism-related functions, it has redefined its mission in terms that fit counterterrorism by emphasizing the capacities of organized drug gangs to "terrorize citizens through fear and intimidation."[31]

The shifting of objectives among law enforcement agencies is not without consequence for their interrelations. While it may be too soon to speak of any new turf wars, what is already clear is that the post–9/11 reorganizations have meant that the FBI is now primarily focused on counterterrorism, although the Bureau is an agency in the Department of Justice with broad criminal justice functions, whereas ICE is broadly involved with migration, customs, smuggling, gangs, sexual crimes, drugs, and other crimes that do not necessarily have a connection to terrorism, although ICE is part of the DHS, a department that has been set up to offer a coordinated counterterrorism response. Thus, what can be ironically noted is the shift away from crimes (other than terrorism) in the FBI and toward crimes (other than terrorism) in ICE.

The Boundaries of Cooperation: Domestic and International Dimensions

Inter-agency partnerships, both domestically and internationally, are an important strategy of counterterrorism policing. Cooperation is achieved among federal and other law enforcement agencies in view of establishing swift systems for information exchange and/or to strengthen selected investigative and intelligence efforts. However, despite such efforts taking place, the mechanisms of cooperation and extra-jurisdictional policing betray a persistence of local and national concerns related to the primary mission of the enforcement agencies that engage in such activities. U.S. federal law enforcement agencies, therefore, generally prefer to operate unilaterally to fulfill organizational tasks. Agencies that are equipped in terms of technology, personnel, and budget to conduct operations without cooperation will undertake efforts alone. The federal status of law enforcement agencies enables a national presence via a decentralized model whereby various field offices are linked with a central headquarters. In terms of cross-jurisdictional and international counterterrorism police work, the preference for unilateral strategies is among U.S. federal law enforcement agencies enabled through the system of legal attachés. The FBI, ICE, CBP, and DS all have agents permanently stationed abroad, with additional options to deploy agents on a need basis.

When counterterrorism cooperation is initiated, it will be limited in scope, restricted to agencies in close functional or national proximity, conducted for a particular investigation and terminated when an inquiry has ended, and/or limited in terms of the number of participating agencies. Thus, bilateral cooperation will be preferred over multilateral initiatives, and cooperation among agencies that are functionally close will be preferred over cooperation between agencies that are remote. These principles help explain that cooperation with participation of U.S. federal law enforcement is predominantly decentralized, for instance in municipalities in the case of the JTTFs and the FBI or at the borders or abroad in the case of CBP. This regional persistence is a function of the fact not only that the United States does not have a national police but that federal agencies too are organizationally decentralized across the territory of the country. The field offices and outposts abroad function as the locales where limited (typically bilateral) partnerships are established. For example, FBI agents at the legat office in London have several meetings every week with British police and intelligence officials.[32]

Police agencies that are organizationally strong are able to play a dominant role in cooperation. A clear manifestation hereof in the case of counterterrorism policing is the force-multiplying function the FBI attributes to the JTTFs. Of a more long-standing nature are the often-reported unwillingness among various agencies to share information and the relative lack of effectiveness of cooperation mechanisms that are organized top-down rather than bottom-up. Even with partnerships organized by police, problems may ensue as differences exist among agencies in the priority that is accorded to terrorism-related activities. The municipal police of a small U.S. town will be more likely to focus on domestic rather than foreign terrorist groups (or not focus much on terrorism at all), but it may also face pressures to cooperate in a JTTF, if only to show a sense of professional commitment. Within a JTTF, however, the perspective of the FBI and other major federal agencies may be dominant. Given the proliferation of JTTFs across the country, no strong conclusions can be reached about the impact of terrorism as a police-relevant problem, and varying local circumstances need to be taken into account as well (see Chapter 5).

Abroad, too, counterterrorist cooperation activities among police institutions are determined by the same forces of relative closeness and distance. The wide-ranging presence of the FBI and the DS across the globe, and of ICE and CBP at and beyond the U.S. border, completely dwarfs the international activities of multilateral organizations. In the area of border control, for instance, CBP is primarily involved in international activities via unilateral and bilateral programs, whereas the globally organized World Customs Organization and its 166 member agencies offer only advisory guidelines on international cooperation. More generally, international police cooperation with U.S. federal law enforcement takes places directly with other police agencies abroad via personal contacts or through the appropriate legat office. Important is that such international cooperation efforts can be established irrespective of the political, legal, and ideological conditions of the nations of participating agencies. The orientation toward efficiency can thus transcend national boundaries when police of different nations share a common understanding of the nature of crime and crime control. In June, 2008, for instance, DS agents along with officers from ICE and CBP cooperated effectively with Cuban police and immigration officials to bring about the return to the United States of a U.S. citizen who was wanted on child sex tourism charges in California and had fled to Cuba.[33]

As the partners of cooperation are considered formally equal, the relative strength of U.S. law enforcement agencies is consequential in determining the agenda and course of international counterterrorism operations. In the case of border controls and migration issues, for instance, the role played by U.S. agencies such as ICE and CBP far outweighs the contributions from their Canadian and, especially, Mexican counterparts (Deflem 2004c). The training programs that are organized by the FBI, CBP, and DS will further contribute to the diffusion of American ideas and techniques in counterterrorism policing on an international scale. Because of the global strength of U.S. policing, an "Americanization" of law enforcement and counterterrorism will take place inasmuch as terrorism issues of concern to the U.S. law enforcement community will, all other conditions being equal, receive more attention than regional and national issues of terrorism elsewhere in the world (Nadelmann 1993). As a result of the preference to work unilaterally or in small, bilateral forms of collaboration, multilateral cooperation efforts in counterterrorism and other police matters are underused by U.S. law enforcement. Besides, as the case of Interpol will show (Chapter 7), multilateral police cooperation is collaborative in nature and thereby reaffirms the roles of participating agencies.

Conclusion

U.S. federal law enforcement agencies in the Justice, Homeland Security, and State departments have long-standing and, since 9/11, greatly expanded roles in the fight against terrorism. Various programs and partnerships have been established to respond to terrorism at the international and domestic level in a manner that is congruent with professional perspectives of crime control. The means of counterterrorism policing are developed on the basis of standards of efficiency to employ technologically advanced methods and other measures based on professional expertise. In terms of its objectives, counterterrorism policing is not involved in a war on terrorism but in counterterrorism as a matter of criminal justice.

Though the transformative powers of September 11 involved distinct attempts to (again) have policing be politically directed, bureaucratic persistence and resistance against such efforts effectively prevented counterterrorist policing from being politicized to instead remain subject to professional expertise and knowledge in terms of means and objectives. Thus, accomplished developments in the institutional autonomy of police bureaucracies and the accompanying evolution of a widespread police culture for well more than a century now can resist politicization attempts to foster a mode of counterterrorist policing that continues to rest on police professionalism rather than political purpose. The professionalism of counterterrorism policing has also influenced the partnerships with federal law enforcement participation to be based on collaborative models of cooperation. In view of the relevance presently accorded to international terrorism, inter-agency cooperation efforts and extra-jurisdictional enforcement tasks comprise international police arrangements. However, police institutions likewise focus on domestic terrorism because they adopt a comprehensive terrorism approach. In domestic matters of counterterrorism policing, regional developments within the United States, at the level of states and municipalities, cannot be ignored.

5

TERRORISM AND THE CITY

The Role of Local Law Enforcement

Counterterrorism policing reaches not only outward from federal agencies to other nations and the international organization of law enforcement, the policing of terrorism also extends inward into the organization of American society at the level of state, county, and municipal governments. To sketch a more comprehensive picture, therefore, a closer look is in order at some of the local components of counterterrorism policing in the United States.[1]

Police functions in the United States have traditionally developed at the local level because of a historically strong opposition against the centralized policing models that were associated with the European autocratic regimes of the eighteenth and nineteenth centuries (Fogelson 1977). At present, there exist almost 18,000 police organizations in the United States, employing more than 800,000 sworn officers.[2] It is obviously impossible to review all the terrorism-related efforts of these agencies in their respective jurisdictions. However, seeking to indicate important trends, this chapter concentrates on some of the issues involved with local police functions in the area of terrorism, with an emphasis on municipal policing. The discussion begins with a review of relevant developments in New York City to reveal the impact of terrorism on policing in the city that, more than any other place in the United States, was impacted by the worst terrorist attack in U.S. history. This chapter next turns to other developments in local counterterrorism policing to estimate broader trends of local counterterrorism policing.

Counterterrorism in New York City

On September 11, 2001, the al-Qaeda terrorist attacks hit the city of New York like no other place in the nation. In the immediate response to the attacks, the city's first-responders, especially firefighters and law enforcement officers, were among those who died during the attacks as they were trying to help others escape the towers. A total of 343 New York firefighters and 23 officers of the New York City Police Department are reported to have died during the rescue efforts.[3]

The largest law enforcement agency in the United States, the NYPD consists of a number of bureaus divided into various divisions, units, and patrol boroughs.[4] Organizationally, the divisions and units are functionally divided, whereas the eight boroughs are geographically differentiated. With respect to terrorism-related issues, the NYPD stepped up its counterterrorism efforts after the attempt to bring down the World Trade Center in 1993. Before the attacks of 9/11 would impact counterterrorism in New York as never before, there had been other, ultimately thwarted terrorist attempts, such as a plan to bomb the Atlantic Avenue subway station in 1997.[5]

Since September 11, counterterrorism policing has become a central part of the overall mission of the NYPD. Areas of New York that are considered particularly vulnerable, such as the financial district, are under constant police surveillance, while tactical teams are held ready to be deployed on a need basis. The NYPD is also keen to visibly deploy surveillance forces across the city, in the form of heavily armed paramilitary-styled units, to "deter terrorists through a show of force."[6] Moreover, training programs are organized to teach officers how to use special counterterrorist tactics, to identify the high-risk infrastructure areas of the city, and to understand the nature of the terrorist threat.

After 9/11, the NYPD created a specialized Counterterrorism Bureau that, led by a Deputy Commissioner for Counterterrorism, works with the patrol boroughs through a network of counterterrorism coordinators. These coordinators are senior uniformed members in each of the eight boroughs, specialized in counterterrorism matters. The NYPD also oversees an Intelligence Division, which was not newly created but was transformed after the events of 9/11 to become primarily focused on counterterrorism rather than general criminal intelligence.

Figure 5.1. Temporary headquarters of the NYPD, New York City, September 13, 2001. The New York Police Department was very directly affected by the terrorist attacks of September 11, in which 23 NYPD officers died. A makeshift NYPD headquarters had to be set up in the premises of a popular hamburger franchise. (Photo by Andrea Booher/FEMA, courtesy of the Federal Emergency Management Agency.)

Among its special counterterrorism measures, the NYPD manages a so-called NYPD Shield program that is focused on the connection between counterterrorism and private-sector security.[7] A private-public partnership established to protect New York City from terrorist attacks, NYPD Shield is meant both for the NYPD to receive information from the private sector and for private sector security to obtain information and cooperation from the police department.

The policing of an American city is a matter not only of municipal policing in the strict sense of the term but of the role of federal and state law enforcement at the level of towns and cities. In the case of New York, the merging of various levels of law enforcement is especially pronounced because of the sheer size of the city and the scope of policing activities. Therefore, the NYPD also partners with federal and other law enforcement agencies, particularly through a Joint Terrorism Task Force (JTTF), allowing for the exchange of intelligence between the local and federal levels of law enforcement. Through its counterterrorism

activities, the NYPD also engages in international cooperation. Akin
to the FBI's legats, a number of NYPD liaison officers are permanently
stationed abroad. Additionally, NYPD agents have been involved on
a temporary basis in various foreign counterterrorism operations. The
NYPD also assisted in interrogations of detainees in Guantanamo Bay
and in Afghanistan. Moreover, the NYPD participates directly in the
electronic communications system managed by Interpol (see Chapter
7).

Professional Perspectives on Local Law Enforcement

The counterterrorism experience of the NYPD after the events of
9/11 indicates certain themes that may be relevant to other local law
enforcement agencies as well. The implications of terrorism for the
organization and functions of local police organizations have been
discussed at some length among law enforcement professionals as part
of a management-oriented literature in police administration.[8] In these
discussions, three themes receive most attention: the localization of
terrorism; the need for inter-agency cooperation; and the relevance of
intelligence and proactive police methods.

First, in the light of prior terrorist attacks on American soil,
including the Oklahoma City Bombing and the attacks of 9/11, law
enforcement professionals emphasize the seriousness of terrorism as an
issue that can strike anywhere, anytime. The notion that terrorism has
come to the United States and that its impact is felt locally, even when
the perpetrators originate from abroad, justifies that decisive action has
to be taken. It is stressed that the distinct possibility has to be taken
into account that terrorist acts can be perpetrated in smaller towns and
jurisdictions, especially because the goal of terrorism—to instill fear—
can be even more efficiently met by targeting unsuspecting communities.
Any "soft targets in the American heartland" are therefore argued to
be in need of special security protection from local law enforcement
(Henry 2005:161).

Second, the most discussed theme among police professionals
addressing counterterrorism among local law enforcement is the need
to establish and/or expand effective systems of cooperation and inter-
agency communication. It is emphasized that police agencies should

transcend their traditionally carefully guarded jurisdictional borders and overcome any existing inter-agency rivalries. The officials involved, therefore, have to come together around a common goal that is built on their shared understanding of the nature of the terrorist threat and the best ways for law enforcement to respond. Such cooperation is favored across the board, that is, among local police agencies, across functionally specialized agencies, such as between police and firefighters, and vertically between local agencies and federal law enforcement. Moreover, law enforcement efforts have to rely on support from civil society as well, both from the community of citizens and from the political leaders in state and local government.

Third, law enforcement professionals emphasize intelligence work as among the key functional adjustments of local policing. All law enforcement is based on information about crimes that have been committed or crimes that are likely to be committed. However, the role of proactive police methods is different in the case of terrorism because counterterrorism intelligence involves a more routine collection of information, irrespective of whether there is a specific threat or occurrence of a crime. Such intelligence capabilities are typically not well developed among police agencies, especially those at the local level. Yet, because of the devastating impact terrorist attacks may have on a community, a focus toward intelligence-led policing involving proactive surveillance and inquiries is emphasized as an important complement to existing reactive measures. Additionally, such intelligence needs to be shared widely in the law enforcement community, both horizontally among local agencies and vertically with relevant federal organizations in the law enforcement and intelligence communities. Gathering intelligence, local law enforcement agencies have the advantage of being in close proximity to their communities, including the neighborhoods where sympathies toward terrorist groups and ideologies are more likely to develop.

Trends and Variations in Local Counterterrorism Policing

Judging from the themes that are emphasized in the professional law enforcement literature, the counterterrorism policing reorganizations that have taken place in New York City perfectly harmonize with the adjustments that are suggested by the law enforcement community. Particularly noticeable are the organization of specialized counterterrorism divisions, the emphasis that is placed on intelligence activities, and the extended cooperation in which the NYPD participates. The case of New York City might thus lead to a conclusion that professional theories of counterterrorism policing have been readily implemented by local law enforcement organizations. However, a more complicated picture must be sketched of the local counterterrorism situation in the United States.

On the basis of available scholarly research, it can be observed that much variation exists in the degree and manner in which local police agencies have responded to the terrorist threat, although there has generally been an increase in counterterrorism activities.[9] During the 1990s, local agencies were generally not prepared to deal with terrorist attacks. However, after the events of September 11, local agencies at the state, county, and municipal levels had made several adjustments to bolster terrorism preparedness. Besides a general increase in counterterrorism activities at the local level, however, many variations can be observed depending on the size and scope of the agency (and the jurisdiction) involved. Generally, the shift towards counterterrorism functions brought about changes in the internal structure of police organizations (specifically the creation of specialized divisions focused on counterterrorism) only in larger cities and at the state level.

The case of New York City is prototypical of the changes that have taken place in counterterrorism policing in other large metropolitan areas of the United States. The Los Angeles Police Department (LAPD), for instance, oversees a specialized Counter Terrorism and Criminal Intelligence Bureau that focuses on terrorism and other major crimes.[10] In 2006, the LAPD was the first municipal police to establish a so-called Joint Regional Intelligence Center (JRIC), in Norwalk just outside of Los Angles, that offers an integrated intelligence network for local and federal agencies.[11] The California JRIC would be the first of 38 such centers across the country, but it remains to date the only one to have been established.[12] In March 2008, the LAPD further bolstered its counterterrorism mission through a National Counterterrorism Academy for the training of personnel from local law enforcement agencies.[13]

Figure 5.2 NYPD officers at the site of the World Trade Center, New York City, October 19, 2001. Despite being directly affected by the terrorist attacks of 9/11, the NYPD also assisted in the recovery and rescue operations at the World Trade Center and additionally worked with other agencies in the criminal investigations. (Photo by Andrea Booher/FEMA, courtesy of the Federal Emergency Management Agency.)

Developments in counterterrorism policing have taken place across the many towns, cities, counties, and states of the United States, in locales ranging from individual states—whether they be big, such as the state of New York,[14] or small, such as South Carolina,[15]—to large cities, such as Philadelphia[16] and Miami,[17] and the smallest of towns[18] and college campuses.[19] Yet, besides New York and Los Angeles, there are very few police forces that have established specialized counterterrorism bureaus of any meaningful significance, with most local police concentrating its counterterrorism role on providing information about terrorism and terrorism preparedness to citizens.

The Dynamics of Local Counterterrorism Policing

Examining the central issues of counterterrorism policing at the local level, some observations can be made that confirm the basic findings about the federal dimension discussed in Chapter 4. This correspondence in findings is not surprising, given that both local and federal agencies form part of a wider professional police culture located in the same national context. However, more peculiar are the similarities and variations that exist among local law enforcement agencies in how they respond to the perceived terrorist threat.

The Coordination of Hometown Security?

In the academic literature, it has occasionally been suggested that the general trend toward the adoption of counterterrorism functions among local police can be attributed to a shift toward the strengthening of national security, centrally directed at the level of the executive branch of U.S. government and the departments of Justice and Homeland Security (Davis *et al.* 2004; McArdle 2006). There are indications, indeed, that there exist pressures to co-opt local law enforcement into a comprehensive nationwide and centrally guided counterterrorism strategy. Under the banner of the "war on terror," this coordination of all levels of law enforcement would also involve a centralization and nationalization of local counterterrorism to be in line and aligned with federal efforts. The Patriot Act, for example, calls for increased information sharing between federal and local police (Henry 2005). With respect to funding, the Act indirectly promotes the integration of local law enforcement within a national counterterrorism program by allowing the Federal Office of Justice programs to offer grants and contracts to local police agencies to identify and fight criminal conspiracies. In the Department of Homeland Security, the Office of Domestic Preparedness also dispenses funds to local counterterrorism efforts (Jones and Newton 2005).

Additionally policies from the U.S. federal government have also sought to promote the development of counterterrorism functions at the local level. In November 2001, Attorney General John Ashcroft distributed memorandums to all U.S. attorneys in which he argued that procedures for information sharing and cooperation among local and federal law enforcement agencies should be developed.[20] A program of inter-agency cooperation, the so-called National Criminal Intelligence Sharing Plan, was worked out autonomously by law enforcement executives and intelligence experts at a "Criminal Intelligence Sharing Summit" organized by the International Association of Chiefs of Police in the spring of 2002.[21] The Plan was eventually launched in 2004, with the approval of Attorney General Ashcroft.[22]

Though lamented by some critics as further proof of the all-overpowering growth of a post-9/11 surveillance state (McArdle 2006) and applauded by others (Davis *et al.* 2004), the underlying assumption in the above explanation of the generalized drift toward counterterrorism functions among local police agencies is that law and policy, formulated at the federal level and additionally coordinated through local governments and offices, effectively determine the course and outcome of related police activities. There is, however, no evidence to suggest that this is the case. On the contrary, though the policy and legal frameworks to promote counterterrorism coordination with local law enforcement are meant to apply across the nation, the variation that exists among local counterterrorism policing is not guided by any legal or political considerations. Instead, rather than being justified on the basis of political directives or legally defined frameworks, the policing of terrorism at the local level is based on a professional understanding of the means and goals of counterterrorism .

Thus, as with the policing of terrorism at the federal level, most conspicuous among local law enforcement agencies is the emphasis on setting up efficient systems of counterterrorism policing. The formal rationalization of counterterrorism tasks within a broader framework of crime control is observed from the creation of specialized counterterrorism bureaus and the assignment of officers to terrorism-related activities, the emphasis on technological systems of counterterrorism, especially with respect to information exchange, and the increased reliance on cooperation agreements with various levels of law enforcement. The targets of these activities are, therefore, conceived in terms of terrorism as crime. As a result of this depoliticized understanding, importantly, local police in different towns, cities, and states will implement counterterrorism measures differentially.

The Localization of Counterterrorism

Research on the variations that exist among local law enforcement agencies in matters of terrorism has identified several aspects of varying local conditions that exist in shaping the law enforcement response.

Specifically, community characteristics (Jones and Newton 2005), funding opportunities (Marks and Sun 2007), locally varying crime conditions (Harris 2006) and, especially, the historical tradition of localism in U.S. policing (Erickson, Carr and Herbert 2006; McArdle 2006; Thacher 2005) have been forwarded to account for variation in local counterterrorism policing. What is particularly noteworthy about these explanations is that legal and political developments are not mentioned. Instead, distinctly societal factors related to crime and crime control, conceived in professional terms from the viewpoint of law enforcement, are argued to shape counterterrorism policing at the local level.

Revealing the relevance of regional persistence in counterterrorism policing, what matters most to local law enforcement are the locally distinct conditions of terrorism as a crime. The police agencies of large metropolitan areas are focused on terrorism because the perceived risk level is high. Conversely, police departments in smaller towns and cities will remain primarily focused on crimes other than terrorism because these concerns are more relevant to the security conditions in their respective communities. Therefore, also, the police departments of some of the largest and most globally oriented cities, in the United States and in other parts of the world (Fussey 2007; Nussbaum 2007), will engage to a considerable extent in international activities as part of their counterterrorism missions. In the case of the NYPD, international counterterrorism efforts are consequently relatively pronounced because of the international nature of the city of New York and its accompanying terrorism concerns. Conversely, U.S. cities that lack the global characteristics of New York may not adopt the counterterrorism principles practiced by the NYPD even though they are confronted with the same political and legal pressures.

Also a function of the relevance of crime conditions rather than political agendas is the fact that crimes other than terrorism remain of much more concern to local police anywhere, even in the case of large metropolitan police departments. From the viewpoint of an efficient management with respect to the central functions of police to control crime and maintain order, it is evident that the counterterrorism functions of local police must be "tempered by the everyday issues confronting the police in communities across the country" (Donnermeyer 2002:348). As

Figure 5.3 Participants of a "Regional Response Coordination Center Top Officials" exercise, Seattle, Washington, October 16, 2007. Officers from municipal and state agencies cooperate with federal agencies in counterterrorism training programs, such as this exercise in Seattle in which some 15,000 officers participated. (Photo by Marvin Nauman/FEMA, courtesy of the Federal Emergency Management Agency.)

in the case of federal enforcement agencies, slogans related to the war on terror are routinely used by local law enforcement officials to publicly express a commitment to the fight against terrorism, but they do not meaningfully contribute to shape the police response. Thus, regional persistence in the case of local counterterrorism policing exists because of the combined influences of "the functional autonomy of these law enforcement agencies and the highly decentralized nature of American policing" (Henry 2005:151).

Resistance as Professionalism

The lack of cooperation in inter-agency arrangements involving local police indicates that variation in counterterrorism activities among local police agencies can also imply resistance against certain efforts. In this respect, a striking event occurred in Portland, Oregon, where the municipal police force in 2005 withdrew from participation in the local JTTF (Erickson *et al.* 2006). Among community groups in Portland, concerns had been raised about the overly broad surveillance powers that would be given to local police officers through participation in the FBI-controlled JTTF and the fact that local officials would not be able to oversee the activities of the city police agents cooperating with the FBI. These feelings were amplified after FBI agents arrested seven Muslim Americans in the Portland area in October 2002 and April 2003.[23] The arrests, now known as the case of the "Portland Seven," not only angered Muslim leaders in the local Oregonian community but also fueled anxieties about the potential of counterterrorism police efforts to violate civil rights and rely on racial profiling tactics, as some analysts have argued (Swan 2006). In 2005, newly elected mayor Tom Potter led an effort to withdraw the Portland Police Bureau's participation from the JTTF, citing "irreconcilable differences with how the Federal Bureau of Investigation has operated in a post–Sept. 11 world."[24]

The Portland case indicating local resistance against cooperation with (and controlled by) federal law enforcement is confirmed by experiences with the use of proactive surveillance methods in Dearborn, Michigan (Thacher 2005). The city of Dearborn has one of the highest concentrations of Arab-Americans in the United States and has therefore been particularly subjected to counterterrorism efforts. In the days after the attacks of 9/11, local police prepared for retaliations against Arab-Americans, a problem that plagued many cities in the United States (Henderson *et al.* 2006). Soon thereafter, however, federal migration officials began intense surveillance programs, including random interviews, of recently arrived immigrants in the Dearborn area. The local police department was generally reluctant to play a part in these efforts, and only one Dearborn police officer was assigned to the local JTTF.

The Portland and Dearborn cases show that there can be resistance from within law enforcement to political and legal plans to direct local counterterrorism. In the case of immigration policy, likewise, politically directed plans in some jurisdictions (with large migrant populations) to influence local counterterrorism policing have met with resistance in opposition to the top-down nature of control (McArdle 2006). The withdrawal of the Portland Police Bureau from the local JTTF is no exception in this case because the actions by mayor Potter (a former Portland police chief) expressed only, at the political level, the professional attitudes that already existed among law enforcement. And as the case of Dearborn showed, local law enforcement will resist cooperation in migration control efforts, even though there are no legal obstacles (Kobach 2005), out of fear for the damage it can bring to their public reputation and legitimacy (Thacher 2005).

The resistance of local law enforcement to cooperate in federally guided counterterrorism efforts can thus be attributed to a general reluctance by police agencies to be dictated by political and legal directives and, additionally, the strong localism that is deeply ingrained in the U.S. system of policing against any intrusion by federal agencies. Whereas the federal level of law enforcement may face pressures only from (federal) law and policy, local police agencies are doubly exposed to pressures from law and policy (at either the federal and/or local level) and from federal law enforcement. It is, therefore, not surprising that complaints are often made against the one-way direction of information flow in cooperation agreements with federal agencies. As the coordination of local law enforcement in counterterrorism cannot be ensured top-down (through legislation, executive action, or federal control), the bureaucratic autonomy of law enforcement necessitates the development of internal policies and guidelines (Donnermeyer 2002). Such agreements would have to be developed on the basis of a condition of equality among the participating agencies if they are to be effective.

Conclusion

How the counterterrorism issues of efficiency, cooperation, and intelligence are articulated in the organization of law enforcement at the local level varies considerably because of locally specific conditions that are relevant from the viewpoint of a professional understanding of crime, including terrorism, and the control thereof. In large metropolitan areas, such as New York and Los Angeles, counterterrorism policing has since 9/11 been approached in more elaborate ways, although other crimes besides terrorism always remain primary. In the jurisdictions of America's towns and smaller cities, there is generally a continuation of police practices focused on crimes other than terrorism. Cooperation with federal law enforcement is welcomed at the local level only when such cooperation exemplifies a state of equality among all participating agencies, a condition that is not always met. In some cases, there can even be resistance from local law enforcement against counterterrorism efforts that are led by federal agencies.

What these findings suggest is not only that counterterrorism is multidimensional in being composed of developments in politics, law, and law enforcement but that there are variations in the extent and nature of counterterrorism practices within the police community. These conditions not only differentiate those agencies that are more engaged in counterterrorism from those that are less involved but indicate the factions that may exist among police because of regionally varying crime conditions and their relevance for police work. The variations in the local police involvement in counterterrorism work is a manifestation of the regional persistence that exists in police cooperation activities and that, as the next chapters will show, is also strongly revealed at the international level.

PART III
INTERNATIONAL DIMENSIONS

6

THE GLOBALIZATION
OF COUNTERTERRORISM
POLICING

Although the attacks of September 11 took place on American soil, the events of that day also resonated on a global scale. This chapter addresses major aspects of national systems of counterterrorism from around the world. Necessarily selective, this analysis focuses on important issues and themes that unite and differentiate national experiences in counterterrorism. The national systems of counterterrorism are reviewed in terms of the totality of their components and their interconnectedness. From this review, it should be possible to tease out the police dimensions in national systems of counterterrorism in relation to their variable political, legal, and other relevant components and, thereby, to draw some sensible conclusions on the global counterterrorism experience since September 11.

At the Borders of 9/11: Canada

One theme that can be observed in virtually all national systems of counterterrorism is the tremendous impact of the events of 9/11. No matter how close or remote a country may be in geographical and other respects to the United States, its counterterrorism approach changed considerably after 9/11. A useful illustration of this phenomenon is the counterterrorism situation in the northern neighbor of the United States. Although Canadian society and government are in many ways different from the United States, Canada has undergone counterterrorism adaptations since September 11 that have involved several similar developments in matters of policy, law, and police.

Canada has historically been relatively free from terrorist problems and, until recently, had not developed major counterterrorism instruments.[1] The main exception to Canada's tranquility in matters of terrorism came from the violent actions of the separatist movement of the Front de Libération du Québec (Front for the Liberation of Quebec) that was particularly active from the early 1960s to the early 1970s. With the general spread of international terrorist movements from the 1990s onward, Canadian institutions redirected and accelerated their counterterrorism missions. Since the attacks of 9/11, furthermore, these efforts have been taken to a new level, including heightened cooperation with the United States, as international (jihadist) terrorism has shifted from the periphery to the center of Canada's security policy.

The major organizations involved in Canada's counterterrorism measures include the Royal Canadian Mounted Police; the Canadian Security Intelligence Service; Citizenship and Immigration Canada; and the Canada Border Services Agency. Since 2003, these agencies are integrated in a newly established ministerial department called Public Safety Canada (French: Sécurité publique Canada).[2] Resembling the U.S. Department of Homeland Security, Public Safety Canada is accompanied on the legal level by an Anti-Terrorism Act that was passed in November of 2001. Generally corresponding to the Patriot Act in the United States, the Act relies on an expanded understanding of terrorism offenses to provide Canadian police and intelligence with new tools of surveillance and investigation.[3]

Though resembling developments in the United States, recent adaptations to Canadian counterterrorism have taken place in a framework that is distinct in terms of the structure of policing and intelligence, specifically the fact that Canada has a national police next to a domestic intelligence service. The Royal Canadian Mounted Police (RCMP) is Canada's police at all governmental levels, national, federal, provincial, and municipal, in all Canadian provinces and territories except for Ontario, Quebec, and Newfoundland and Labrador, which have their own police.[4] The RCMP resided in the Department of Justice until it was transferred to Public Safety Canada when that department was created. Exemplifying its move toward counterterrorism, the RCMP presently lists terrorism as one of its priority assignments, second only to organized crime.

The domestic intelligence function in Canada is since 1984 secured by the Canadian Security Intelligence Service (CSIS).[5] The relation between Canada's domestic intelligence and police functions is primarily shaped by the intelligence service's lack of arrest powers, for which it must rely on the police. Until 9/11, the CSIS would work exclusively with the RCMP, but it currently also collaborates directly with local police forces. It is not only different from the situation in the United States that Canada has a domestic intelligence service separated from law enforcement (unlike the integration of both functions in the FBI), Canada also has no specialized exterior intelligence force (like the CIA), although the CSIS has acknowledged to operate outside Canadian borders as well.

Besides having augmented their intelligence and investigative activities, Canadian counterterrorism agencies have also strengthened inter-agency cooperation. Within Public Safety Canada, newly formed Integrated National Security Enforcement Teams (French: Équipes Intégrées de la Sécurité Nationale) bring together officials from various Canadian police forces at the national and local level. Internationally, Canadian security organizations also engage in cooperative arrangements, especially with U.S. agencies, in matters of immigration and border security. Canada thus acts as a partner in collaborative bilateral efforts that, as discussed in Chapter 4, are also favored in the United States. However, besides cooperation with the United States, Canada is also involved in multilateral counterterrorism partnerships and has generally been favorable to diplomatic efforts or military interventions that meet with broad international support, such as in Afghanistan (see Chapter 10).

Domestic Intelligence and Police: The United Kingdom and France

Besides Canada, there are other countries that have domestic intelligence services that are organizationally separated from law enforcement and external intelligence and military institutions. These domestic intelligence services are typically also involved with proactive work oriented at preventing terrorism and other forms of public unrest. The most outstanding characteristic of these services is not only that they focus on intelligence-gathering activities within a country's borders but that they have no police powers of arrest. The latter authority remains reserved for law enforcement agencies, with which domestic intelligence services entertain special relations. Two interesting cases of such an organization of intelligence and law enforcement are the United Kingdom and France.

In the United Kingdom, terrorism issues were for a long time dominated by the problem of nationalist groups seeking Irish independence, in particular the violent exploits of the Irish Republican Army.[6] Since 9/11, however, there has been a distinct shift in counterterrorism policies and practices toward a focus on Muslim extremists and jihadist groups related to or inspired by al-Qaeda. The reality of these concerns was most tragically revealed on July 7, 2005, when bombs exploded on three London underground trains and a city bus. Followed by other incidents, such as the second series of bombings targeted at London's transportation system on July 21, 2005, which claimed no casualties, the plot to blow up jet airliners from the United Kingdom to the United States, which was foiled by UK police on August 6, 2006, and the Glasgow International Airport attack on June 30, 2007, whereby a car loaded with gas canisters was driven into the airport's main terminal, it is clear that jihadist terrorism has found roots in the United Kingdom. Yet, as in many other countries, it was nonetheless the impact of 9/11 that was felt most strongly in shaping the United Kingdom's counterterrorism strategies.

Although the United Kingdom has had long-standing legal instruments in place to deal with terrorism (especially in view of the Irish problem), the events of 9/11 heavily influenced British counterterrorism law and policy. A new Anti-Terrorism, Crime and Security Act was passed by the British Parliament in November, 2001 as a direct result of the September 11 attacks. The Act allows for an expansion of various counterterrorism powers. Since the Act became law, additional legal measures have been taken in the United Kingdom to further strengthen counterterrorism activities. In 2006, a new Terrorism Act, initially drafted in the aftermath of the 7/7 London bombings, became law to create additional terrorism-related offenses.

Unlike the United States and Canada, the United Kingdom has not developed a new coordinating counterterrorism department at the cabinet level. However, special policy measures have been taken to streamline the counterterrorism activities of relevant British agencies, especially through the Counterterrorism Strategy that is overseen by the Home Office to coordinate a multitude of agencies involved with various aspects of counterterrorism.[7] Also resembling the situation in the United States, the United Kingdom has implemented a threat level warning system (that differentiates between low, moderate, substantial, severe, and critical levels).

As in Canada, counterterrorism functions in the United Kingdom are handled by a domestic intelligence agency and by the police. The United Kingdom's domestic intelligence service, the Security Service (better known as MI5), is part of a group of intelligence agencies that also comprise the Secret Intelligence Service (MI6), which is responsible for intelligence from abroad, and the Government Communications Headquarters, which specializes in the interception and decoding of electronic communications with intelligence significance.[8] In the 1970s and 1980s, when counterterrorism efforts were primarily focused on Irish separatist terrorism, the United Kingdom's intelligence services and police (and military) forces had responsibilities in counterterrorism. Police functions in the United Kingdom are decentralized into a multitude of territorial police agencies. Most famous among these regional police forces is the Metropolitan Police Service, headquartered at New Scotland Yard, which is responsible for the greater London area.

Since the events of 9/11 and the rising concern over jihadist terrorism, UK counterterrorism efforts have developed greatly in both intelligence and law enforcement. MI5 has expanded its counterterrorism focus to include a multitude of extremist groups and threats to national security. In the post–9/11 era, also, local police forces across the United Kingdom have been focusing in varying degrees on terrorism matters. Absent a national police, the Metropolitan Police Service has strengthened its coordinating and investigative roles in counterterrorism, particularly through a newly created Counter Terrorism Command.[9] Also known as SO15, the Counter Terrorism Command is not only involved with investigating terrorist incidents but adopts a proactive approach by gathering and analyzing intelligence on terrorism and extremism.

As in Canada and the United Kingdom, France also has a domestic intelligence service with counterterrorism functions separate from

Figure 6.1 Members of the City of Montreal Police Service at an anti–police brutality demonstration in Montreal, Quebec, March 15, 2009. As in the United States, coordination among local and federal or national police is a central concern in many nations. Critics fear that such a coordination for counterterrorism purposes might also affect other police tasks, such as crowd control during public demonstrations, which thereby may become seen as terrorist-like behavior. (Photo by the author.)

law enforcement. However, specific to the French situation is that domestic intelligence coexists with a national and strongly centralized police system.[10] The country wherein the term *terrorism* was originally introduced during the Reign of Terror after the French Revolution, France has had (more recent) experiences with terrorism since the 1960s and 1970s, when various separatist movements and politically extremist groups caused unrest. Because of the French colonial involvement in Algiers, terrorism with ties to Islamic groups has also been a relatively long-standing concern.

In matters of counterterrorism law and policy, France has generally moved from a reactive strategy to a preventive approach in the wake of growing concerns over Islamist fundamentalist groups since the 1990s. In 1995, for example, three separate bombing incidents took place in France, killing eight people and injuring more than 100, activities that were claimed by the Groupe Islamique Armé (Armed Islamic Group). On September 10, 2001, French authorities began inquiries into a suspected terrorist attack against the United States embassy in Paris and a munitions depot in Belgium, leading to several arrests later that month. In line with these internal developments but especially after the terrorist attacks of September 11, new counterterrorism measures have been taken, and existing measures have been expanded.

French counterterrorism legislation dates back to a 1986 law specifically addressing the fight against terrorism, which was passed as part of the French penal code.[11] The law was amended in 1996 after the 1995 bombings and again after the attacks of 9/11, in November 2001, when a separate law on "everyday security" (*sécurité quotidienne*) was passed. The French law generally authorizes broad surveillance and investigative measures. After the bombings on mass transit systems in Madrid, Spain, on March 11, 2004, and in London on July 7, 2005, an additional law was passed concerning the terrorism and new security measures.

The central agencies involved in implementing France's counterterrorism policy are both intelligence and police organizations. Unlike the Canadian model, the French national police is highly centralized in two forces. The Police Nationale (National Police), which used to be called the Sûreté Nationale (National Security), is the major civilian police agency, with primary jurisdiction in cities and large towns.[12] The Gendarmerie Nationale is more military in style and has primary jurisdiction in France's smaller towns and rural areas. It is administratively part of France's armed forces under the Ministry of Defense, although it is since 2002 operationally attached to the Ministry of the Interior for its activities within French borders.[13]

France's domestic intelligence agency is the Direction de la Surveillance du Territoire (DST, Directorate of Territorial Surveillance).[14] Its Central Intelligence Directorate, which is responsible for terrorism, cooperates with central command of the national police and with its equivalent in the Gendarmerie. Cooperation between domestic intelligence and police is coordinated through a central Anti-Terrorist Fight Coordination Unit (Unité de Coordination de la Lutte Anti-Terroriste).

Counterterrorism functions are also independently taken on by France's police forces. Besides the DST, the French National Police oversees a Central Directorate of the Judicial Police (Direction Centrale de la Police Judiciaire), one division of which is responsible for counterterrorism. Further, within the two national police systems of France there are special units for terrorism intervention: the Groupes d'Intervention (Intervention Groups) and Recherche Assistance Intervention Dissuasion (Research, Assistance, Intervention, Deterrence) in the National Police, and the Groupe d'Intervention in the Gendarmerie.

With a centralized security system dating back to Napoleonic times, French law enforcement and intelligence activities in terrorism-related affairs have generally not received much popular resistance or public concerns over civil liberties and individual rights.[15] Accounting for this curious passivity are the emphasis placed on strengthening France's security and affirming French national identity and the dual influences of the growth of Muslim or Arab populations in France and the rise of so-called Islamophobia.

European Variations: The Netherlands and Spain

The cases of Canada, the United Kingdom, and France reveal that local conditions in the perceptions of the terrorist threat and differences in the existing security instruments within nations affect the measures that are developed. On the European continent, the Netherlands and Spain present interesting cases of national systems of counterterrorism because of these countries' very different historical experiences with terrorism.

The Netherlands has historically been among the nations of Europe that did not experience any major terrorist issues and, therefore, also had not developed significant counterterrorism measures.[16] However, this situation has changed since the terrorist attacks of 9/11, when the Dutch government announced a comprehensive Action Plan on Counterterrorism and Security (Actieplan Terrorismebestrijding en Veiligheid). In response, the Dutch national police of the Royal Military Constabulary (Koninklijke Marechaussee) was strengthened to step up its border-control activities.

In 2004, after the murders of Pim Fortuyn and Theo van Gogh, Dutch counterterrorism efforts were further formalized. The Dutch politician Pim Fortuyn was assassinated in 2002 by a radical animal rights activist because of Fortuyn's purported anti-Islamic views. Theo van Gogh, a filmmaker and friend of Fortuyn, was killed in 2004 for the same reason by Mohammed Bouyeri, a Dutch citizen of Moroccan descent. Later that year, the Netherlands adopted a new terrorism law, the Law on Terrorist Crimes (Wet Terroristische Misdrijven), in line with terrorism-related decisions by the European Union (see Chapter 8). Both Dutch police and intelligence forces have since expanded their counterterrorism capabilities, particularly in view of jihadist terrorism.

As elsewhere, counterterrorism coordination has been a key concern in the Netherlands. A new position of National Anti-Terrorism Coordinator (Nationaal Coordinator Terrorismebestrijding) was established in 2004 to analyze intelligence and develop policies on terrorism. To facilitate inter-agency communications, furthermore, two coordinating committees have been created: the Joint Committee for Combating Terrorism (Gezamenlijk Comité Terrorismebestrijding) to coordinate counterterrorism policy and the Coordinating Committee for Combating Terrorism (Coordinerend Overleg Terrorismebestrijding), which is centered on operational coordination.

In sum, unlike nations that strengthened their already existing counterterrorism measures after 9/11, an entirely new model of counterterrorism was built up in the Netherlands. The traditional image of the Dutch police as a service agency has thereby been subject to a sharpening of its security functions. The situation is quite different in Spain, where terrorism has been an enduring concern, especially because of the activities of the Basque separatist group ETA (Euskadi ta Askatasuna, meaning Basque Homeland and Freedom).[17] Since its establishment in 1959, members of ETA have engaged in violent actions at least until 2003, causing many hundreds of fatalities. Besides continued actions from ETA, Spain experienced a devastating terrorist attack on March 11, 2004, when jihadist extremists exploded a series of bombs on the Madrid railway system.

After the transition to democracy after the end of the Franco dictatorship in 1975, terrorism is in Spain constitutionally regulated in Article 55 of the Spanish Constitution, which states that fundamental rights and liberties can be suspended in case of a state of emergency or during terrorism investigations. The attacks of 9/11 led to new legislative efforts, although Spain already had counterterrorism laws in place well before that time, mostly to deal with ETA. In the post–

9/11 climate, Spanish counterterrorism laws have remained focused on Basque separatism.

The Spanish system of policing consists of three relatively uncoordinated forces. The Civil Guard (Guardia Civil) is primarily responsible for law enforcement in rural areas. The National Police Corps (Cuerpo national de Policia) is responsible for urban areas and engages in major detective and investigative activities. The Municipal Police (Policia Municipal) is organized locally and deals predominantly with minor offenses. Before 9/11, counterterrorism police measures in Spain were already intense, involving both monitoring activities and repressive law enforcement actions. Special counterterrorism units were established in the National Police (the Grupos Especiales de Operaciones) and the Guardia Civil (the Unidades Antiterroristas Rurales). Occasionally, counterterrorism duties in Spain have also been assigned to military forces but not for internal security issues. From the early 1980s onward, the Guardia Civil has been favored as the preferred counterterrorism agency.

Since the Madrid bombings, Spain's multiple counterterrorism institutions are directed through a national center for anti-terrorism coordination. After 9/11, the focus shifted somewhat toward proactive measures and, since the Madrid bombings, toward jihadist terrorism, although the response remains largely focused on violent Basque separatism. Interestingly, although Spain elaborated its terrorism laws after September 11, it did not take any additional legislative steps after the Madrid bombings.

Inside the Muslim World: Turkey and the Arab States

As international terrorism has today come to be conceived primarily in terms of the threat from jihadist extremism, it is useful to expand the international scope of this investigation to countries in which the majority of the population is Islamic and national history has been shaped by the Muslim religion. It is in this respect interesting to contrast the secular state of Turkey with some of the Arab states of the Middle East.

Beyond the Bosporus, the state of Turkey has a long history of dealing with terrorism, primarily because of the activities of the

Kurdish separatist movement PKK (Partiya Karkerên Kurdistan, meaning Kurdistan Workers' Party), the extreme-left Revolutionary People's Liberation Party/Front, and jihadist groups such as the Turkish Hezbollah.[18] Among Turkey's counterterrorism measures, the "Law No. 3713 on the Struggle Against Terrorism" was passed in 1991. Because the 1991 law already defined terrorism very broadly and had enabled the development and use of counterterrorism measures by many security institutions, the September 11 attacks did not lead to any legal adaptations in Turkey. What Turkey's government has done in recent years, in fact, is to legally guarantee more freedoms to bring the Turkish legal system closer to the standards of the European Union, in which Turkey is seeking membership.

Counterterrorism tasks in Turkey are assigned to law enforcement, intelligence services, and the armed forces. The Turkish system of law enforcement consists of the Turkish National Police, which has law enforcement jurisdiction in the cities, and the military law enforcement force of the Jandarma, which is primarily responsible for the rural areas. Both the Turkish Police and the Jandarma have counterterrorism functions, whereas intelligence functions are maintained by a separate National Intelligence Agency (Milli Istihbarat Teskilati). Turkey's armed forces also engage in counterterrorism activities, mainly against the PKK.

The secularism of the Turkish state and the country's predominantly Muslim population consisting of Kurdish and other ethnic groups have combined to create peculiar difficulties in Turkey's counterterrorism. Within Turkey, special cooperation problems exist because the strongly secularist military generally distrusts the Turkish National Police, which it suspects of harboring Islamic sympathizers. Members of the police, in turn, resent the condescension they feel from the military.

Internationally, counterterrorism cooperation between Turkey and other nations has suffered because of the generally ruthless, if effective, manner in which Turkish institutions have suppressed terrorist activities at the expense of respect for human rights and freedoms.[19] Yet, effectively bringing the Turkish terrorism experience closer to the concerns of other nations has been the fact that Turkey has been involved in counterterrorism operations against al-Qaeda. The reality of the jihadist terrorist threat hit Turkey most distinctly

Figure 6.2 Bombing of the Khobar Towers in Dhahran, Saudi Arabia, June 25, 1996. Terrorism is a concern that many nations across the world are confronted with. Creating a scene of destruction eerily similar to the Oklahoma City bombing, the terrorist attack against the Khobar Towers was targeted at the foreign military personnel that were housed there. It was also among the first attacks by Islamic fundamentalist groups on Arab soil. (Photo courtesy of the U.S. Department of Defense.)

on November 15 and 20 of 2003, when al-Qaeda militants exploded four truck bombs at two synagogues and a bank in Istanbul, killing 57 and wounding 700.

The current fight against international terrorism has a special relevance to the Arab states of the Middle East and Northern Africa. Especially the region of the Middle East, including the post-invasion turmoil in Iraq and the precarious relation between the Arab states and Israel, is of central concern in the internationally oriented counterterrorism strategies that are presently formulated in many, predominantly Western, nations. From the viewpoint of the Arab world, terrorism has also been, and continues to be, of considerable domestic concern, often as a result of actions by the same groups that have engaged in attacks in the West, as a matter there perceived as international terrorism. After the events of September 11, major terrorist attacks have taken place across the Middle East (and elsewhere in the world). Restricted to attacks attributed to al-Qaeda alone, for example, major terrorist activities have been committed in the Arab nations of Saudi Arabia, Egypt, Yemen, Tunisia, Morocco, and Qatar. Arab states have responded to terrorism at the national and regional level by means of legislative efforts and a variety of security practices.[20]

At the regional level, an Arab Convention on the Suppression of Terrorism was adopted by the members of the Arab League in 1998.[21] Yet, there is some variation among Arab nations' respective national laws on terrorism. Some Arab states had already developed anti-terrorist legislation before the Arab Convention. The 1992 anti-terrorist law of Egypt in fact served as a model for the Convention. Likewise, the country of Syria, which the United States considers one of currently six state sponsors of terrorism (along with Cuba, Iran, North Korea, and Sudan),[22] already has had anti-terrorism legislation in place since 1949.

Other Arab states have made modifications to their legislative efforts against terrorism since the terrorist attacks of 9/11. Jordan, for instance, made amendments to its Penal Code in October 2001 by broadening the definition of terrorism adopted from the Arab Convention. Morocco similarly introduced a Law on the Fight Against Terrorism in 2003 that criminalizes terrorism as acts aimed at prejudicing public order by means of intimidation, terrorization, or violence. Also adjusting its criminal code, Tunisia enacted a new anti-terrorist law in 2003, after the 2002 terrorist bombing of a synagogue in the Turkish city of Ghriba, whereby 21 people were killed.

Reviewing terrorism legislation in the Arab world, the national laws that are in place generally correspond, despite some variations, to many of the same principles that can be observed in other nations as well. Terrorism is broadly defined, and corresponding police powers are liberally authorized. However, in view of the generally undemocratic nature of many Arab states, the anti-terrorism laws have been implemented much more resolutely and without many restrictions in terms of civil liberties and individual rights. Still, there has been cooperation between the security agencies of the Arab world and those of Western nations. The U.S. Department of State, for instance, has reported that the United States cooperates in counterterrorism investigations with many countries in the Middle East, including cooperation at the level of law enforcement.[23] Even security forces of Syria (one of the countries on the U.S.–designated state sponsors of terrorism) have been reported to have cooperated with U.S. authorities.

Moreover, besides such bilateral arrangements, cooperation with Arab security forces also occurs on a multilateral scale, for instance through Interpol (see Chapter 7).

Repressive Counterterrorism: Russia

Even more than is the case in some of the Arab states, Russia's counterterrorism practices are extremely repressive.[24] Counterterrorism policing and security measures are in the Russian context steered top-down through a system of strongly centralized political command, vested in the position of the President of the Russian Federation.[25]

Contemporary Russian counterterrorism policies and measures are almost completely oriented at unrests in Chechnya, located in the southwestern part of the former Soviet Union. Chechnya first sought to gain political independence after the collapse of the Soviet Union. The Russian government opposed the move, leading to the first Chechen war between 1994 and 1996. The war led to a factual independence of the Chechen Republic of Ichkeria, but since the second Chechen war, ongoing since 1999, Russia has again taken control of the region and installed a local government favorable to Moscow. The second phase in the Chechen conflict was the result of a series of bombings on apartments in Moscow and the Russian towns of Volgodonsk and Buinaksk in September 1999, whereby 300 people were killed. Russian authorities blamed Chechen militants for the attacks, although no Chechen group has claimed responsibility.

Fighting Russian control in a twilight zone of legitimate rebellion and violent terrorism, Chechen rebels have engaged in violent activities in and against Russia in the form of hostage-takings and bombings. Among the most violent incidents were those in Moscow in 2002 and in Beslan in 2004. On October 23, 2002, pro-Chechen militants took 700 people hostage at a Moscow theater. The situation ended violently 3 days later when Russian forces stormed the building, killing most militants and more than 100 of the hostages. On September 1, 2004, Chechen gunmen occupied a school in Beslan and held more than 1,000 people hostage, most of them children between the ages of 6 and 16 years. Three days later, Russian police and military troops stormed the school, killing many of the rebels and more than 300 civilians.

After the hostage crises in Moscow and Beslan, a new and more stringent anti-terrorism law went into effect in Russia in March, 2006. The new law authorizes the President of the Russian Federation to rely on the military and the Federal Security Service to fight terrorism. The lead role in Russian counterterrorism investigations is placed in the Federal Security Service (Federal'naya Sluzhba Bezopasnosti [FSB]), the successor of the Committee for State Security, better known as the KGB (Komityet Gosudarstvennoy Bezopasnosti). Responsible for intelligence and internal and border security, including counterterrorism, the FSB combines domestic intelligence, police, and border control powers.

Despite the relative harshness of Russian counterterrorism practices, Russian institutions have been able to engage in international cooperation. The FSB is specifically reported to regularly exchange information with the FBI in the United States. In 2004, FBI Director Robert Mueller and FSB Director Nikolai Patrushev signed a memorandum of agreement on counterterrorism to increase information exchange between the two agencies.[26] Besides cooperation at the bilateral level, also, the Russian police engages in multilateral cooperation through Interpol.

The Dynamics of Global Counterterrorism

A number of themes emerge in the global reality of counterterrorism policing. At least two issues deserve special attention. One, the relationship between political and legal measures of counterterrorism on the one hand and the role of law enforcement and intelligence agencies therein on the other are critical in shaping the manner in which counterterrorism measures are implemented. Two, the course and outcome of counterterrorism practices within nations is also greatly influenced by the relationships across nations in matters of the extent and manner in which they cooperate at various levels of counterterrorism. No nation's counterterrorism system today can be discussed in isolation.

The Relative Relevance of Policy and Law

It is important to consider the political, legal, and policing frameworks of individual nations in the global constellation of counterterrorism. It

Figure 6.3 A Russian military honor guard during a wreath-laying ceremony at the Tomb of the Unknown Soldier in Moscow, June 26, 2009. The historical tradition of a strong military in Russia, dating back to Tsarist times and extended during the Soviet era, combines with a heavily centralized political system to produce a very pronounced militaristic style of Russian counterterrorism operations. Even more than is the case in other parts of the world, Russian counterterrorism functions are often overseen by the military rather than the police. (Photo by Chad J. McNeeley, courtesy of the U.S. Department of Defense.)

can generally be observed that the nations of the world have special legislation in place on terrorism. In some nations, anti-terrorism laws have existed for a long time, whereas in other countries, they are of more recent date. Indicating the extent to which these differences in the legal response to terrorism are shaped by local situational factors, nations whose counterterrorism laws are longstanding (e.g., Syria, Egypt, Spain, Turkey) and those where legal developments are relatively new or have been greatly modified in recent years (e.g., Canada, The Netherlands, Russia) may otherwise have very little in common.

Moreover, although variations exist in the precise manner in which terrorism is framed in national systems of legislation and/or constitutional law, terrorism is in the contemporary post–9/11 era almost invariably defined very broadly in terms of violent acts, or the threat of or incitement to violence, that is aimed at a destabilization of the public order. As such, the legal systems in countries that otherwise do not have much in common, such as the Western nations of Europe and the Arab states of the Middle East, have in terrorism found a common theme. Likewise indicating a global trend, more specific descriptions of terrorism are typically not legally formulated, so that terrorism in any nation can be liberally applied to certain groups and activities.

Politically, the nations of the world harbor great differences, ranging from liberal democratic regimes to transitional-mixed systems and various forms of autocratic rule. Important is that, as the foregoing review has shown, these political differences not only shape counterterrorism policies and laws, they impact the implementation of counterterrorism policies because of the variable police and security structures that they bring about. Thus, for instance, the global war on terror as it is conceived in the United States does not differ much from the formally established policies that have been established in countries as different as Russia, the United Kingdom, Turkey, Spain, or France.

However, there is much variation among nations in terms of the manner in which their respective national policies are applied in concrete actions by various agencies. In the United States and in other democracies across much of the Western world, counterterrorist policing practices are framed and bound by restrictions in terms of civil liberties and individual freedoms. No matter the criticisms that can be legitimately raised against counterterrorism policing in countries such as the United States, France, and the United Kingdom, the counterterrorism practices of security and police agencies there do not come close to attaining the level of repression and ruthlessness of counterterrorist practices in states that are less committed to democratic principles of government, such as Russia, Turkey, and many of the Arab states. The global fight against terrorism functions very differently across nations depending on how political and legal objectives can be implemented at the level of policing and security agencies.

Important also is that political variations among the nations of the world account for the degree of bureaucratization police institutions within each nation can enjoy. Therefore, counterterrorism policing is in some nations heavily politicized, whereas police systems in other nations have developed much more autonomously. The dynamics of counterterrorism policing in Western democracies, in particular, harmonize with the principles of bureaucratized institutions, both in terms of the means and objectives of police work. Yet in other states, counterterrorist police practices are heavily determined and controlled by political directives. The clearest case is arguably Russia, where counterterrorism is centrally dictated by the President, but similar conditions can also be observed in Turkey and many of the Arab states. In these countries, counterterrorism often is a tool of political oppression. Counterterrorism police activities in these nations, therefore, also take on a highly militaristic character and are often accompanied, or even dominated, by military operations. Consequently, counterterrorism as a whole is more integrated in those societies wherein military forces, intelligence agencies, and police and other security institutions are under great central political control, unlike the multi-level approaches that are characteristic of democratic societies, wherein multiple organizations are involved in various aspects of counterterrorism with a relatively moderate degree of coordination.

An additional variable in the organization of policing across the world concerns the relation between the functions and organizations of intelligence and law enforcement. The relation between intelligence and police agencies is variable within democratic states and across democratic and autocratic regimes. The existence of separate domestic intelligence services in some states brings about a clearer separation between intelligence and law enforcement activities that is not observed elsewhere. In some nations, moreover, intelligence functions in terrorism matters are additionally subsumed under a military model of counterterrorism as a national security concern. Next to Russia, a typical case of this approach is Israel, where law enforcement and national security goals are very closely interwoven (see Chapter 9). Yet, despite such variations, it is important to note that counterterrorism measures in any one nation always involve both intelligence and law enforcement components, whether they are or are not organized in separate agencies.

September 11 as World Event

Despite variations in the global constellation of counterterrorism, the 9/11 attacks have served as a powerful symbol to step up political, legislative, and police efforts in the fight against terrorism in many countries of the world and, relatedly, to increase international cooperation. After

Figure 6.4 Participants of a global forum on counterterrorism at the Group of Eight (G8) summit, Moscow, November 2006. To the extent that terrorism is perceived as a global problem confronting many nations, it can serve as a catalyst for cooperation. Such partnerships take place intergovernmentally (among the governments of different nations, such as the G8 countries), separate from the counterterrorism strategies that exist at the level of security and police agencies. (Photo courtesy of the website of the G8 Presidency of the Russian Federation in 2006, http://en.g8russia.ru/.)

September 11, most nations passed new counterterrorist agreements and legislation or adjusted existing laws. Reorganizations also took place in counterterrorist policing practices, almost invariably involving an expansion of police powers in terrorism-related investigations and a prioritization of counterterrorism as a mission of enforcement and other security organizations.

Also uniting the countries of the world in a global fight against terrorism, the focus of counterterrorism measures has largely, though never exclusively, shifted toward jihadist extremism, even in the predominantly Muslim countries of the Middle East. As such, the world of national counterterrorism systems indicates the existence of a global constellation of interacting national (and international) systems.

National adjustments in counterterrorism take shape in specific historical settings. Thus, local developments in the terrorist experience, ranging from continued violence from Basque extremists in Spain to sporadic incidents of jihadist-inspired individual killings in the Netherlands, will inevitably determine the extent to which counterterrorism practices are engaged in. Yet, in spite of the relevance of situational differences in terrorist activity, September 11 was a global event. For even those nations that experienced their own high-profile terrorist attacks, such as Spain in March 2004 and the United Kingdom in July 2005, have been influenced more by September 11 in shaping their respective counterterrorism responses.

The attacks of 9/11 have not only shaped the global constellation of counterterrorism in view of the international impact of terrorist activities by members and sympathizers of al-Qaeda but have additionally served as a highly symbolic event that has been used across the globe to conduct counterterrorism actions of distinctly local import within each nation. Revealing a persistence of nationally variable concerns, the nations of the world have each made September 11 their own as a nationalization of a global event that is given meaning in the specific context of the counterterrorism experience within nations.

The need for cooperation and information exchange is an important consideration in counterterrorism activities that is emphasized across the world, both within nations and internationally. Cooperation within nations takes places across and among intelligence and police institutions and related policy and legal institutions. Whether states are more or less centrally organized and more or less democratic in nature, coordinating institutions exist at the governmental and inter-agency level. At least two nations, the United States and Canada, have established new ministerial departments specifically for the purpose of security coordination, whereas most nations have set up coordinating mechanisms within the existing governmental structure. Inter-agency coordination is directed by means of political coordinating bodies in those states where the political control of police and security agencies is high, whereas such coordination is more independently accomplished in nations with highly bureaucratized police agencies.

Internationally, counterterrorism involves mechanisms of cooperation at a variety of levels. A number of legal and political developments have taken place at the level of international governing bodies, such as the United Nations, to shape the move toward a global regime of counterterrorism.[27] Yet, what is particularly noteworthy about these developments of international law is that they have not brought about a standardization of counterterrorism laws across the world and, furthermore, that they have not been influential in determining counterterrorism police operations. With respect to international police cooperation, likewise, United Nations resolutions remain inconsequential, as such cooperation is independently brought about on the basis of the development of counterterrorism strategies at the level of law enforcement and security agencies.

Conclusion

This chapter has reviewed the counterterrorism measures that exist in a number of nations across the world. Despite local and regional variations, the events of September 11 have greatly influenced counterterrorism efforts, even in countries that had no direct connection with the attacks or the subsequent investigations. A trend can be observed toward a greater authorization of special measures to investigate terrorism and gather necessary intelligence. Considering the mechanisms that drive international cooperation against terrorism at the level of policing, emphasis is placed on effectiveness and speed in cooperation, in spite of differences across nations in the structure and form of policing and counterterrorism policies and practices.

Terrorism has in the post–9/11 era served as a symbol that unites nations, even when they otherwise differ from one another in political, legal, cultural, and other relevant respects. The argument forwarded by Peter Manning (2005:24) that democratic policing "eschews torture, terrorism, and counterterrorism" is nonsensical and merely reflects a normative opinion grounded in ideology. In truth, counterterrorism responsibilities in existing democratic and otherwise organized political communities are shared among police, military, and intelligence agencies. Yet, terrorism can hereby not be understood as a uniform construct that is simply shared across the world. Instead, nationally varying conditions of the (domestic) terrorist threat shape the counterterrorist experience along with a nationalization of (international) terrorism as a global reality. In view of the border-transcending nature of terrorism as a problem affecting many nations, international cooperation takes on special significance. Cooperation among police in terrorism matters is in part accomplished by international police organizations, such as Interpol and Europol, which Chapters 7 and 8 examine.

7

POLICING WORLD TERRORISM

The Role of Interpol

As Chapter 6 revealed, the September 11 terrorist attacks in the United States had a ripple effect that could be felt across the world and led to major reorganizations of counterterrorist policing (and other components of counterterrorism) in many countries. Although the nations of the world each have distinct histories with respect to terrorism, the events of 9/11 have served as a critical catalyst for global police reform in matters of counterterrorism. On the international level, these developments can also be observed by the changes that have taken place in matters of international police cooperation at both the bilateral level, directly among police of different nations, and at the multilateral level, as organized through international police organizations. In this chapter, an analysis is presented of the organization and practices of counterterrorism that have been instituted by the International Criminal Police Organization, the organization better known as Interpol.

Interpol and International Terrorism: A Brief History

Interpol is an organization that aims to provide and promote mutual assistance between criminal police authorities within the limits of national laws and the Universal Declaration of Human Rights. Originally formed in Vienna in 1923 as the International Criminal Police Commission, the organization has steadily grown in membership (currently totaling police from 187 nations) but never substantially changed in its structure and objectives (Deflem 2002). By the late 1930s, police officials of the German Nazi regime gradually took control of the organization, and its headquarters was eventually moved to Berlin, where it was institutionally linked to the SS police structure. Absent any meaningful form of international cooperation during World War II, the organization was revived in 1946 at an international police meeting in Brussels, Belgium. The headquarters was then moved to France, where it has since been located, first in Paris and, since 1989, in Lyon. The formal name change to the International Criminal Police Organization, abbreviated as ICPO-Interpol, came about in 1956.

From its inception, Interpol has not been conceived as a supranational police agency with investigative powers but as a cooperative network intended to foster collaboration and to provide assistance in police work among law enforcement agencies in many nations.[1] To this end, Interpol links the central headquarters in Lyon, France, with specialized bureaus, the so-called National Central Bureaus (NCBs), in the countries of participating police agencies. Besides the Lyon headquarters, Interpol also has six regional offices, in Argentina, the Ivory Coast, El Salvador, Kenya, Thailand, and Zimbabwe, in addition to a liaison office at the United Nations in New York.

Communications between the NCBs and the headquarters are conducted on the basis of a specialized color-coded notification system whereby each one of six possible colors represents a specific type of request. Most commonly used are the Red Notices, to request the arrest of a wanted person with a view to extradition, and the Blue Notices, to request information about a person's identity or activities in relation to a crime. Since 2005, an Interpol–United Nations Special Notice has been added for requests concerning groups or individuals subject to United Nations sanctions against al-Qaeda and the Taliban. Although Interpol is a nongovernmental organization, the cooperation with the United Nations through the Special Notice program is enabled on the basis of a 1996 agreement that grants observer status to both organizations in the sessions of their respective general assemblies. Interpol has reached similar cooperation agreements with Europol, the International Criminal Court, and other police and legal organizations.

The objectives of Interpol are confined to criminal enforcement duties at the exclusion of "any intervention or activities of a political, military, religious or racial character," as specified in Article 3 of Interpol's constitution.[2] Despite this restriction, Interpol passed various counterterrorism resolutions to combat terrorism and terrorism-related activities. During the 1970s, Interpol resolutions focused on terrorism-related issues, such as criminal acts conducted against international civil aviation and acts of violence that could "seriously jeopardise general public safety."[3]

Interpol took a more explicit move toward the policing of terrorism in 1983 when the General Assembly meeting in Cannes, France, resolved that a study would be conducted to define Interpol's position regarding criminal acts that resulted in many victims, are committed by organized groups, and "which are usually covered by the general term 'terrorism.'"[4] In 1984, an Interpol resolution passed on "Violent Crime Commonly Referred to as Terrorism" to encourage the member agencies to cooperate and "combat terrorism as far as their national laws permit."[5]

In 1985, an Interpol resolution led to the creation of a specialized "Public Safety and Terrorism" sub-directorate to coordinate and enhance cooperation in "combating international terrorism."[6] After the apparent escalation of terrorism during the 1990s, Interpol stepped up its counterterrorism initiatives. In 1998, at the General Assembly meeting in Cairo, Egypt, Interpol's commitment to combat international terrorism was explicitly confirmed in a "Declaration Against Terrorism," condemning terrorism because of the threat it poses "not only with regard to security and stability, but also to the State of Law, to democracy and to human rights."[7]

Interpol and Counterterrorism Since 9/11

Although terrorism has been on the agenda of Interpol for some time, the terrorist attacks of September 11 have brought about important changes in Interpol's counterterrorism strategies. Interpol has developed a number of new policies that are specifically aimed at terrorism-related investigations. The Interpol headquarters and its relations with the member agencies have accordingly also been reorganized.

Interpol Counterterrorism Policies

A few weeks after the terrorist attacks in the United States, from September 24 to 28, 2001, the Interpol General Assembly held its seventieth meeting in Budapest, Hungary. At the meeting, the General Assembly passed Resolution AG-2001-RES-05 on the "Terrorist Attack of 11 September 2001" to condemn the "murderous attacks perpetrated against the world's citizens in the United States of America on 11 September 2001" as "an abhorrent violation of law and of the standards of human decency" that constitute "cold-blooded mass murder [and] a crime against humanity."[8] It was decided that Interpol and its member agencies should seek to tackle terrorism and organized crime more effectively and that the highest priority be given to the issuance of so-called Red Notices (international Interpol warrants to seek arrest and extradition) for terrorists sought in connection with the attacks.

In October 2001, Interpol held its Sixteenth Annual Symposium on Terrorism, the first Interpol meeting on terrorism after the events of September 11. It was attended by some 110 experts from 51 countries, and various new long-term counterterrorism initiatives were discussed. The renewed focus toward terrorism was confirmed in October 2002, at the Seventy-First General Assembly meeting in Yaoundé, Cameroon. Acknowledging September 11 as a catalyst in the development of global approaches to crime, the Assembly attendants agreed to draft a list of security precautions for the handling of potentially dangerous materials (such as letters and parcels that might contain anthrax), and bio-terrorism was specified as deserving special attention.

Interpol's current policies on terrorism build on a formal set of "New Guidelines for Co-operation in Combating International Terrorism" that was drawn up in 1998 to explicitly address the relationship of terrorism to Article 3 of Interpol's Constitution, forbidding Interpol to undertake matters of a political, military, religious, or racial character.[9] The key element of the guidelines is that terrorist incidents are broken down into their constituent parts, only the criminal elements of which can be subject to police investigations.[10]

Additionally indicating the inclusive manner in which Interpol treats terrorism is its current policy on membership in a terrorist organization. Until a few years ago, Interpol had a policy in place that specified that the decision to circulate information via the Interpol headquarters always had to be based on intelligence indicating that an individual might be involved in a terrorist offense, rather than that the individual merely was a member of some particular group. Effective November 18, 2003, however, it was decided that a Red Notice for arrest and extradition can be issued for suspected members of a terrorist group, providing strong evidence of such membership. The policy change has been justified because membership in a terrorist organization is by itself considered a criminal offense in an increasing number of nations.

To achieve its counterterrorism aims, Interpol has set up a number of new specialized programs.[11] Interpol can deploy an Incident Response Team from the headquarters to provide investigative and analytical support services upon the request of a member agency. Additionally, a Fusion Task Force was established in September 2002 to assist member agencies in terrorism-related investigations, particularly by identifying members of terrorist organizations, collecting intelligence, and providing analytical support on wanted and suspected terrorists.

Interpol also pays special attention to the financing of terrorist activities, because it is assumed that the frequency and seriousness of terrorist attacks are often proportionate to the amount of financing terrorists receive. Interpol's emphasis on financing is aided by the fact that Interpol Secretary General Ronald K. Noble, the organization's chief executive (and an NYU Law School professor), has a long-standing interest in monetary crimes as former Undersecretary for Enforcement of the U.S. Department of the Treasury and president of the Financial Action Task Force, a 26-nation agency established to fight money laundering.

Among Interpol's most recent policies concerning terrorism, it was decided at the Interpol meeting in Berlin, Germany, in 2005 to draw special attention to the use of the Internet by terrorist groups and individuals.[12] Interpol encourages the international coordination of communications concerning police investigations on Web sites used for terrorism-related purposes. At the General Assembly meeting in Rio de Janeiro, Brazil, in 2006, furthermore, it was decided to strengthen international police cooperation in matters pertaining to the global spread of al-Qaeda–linked or al-Qaeda–inspired terrorist groups and individuals.[13] The Interpol headquarters are particularly encouraged to

Figure 7.1 Interpol wanted notice, September 2006. Among its activities, Interpol issues Special Notices for individuals and groups associated with al-Qaeda and the Taliban. Listed in the middle at the top of the list shown here is Osama bin Laden, who is mentioned as being wanted by the United States, Spain, and Libya. (Photo courtesy of Interpol.)

be used by the member agencies to request assistance from the Incident Response Team.

The Impact of September 11

How did the terrorist attacks of September 11 fall within the scope of Interpol's objectives? The clearest answer to this question came from Interpol's Secretary General, Ronald Noble, who in his opening speech to the Seventieth General Assembly in Budapest emphasized the global, non-political dimensions of the September 11 attacks. Noble not only referred to the fact that citizens from more than 80 countries were among the casualties but argued that though the terrorist attacks took place on U.S. soil, "they constituted attacks against the entire world and its citizens."[14] Likewise, the Interpol Resolution agreed upon in Budapest also made reference to the September 11 attacks as having been directed "against the world's citizens."[15] At a special session of the Financial Action Task Force in Washington, DC, on October 29, 2001, Noble emphasized that the attacks targeted the World Trade Center, which "thus represented the world by name."[16]

Although Interpol recognized that the FBI was handling the primary investigation of the acts of September 11, many investigative leads spanned the globe, and many of Interpol's member agencies have been involved with the investigations. Interpol members have issued Red Notices for a number of terrorist suspects through Interpol's international communication network and have published them on the organization's Web site to give them as wide a circulation as possible. Immediately after the events of September 11, Interpol issued 55 Red Notices for terrorists believed to have been connected to the attacks. After 9/11, Interpol also increased its circulation of Blue Notices, of which 19 concerned the hijackers who carried out the September 11 attacks. At least some national police agencies cooperated with Interpol's requests. On September 25, 2001, for instance, Egyptian police authorities posted a Red Notice for Aiman Al Zawahry, a leader of the Al Jihad terrorist group and considered bin Laden's right hand man.[17]

After September 11, Interpol reorganized in several key respects, although some of these organizational changes had already been planned some time before. After the creation of an "11 September Task Force" at the Interpol headquarters to ensure cooperation with the FBI, a permanent General Secretariat Command and Co-ordination Center was instituted. Additionally, a new Financial and High Tech Crimes Sub-Directorate was created that specialized in money laundering.

In April 2002, the Interpol headquarters announced the creation of an Interpol Terrorism Watch List to provide direct access for police agencies to information on fugitive and suspected terrorists who are subject to Red, Blue, and other notices. On June 22, 2001, Interpol established a system for member agencies to automatically enter information into and retrieve information from a database on stolen blank travel documents. Additionally established is an Interpol "Stolen and Lost Travel Document" database, presently containing some 11 million documents from 97 countries.[18] The database is accorded special significance as a tool useful to track down the movement of terrorists across national borders.

Further seeking to enhance its information-sharing capabilities in the wake of 9/11, Interpol has established a new encrypted Internet-based Global Communications System, called "I-24/7." This communication system is meant to provide for a rapid and secure exchange of data among Interpol's member agencies. Operational since 2003, the I-24/7 system allows for the searching and cross-checking of data submitted to Interpol by the organization's members over a private network system that transmits encrypted information via the Internet.

The I-24/7 communications system supplements the agreements Interpol has reached with other international police and security organizations to extend the reach of their respective efforts. In November 2001, for example, Interpol signed an agreement with Europol to foster cooperation in the policing of terrorism and other international crimes. In December 2001, Interpol and the U.S. Department of the Treasury similarly pledged to cooperate more closely and create an international database of organizations and persons identified as providing financial assistance to terrorist groups. In March 2002, Interpol reached an agreement to cooperate closely with the Arab Interior Ministers' Council to facilitate the exchange of information with the Arab police community. Other such cooperative agreements have been established with local police organizations, such as the New York Police Department.[19] And since 2008, Interpol cooperates with the two counterterrorism units that were established in the *Domenico Gianai*, the gendarme corps of the Vatican.[20]

The Dynamics of Interpol Counterterrorism

Related to the perspective introduced in this book that police agencies are subject to bureaucratization processes and that there is a persistence of nationally variable concerns in international police work, two issues emerge as central from this analysis. One, because of Interpol's structure as a cooperative organization, the limitations and characteristics of the various police systems of different nations continue to be revealed when they engage in border-transcending international work. And, two, technological developments and concerns of efficiency are primary considerations in establishing international organizational structures of counterterrorism, oftentimes even overriding the ideological antagonisms on terrorism as a politically volatile issue.

The Boundaries of Interpol

The fact that Interpol brings together police of different nations without creating a supranational police force demonstrates that national concerns affect international cooperation among police of different nations. By its very nature, Interpol serves in the "limited capacity of a communication network system to assist local law enforcement in locating terrorists" (Carberry 1999:706). Additionally, local developments and unilaterally executed transnational police operations typically outweigh international police cooperation on a multilateral scale. As a result, the famous international criminal law scholar, Cherif Bassiouni (2002), argues that Interpol is simply not effective because "major powers, like the United States, do not fully trust it" (p. 93). In the days after the attacks of 9/11, FBI officials were indeed reported to "have been loathe to share sensitive information" with Interpol, instead preferring unilaterally conducted operations.[21] Furthermore, the fight against international terrorism is less likely to be effective when no or only limited cooperation exists with the intelligence community and counterterrorism instead remains restricted, as in the case of Interpol, to police agencies.

Recognizing these limitations, Interpol places most emphasis on a smooth coordination of and direct contacts between the various participating police agencies. Only a few days after September 11, Interpol Secretary General Noble flew to New York and Washington to meet with U.S. police chiefs and plead for international cooperation. Also, during his speech in Budapest, Noble stressed that the concrete steps that had to be taken to expand Interpol's counterterrorist role would have to be "beginning in each of our home countries."[22] He added that Interpol needed "each country's commitment to use our systems and to fill our databases," but that, regrettably, "many countries consider

Interpol too slow." Despite repeated pleas to member agencies to take more advantage of Interpol's databases, cooperation has generally been limited.[23]

Police support at the national level is not self-evident, particularly not in cases involving politically sensitive matters. This was clearly shown in the case of a former Chechen government representative, Akhmed Zakayev, for whom an Interpol warrant on charges of terrorism was distributed on the request of Russian authorities. The Chechen envoy was released by Danish authorities in 2002, because no evidence was found against him. Thereafter, the Chechen citizen was also released on bail from a London prison.[24] In spite of such cases of international friction, however, Interpol emphasizes the cooperation that can exist among the police of nations that are very divided in political respects. For example, when Argentinean officials in 2007 sought the arrest of six Iranians in connection with the 1994 bombing of a Jewish community center in Buenos Aires, in which 85 people were killed, Interpol issued Red Notices.[25] Although Iranian authorities condemned Interpol's action as having been pressured by the United States and Israel, Interpol Secretary General Noble praised Iran for its cooperation.[26]

An additional consequence of the persistence of nationality in international police work is the fact that international terrorism has mostly remained a matter regulated, policed, and prosecuted at the national level or on a more limited multilateral scale. This accounts for the development of international counterterrorist initiatives that are independent from Interpol, such as those instituted by Europol, and the international efforts that originate from within individual nations. Although Interpol's role in counterterrorism is more significant today than it ever was before, the police agencies of many countries tend to prefer working on a unilateral or limited cooperative basis rather than taking advantage of participation in the international organization.

In multilateral matters of counterterrorism policing, the United States has typically played a leading and dominant role that has also affected the work of Interpol. As Ethan Nadelmann (1993) argues, U.S. police agencies have influenced Interpol to become a more effective organization and promote U.S. law enforcement concerns, including improvement of international cooperation in Interpol and its member agencies in matters of "terrorism and the financial aspects of drug trafficking" (p. 185). Police agencies from the Western industrialized world also strongly influence Interpol's agenda on terrorism, specifically by shaping its focus on jihadist extremists. Strikingly, for instance, in the immediate period after September 11, documents in the Arabic language were always listed first on the pages of the Interpol Web site and all of its official reports. Although Arabic was together with English, French, and Spanish already one of Interpol's official languages, the prominence accorded to the language in the post–9/11 years clearly shows that international police organizations such as Interpol reflect the relative weight of national police agencies on the international scene and the resulting focus on terrorist groups of Arab descent. This focus on Islamic terrorist groups has led to an emphasis in Interpol's counterterrorism programs on citizens of certain countries, often with distinct ethnic characteristics, which in turn can bring about problems with respect to civil and human rights.

Figure 7.2 Interpol Secretary General Ronald Noble attending a meeting of the G8, St. Petersburg, 2006. Interpol's chief executive, Ronald Noble, has ironically been among the victims of an ethnic bias in counterterrorism operations as he has experienced having been singled out at airport checks because of his appearance as an African-American. In a 2003 interview, Noble explained: "I know that I've been searched because I look like a person who could be Arabic if I'm traveling from an Arab country—or I could be a drug-trafficker if I'm coming from a drug-trafficking country" ("Interpol Chief Slams Abuses in War on Terror," by Mark Trevelyan, Reuters, October 2, 2003). (Photo courtesy of the Web site of the G8 Presidency of the Russian Federation in 2006, http://en.g8russia.ru/.)

Toward Global Police Efficiency

Looking at Interpol's counterterrorism policies, a remarkable emphasis is placed on technology in formulating the proper police response to international terrorism. The centrality of technology in international counterterrorist policing is seen as a necessity in response to the use of new technologies by contemporary terrorist organizations, which are argued to be highly sophisticated in terms of scope and methods of operation and are also said to rely on high-tech means of communication and financing to recruit new members and organize attacks. Aided by such technical developments, a relatively high degree of internationalism and cross-border activity characterizes many present-day terrorist groups.

Additionally, there is an independent technological drive in (international) police work based on the means rather than the objectives of policing. Language barriers, poor inter-agency communications, and aged equipment among police are seen as hindering police investigations. Likewise indicating the sharp emphasis on technological issues, separate concern in counterterrorism goes to bio-terrorism, the use of computers, and the financial assets of terrorist groupings. All these factors betray an emphasis on the technological means at the disposal of terrorist groups and the likewise technically sophisticated manner in which counterterrorist police strategies should respond.

Demonstrating the emphasis on technology at Interpol is the creation of the specialized counterterrorism Command and Coordination Center, the new sub-directorate specialized in sophisticated financial crimes, new computerized databases, and the newly instituted I-24/7 communications system. The technological focus in counterterrorism does not necessarily imply that employed means are effective and that the instruments Interpol has developed to promote cooperation are actually used by participating agencies. Interpol Secretary General Noble has in fact admitted that the sharing of information among the police agencies throughout the world is not always easy, because national agencies do not want to jeopardize their investigations.

Noble further acknowledged that Interpol's "communication system... is antiquated, clumsy to use."[27] Until recently, the circulation of Red Notices occurred by regular mail. Even though a received Red Notice could be processed and translated into Interpol's four languages within a day, the Interpol headquarters would then mail photocopies back to member agencies, using the cheapest and lowest-priority mail service. It could take weeks, even months, before the Red Notices would reach their destination. Changes were made after September 11 to move to an electronic communications system. During the first 10 months of 2002, about half of all (968) Red Notices were transmitted electronically, albeit to only 42 member agencies. Some NCBs are not aware of the benefits of the electronic system, and others do not have the necessary technical infrastructure.

Related to the technological emphasis in the means of counterterrorist policing is a de-politicization of terrorism as the target of police activities. Because terrorist activities by definition contain a political element in terms of their motive, it has been argued that Interpol cannot be authorized within the parameter of its own constitution, especially Article 3, to exchange information regarding political terrorists (Bassiouni 2002). However, terrorist incidents are de-politicized by Interpol (and its participating police agencies) to become the foundation of shared systems of information on which international cooperation can be based. Politically sensitive crimes, such as terrorism, can also be broken down into several components, only the criminal elements of which (e.g., homicide, bombings, illegal weapons trade) are taken as the focus of international police investigations. Therefore, though it is legally problematic that terrorism is defined differently across the nations of the world, police agencies of various countries can agree to accept their common task to focus on terrorism, whatever its more precise legal specification in any one country.

From the perspective of a de-politicized understanding of terrorism, it becomes understandable why Interpol manages to attract cooperation from police agencies representing nations that are ideologically very diverse and not always on friendly terms in political respects. In January 2002, for example, Interpol decided to donate communications equipment to the Cuban police to better coordinate its counterterrorist operations. According to Secretary General Noble, the technology transfer was in part the result of the cooperation agreement Interpol had signed with the U.S. Treasury Department concerning matters of the financing of terrorism.[28]

Similarly revealing the politics-transcending nature of international counterterrorist police work is the fact that shortly after the Iraqi invasion, authorities from France and the United States agreed to cooperate toward the development of biometric techniques to prevent the forgery of passports as part of their efforts against terrorism, despite these countries' profound disagreements over the Iraqi conflict.[29] On the occasion of the signing of the agreement, U.S. Attorney General John Ashcroft also visited the Interpol Headquarters in Lyon to attend an international conference aimed at stepping up the recovery of Iraqi works of art stolen in the aftermath of the fall of the Saddam regime. Thus, international efforts at the level of police agencies and organizations, such as Interpol and its member agencies, can be based on a common ground surrounding terrorism through its treatment as a de-politicized crime.

Conclusion

Interpol has undergone significant changes since September 11 as part of a renewed and vigorous effort to more efficiently organize international police cooperation against the terrorist threat. New systems of information exchange among police across the world have been instituted, and policy resolutions have been developed to offer a foundation to these new counterterrorist arrangements. Important is that concerns of efficiency and technical sophistication in international police work are emphasized. In the wake of September 11, Interpol drastically modernized some of its technical apparatus and further built on the communications facilities it has been developing for many decades among a growing number of member agencies. By criminalizing terrorism, furthermore, Interpol seeks to develop counterterrorist programs that can be participated in by police institutions from countries across the world irrespective of the ideological justifications of and sentiments about terrorist activities. Interpol's treatment of terrorism as a criminal matter reflects the impact of a professionalized global police culture.

Given the collaborative model in which Interpol's 187 member agencies participate, it remains unclear to what extent the organization can effectively determine the course and outcome of counterterrorist police efforts. Relative to the activities undertaken by the police agencies of the more powerful nations across the world, Interpol's efforts are rather minimal. Particularly in matters of terrorism, police organizations prefer unilateral strategies and cooperative efforts on a more limited scale. Additionally, Interpol also coexists on the international level of counterterrorism policing with other, regional police organizations such as Europol.

8

POLICING TERRORISM IN EUROPE

The Role of Europol

Besides Interpol, other international police organizations also focus on terrorism-related investigations, the development of which has been considerably impacted since the events of 9/11. Among the regional organizations aimed at fostering international police cooperation is the European Police Office (Europol), the police organization that was established to promote cooperation among the law enforcement agencies of the European Union (EU). The idea of a European police was originally conceived in the Treaty on the European Union in 1992. Limited operations of a European police office began in 1994 with an emphasis on drug enforcement, which was later extended to cover organized crime. In 1998, the Council of European Union Ministers formally approved an extension of Europol's mandate to include counterterrorism. Also already agreed upon was the creation of a specialized counterterrorism unit within Europol, which eventually was set up shortly after 9/11.

Europol presents an interesting case because of the dual forces that affect the organization in terms of the political control that is exerted via the regulative bodies of the EU on the one hand and the institutional autonomy and professional expertise that marks the international police organization and its participating police agencies on the other. Unlike other international police organizations, Europol was not formed from the bottom up by police professionals but was the result of a top-down decision by the political and legislative bodies of the EU. Europol's operations are also supervised by the political representatives of the EU.

Yet, despite Europol's unique status, this analysis will show that the police organization is nonetheless characterized by a high degree of autonomy to determine the means and specify the objectives of its policing and counterterrorist programs. Primarily geared at instituting an efficient system of information sharing among police, Europol conceives of its counterterrorism functions on the basis of professional standards of policing. Before analyzing Europol's counterterrorism activities, it will be useful to first briefly describe its history and structure.

The Organization of Europol

The establishment of Europol was first agreed upon on February 7, 1992, in the Treaty on the European Union, also called the Maastricht Treaty after the town in The Netherlands where the treaty was signed.[1] Article K.3 of the Treaty concerned the "Establishment of a European Police Office," specifying the new body's governance structure and its function to facilitate cooperation among the police of the EU member-states. On January 3, 1994, Europol started limited operations in The Hague, The Netherlands. On July 18, 1995, a Europol Convention was formally drawn up in Brussels, and the Convention came into force on October 1, 1998 upon ratification by all member states.[2] Europol commenced its full range of activities on July 1, 1999.

Based on the provisions of the Europol Convention, Europol aims to improve the effectiveness of and cooperation among the police authorities of the EU member-states to prevent and combat serious international organized crime. Europol's specific areas of criminal investigation include the illicit trafficking of drugs, vehicles, and human beings (including child pornography); the forgery of money; money laundering; and terrorism. Priority is given to these crimes when an organized criminal structure is involved and when the criminal activity involves two or more member-states of the EU. As of January 1, 2002, the mandate of Europol has been expanded to deal with "all serious forms of international crime," including organized robbery, swindling and fraud, computer crime, and corruption.[3]

Similar to the structure of other international police organizations, Europol is not an executive police force with autonomous investigative powers. Instead, Europol's activities are oriented at facilitating communications among, and supporting selected activities of, the police organizations in the participating states. To this end, so-called Europol Liaison Officers are seconded to the Europol headquarters in The Hague, whereas each member-state of the EU designates a particular agency to act as the Europol National Unit or contact point for Europol communications.

Among its most important instruments, Europol manages "The Europol Computer System," which was set up in accordance with the Europol Convention's specification that Europol would maintain a computerized system for the analysis of data within a framework that would also include protections in terms of human rights and a proper supervision of the stored data.[4] Additional databases include the EU Customs Information System, which provides customs agencies the ability to exchange information on smuggling, and the FIDE (an acronym for "Fichier d'identification des dossiers d'enquêtes douanières," Identification File of Customs Investigations), which provides information on subjects involved in a criminal investigation.

Europol ensures cooperation among police of all 27 EU member-states, although participation in Europol is not automatic upon membership in the EU. A new member-state must first adopt the Europol Convention and subsequently send notification of its intention to join Europol to the EU. The 10 states that joined the EU in May 2004, for example, did not all become members of Europol until July 1, 2005, when Estonia formally joined the police organization. Each member state sets up a Europol National Unit and seconds officers to the Europol headquarters in The Hague.

Europol is governed by a directorate consisting of a director and three deputy directors. The EU Council of Ministers for Justice and Home Affairs appoints the director for a 5-year period, renewable once for 4 years, and the deputy directors for a once-renewable 4-year period. The Council also adopts the Europol budget and acts as a control and regulatory body over Europol by each year forwarding a report to the European Parliament to document the work of Europol. The European Parliament must also be consulted if provisions of the Europol Convention or any other Europol regulations are to be amended.

Supervision of Europol's day-to-day operations is undertaken by a management board, which reports to the EU Council of Ministers of

Figure 8.1 Max-Peter Ratzel (third from left), then Director of Europol, meets with EU political leaders, May 2005. Unlike other international police organizations, most notably Interpol, the activities of Europol are directly overseen by the political body of the European Union. Europol is thus a unique police organization in being placed between politics and bureaucracy. (Photo copyright Europol, courtesy of the European Communities).

Justice and Home Affairs. Finally, Europol is also guided by a Joint Supervisory Body that is composed of appointed representatives of the national supervisory bodies in the member states. The task of the Joint Supervisory Board is to ensure that the rights of the individual are not violated by the handling of data that are managed through the Europol channels.

Europol and Counterterrorism

European efforts to control terrorism have a relatively long history.[5] In 1975, the Terrorism, Radicalism, Extremism, and International Violence group (or TREVI group) was formed by European police officials to exchange information and provide mutual assistance on terrorism and related international crimes. Beyond TREVI, unified Europe created additional cooperative arrangements to combat terrorism, such as the Police Working Group on Terrorism and the Counter Terrorist Group (CTG) or so-called Club of Berne, both of which provide for cooperation in terrorism matters next to Europol.

Corresponding to the developments in the United States and many other nations across the world, the events of September 11, 2001 served as an important catalyst in the development of Europol's counterterrorism programs. A few months after 9/11, a specialized counterterrorism unit, the Counterterrorism Task Force (at some point called the Task Force Terrorism) became operational at the Europol headquarters. A year later, the specialized unit was incorporated into Europol's Serious Crime Department, but after the terrorist bombings in Madrid on March 11, 2004, the Task Force was reestablished as a separate entity. It has since again been brought under the Serious Crime Department as the (Europol) Counter Terrorism Unit.[6]

The events of 9/11 heavily influenced formal counterterrorism policy in the EU. Among the most important of the newly instituted EU policies are the so-called framework decisions on terrorism and related matters, such as joint investigation teams and mutual legal assistance, that were agreed upon by the Council of the European Union in June 2002.[7] The Council framework decisions define terrorist offences as criminal activities, or the threat to commit them, aimed at seriously intimidating a population, unduly compelling a government or international organization from performing or abstaining from any act, and/or seriously destabilizing or destroying the fundamental structures of a country or of an international organization. In matters of police cooperation, the EU framework decisions call for an improvement of cooperation among the counterterrorism units of the EU member-states. To this end, joint investigation teams can be set up by the security forces of two or more EU member states for a specific purpose and for a limited period. Among the requirements, the leader of the team operating in any one EU country must be from that country, and the team must always abide by the laws of the member state in which it operates. A newly introduced European Arrest Warrant allows for the handing over of wanted persons directly from one member-states' judicial authority to that of any other EU state.[8]

The EU framework decisions of 2002 also proposed an elaboration of Europol's counterterrorism mandate and related international cooperation activities. The international police organization has since been formally allowed to maintain relations with police and security forces outside the EU. At present, Europol maintains agreements with Interpol and several countries, including Canada, the United States, Russia, and Turkey. Some of the non-EU agencies cooperating with Europol have liaison officers at the headquarters in The Hague, whereas Europol, in turn, maintains liaison offices abroad, such as in Washington, DC. The agreement between the United States and Europol was originally drafted after September 11 and renewed after the March 11 terrorist bombings in Madrid, when the EU drafted a new "Declaration on Combating Terrorism" that reaffirmed the 2002 framework decisions.[9] Additional counterterrorism police powers were formally approved by the EU in April 2008, when measures were agreed upon to allow police to cooperate with Internet service providers to shut down Web sites that have been used to incite violence.[10]

The Dynamics of Europol Counterterrorism

Reviewing the structure and activities of Europol, an important duality can be noted in the manner in which the police organization relates to the formal political structure of the EU on the one hand and the organizational and operational components of the organization on the other. Europol is an international police organization that is formally mandated by the EU and overseen by the regulatory bodies of the EU. At the same time, Europol coordinates activities among National Units drawn from existing police and security agencies in the EU member-states. These agencies are highly bureaucratized in respect of the knowledge and know-how of their enforcement duties, which will also influence the workings of Europol as a collaborative organization. In terms of its operations and objectives, Europol's activities are indeed primarily guided by concerns over efficiency on the basis of a broadly understood mandate. Europol's operations, furthermore, are framed within the context of the interests of the EU and its participating national states, involving a "Europeanization" of counterterrorism.

Europol in the European Union: Legality and Expertise

The framework of Europol as a body formally sanctioned within the political structures of the EU creates certain opportunities that other international police organizations lack. Most distinctly, inasmuch as

Europol's mandate is legally specified, the organization has a clearly defined and limited field of operations. Relatedly, Europol can also rely on formal agreements of cooperation with the various participating police institutions and their respective national governments and formally maintain external agreements with non-EU states. In the history of international policing, the formal status of membership in Europol is one of the organization's most outstanding characteristics, as other organizations of international policing, such as Interpol, rely only on informal resolutions, typically in the form of a memorandum of understanding.

The formal legality of Europol also poses restrictions to the organization's operations. In the aftermath of the terrorist bombings that hit Madrid in March 2004 and London in July 2005, for instance, the Council of the European Union failed to have several proposals to enhance counterterrorism implemented at the level of the member states. Among the few concrete results of the EU Ministers' counterterrorism efforts has been the creation of a new "EU Counterterrorism Coordinator," a position currently held by the Belgian Gilles de Kerchove d'Ousselghem.[11] However, though counterterrorism cooperation at the political level may remain an expression of goodwill with little consequences, police and security agencies can and do achieve cooperation in practical matters. These accomplishments are in part achieved by European counterterrorism officials gathering at meetings separate from the EU Ministers, such as those that were held after the Madrid and London bombings.[12]

Though the formal legal framework set by the EU's governing bodies places limits on the autonomy of Europol, the organization also maintains relations with countries outside the EU. Although Europol's international cooperation agreements have to be approved by the EU Justice and Home Affairs Ministers, they are initiated by Europol's Management Board. Europol's agreements with other police organizations have distinct implications in terms of the organization's autonomy as an international police body. The cooperation between Europol and Eurojust, the European prosecutorial office, originally located in Brussels, Belgium, and now moved permanently to The Hague, harmonizes with the fact that Europol and Eurojust are both formal EU-sanctioned organizations.[13] However, other cooperation agreements enable Europol to expand its scope beyond the formally proscribed mandate of the EU. For example, Europol cooperates with the CTG that was formed after 9/11.[14] Unlike Europol, the CTG was formed at a professional level by the heads of the police and intelligence services of the EU member-states. Importantly, the CTG does not operate in terms of a formal mandate by the EU but on the basis of a memorandum of understanding that was drafted and agreed upon by the participating heads of police. Cooperating with the CTG, Europol can, therefore, route information more quickly.

Europol entertains agreements (similar to the one it has with the CTG) with other police organizations that are marked by a high degree of bureaucratic autonomy, such as Interpol and the (European) Police Chiefs Task Force (PCTF).[15] The PCTF is a European police cooperation network that (like the CTG) is not regulated on the basis of an explicit EU treaty and has no formal accountability to the Union but was instead formed on the basis of a recommendation from the European Council in October 1999. The cooperation between Europol and the PCTF concerns several counterterrorism issues, such as the operational analysis of "Islamic Extremist Terrorism," terrorism threat assessments, the financing of terrorism, and weapons of mass destruction. As such, Europol's formal status as an international organization in the political framework of the EU is supplemented by an independent structure of international cooperation at the bureaucratic level of police institutions. Besides cooperation agreements, the interlinking of multiple international police organizations is also accomplished by overlapping memberships in their respective leadership structures as members of national police forces in Europe also simultaneously serve in international organizations such as Europol and the PCTF.

Europol as Bureaucracy

Despite Europol's origins in the context of an international political union, the organization's policing and counterterrorism operations are organized in the rationalized terms of an efficient crime control model. Europol relies on the participation of existing police institutions in the EU for the staffing of the headquarters and the Europol National Units in the 25 member states. Personnel at the headquarters and in the

Figure 8.2 Informal meeting of the EU Ministers of Justice and Home Affairs, January 2005. As the European Union is primarily a political organization that unites the governments of 27 European states, its ministers meet regularly to address important issues. In matters of forging counterterrorism cooperation, however, these ministerial meetings are often not effective in shaping counterterrorism strategies at the level of police and security. One of the investigating judges in the 2004 Madrid terrorist bombings summed up the problem well when he complained that the political goodwill to enhance "cooperation and coordination in the fight against terrorism... generally lasts no longer than the duration of the symposium" ("EU Terror Chief Positive on Improving Cooperation," BBC Monitoring International Reports, October 7, 2004). (Photo copyright www.eu2005.lu/Luc Deflorenne, courtesy of the European Communities).

National Units is typically made up of experts in international policing with prior experience participating in nongovernmental international police organizations. Europol's recruitment of police professionals from existing national police and intelligence agencies may seem obvious, but the implication of this reliance is nonetheless that the international organization can operate only within the context of an existing professional culture of policing.

Besides the creation of a specialized Counter Terrorism Unit, the relevance of instrumental rationality in Europol can also be observed in the organization's emphasis on efficiency in police operations. Primary emphasis is placed in Europol's crime-fighting activities on establishing swift methods of communication and information exchange among the participating agencies. Most distinct in this respect has been the creation of Europol as a cooperative network with a central headquarters that functions to enable rapid communications among the various National Units. The practical advantages of such a structure are considerable from an efficiency-oriented viewpoint as the participating agencies need not contact one another directly but can route information via The Hague to be passed on to all other member-agencies. Europol communications with the National Units rely on the latest advances in technology by means of an "Information Exchange System" that enables encrypted electronic messages.

Europol's emphasis on efficiency in cooperative matters can also be observed in the various agreements the organization oversees with non-EU states. Europol's liaison office in Washington, DC, for instance, functions to ease cooperation with the various law enforcement agencies in the United States. It does so directly in police matters that concern the United States and two or more member-states, and it handles requests to U.S. police from the National Units in the EU member-states. Europol cooperation with local and state police agencies in the United States is accomplished via the U.S. National Central Bureau, the U.S. representative of Interpol.[16] Similarly indicating the concern with efficiency in communications, Europol officials have expressed concerns that some of the newest member-states (the so-called accession states, such as Estonia and Lithuania) do not possess the necessary infrastructure to effectively participate in international police cooperation (Storbeck 2003).

Among the implications of police bureaucratization in terms of efficiency, it is important to note that police agencies cannot only independently determine the proper means of policing, they can specify the objectives of police work given a broad and generally formulated mandate of crime control. In the case of Europol, the relative restrictiveness of the organization's formal mandate can be evaded by relying on existing police agencies in the EU and broadening the organization's membership by cooperating with other international police organizations and the agencies of non-EU nations. As a result, Europol can rely on a well-developed international police culture, in Europe and across the world, which has for a long time forged international relations on the basis of a common understanding of the function of police. Therefore, also, Europol's participating agencies and those with whom Europol cooperates will typically be able to agree on the scope of terrorism-related activities, despite the diversity of the legal systems of the EU member-states (Tak 2000).

What is most remarkable given the range of institutions that cooperate with Europol is not that problems occasionally ensue but that there has been a trend toward the development of a shared understanding of terrorism across European police, especially since the events of 9/11. Much as has been the case with police organizations in the United States and other parts of the world, Europol's counterterrorism focus has gone most centrally to "Islamic extremist terrorism" or "fundamentalist jihadist terrorism."[17] In a Europol terrorism-trends report of December 2004, al-Qaeda and its affiliates are mentioned as a main security concern against European and Western interests.[18] Other terrorist groups Europol focuses on include the separatist Basque group ETA, the Real IRA, Bosnian and Chechen nationalist groups that organize in Austria, and extreme leftists and anarchist groups in Italy, Germany, and elsewhere. These assorted terrorist groups are similarly targeted by Europol because of the impact their activities have on European societies, irrespective of any political motivations. Harmonizing with the comprehensive definition of terrorism in the EU framework decisions, Europol and its participating agencies focus on terrorism very broadly in terms of the commonalities terrorist activities have as crimes rather than political offenses.

Europol in Europe: The Boundaries of International Cooperation

A marked persistence of nationality in international policing affects Europol's cooperation efforts. Although the establishment of a Europol National Unit is required for all EU member-states once they have joined Europol, the organization and staffing of the Units are entirely up to the member-states. Information exchange with the Europol headquarters, also, is voluntary, and the level of involvement from the various National Units in Europol varies greatly from one country to the next.

Differences in the level of participation in Europol are not surprising inasmuch as police agencies can be expected to be involved in international activities to a degree that is determined by their experience with relevant criminal problems. However, indications are that other factors play a role as well and that even in the case of international terrorism and organized crime—problems that effectively cross national boundaries—cooperation is not always easily accomplished. A sense of trust among police and an expectation of positive outcomes are among the central concerns in international cooperation irrespective of the availability of technologically advanced communication systems. In the absence of these prerequisites, police agencies may be reluctant to share information even when they formally participate in international organizations such as Europol. Europol officials themselves have conceded that cooperation could be improved. After the 2004 bombings in Madrid, then–Europol Director Jürgen Storbeck criticized the EU member states for paying mostly "lip service" to the international organization.[19]

A lack of cooperation among Europe's counterterrorism forces has occasionally been revealed. For instance, after a Moroccan citizen who used to live in Hamburg, Germany, was arrested by Italian authorities in April 2003 because of his association with a Milan-based al-Qaeda cell, it turned out that the man had already been questioned by German police just a few weeks after the 9/11 attacks. Information about the suspect, however, had not been shared among Europe's police.[20] Such findings indicate that police agencies remain concerned primarily with nationally defined enforcement tasks, even when these tasks involve crimes of an international nature.

Though indications are that Europe is facing a growing number of internationally organized militant organizations, agencies in the EU states are generally reluctant to share information on a multilateral scale and instead tend to engage in more limited bilateral cooperation. The preference for bilateral cooperation is most noticeable in the relations between Europol and the FBI. Despite the cooperation agreement between Europol and the United States, the FBI prefers to conduct its international cooperation directly with the police of the EU member-states in a bilateral context. Whenever a EU member-state contacts Europol with a request to the FBI, the message is not passed on via the Europol Liaison Office in Washington but is routed to the FBI legal attaché in the EU member-state from which the request originates. The police agencies of some member-states, furthermore, have their own liaison officers stationed in Washington, DC, and supplement the Europol system by means of bilateral cooperation with U.S. agencies.

Finally, national and regional persistence in international policing is also reflected in Europol's focus on those terrorist and other criminal conditions that are specific to the EU. The "Europeanization" of international counterterrorism policing is not surprising as the disappearance of Europe's internal borders with the European unification was the primary motivating factors in developing enhanced police cooperation (den Boer 2003). Europol concentrates its efforts, therefore, on Islamic fundamentalist terrorist groups inasmuch as they are active in or otherwise relevant to Europe. In the EU, some countries are targeted because of their involvement in the wars in Iraq or Afghanistan or because of some specific regional factor, such as the ban on wearing conspicuous religious symbols, including the hijab, in French schools. Other counterterrorism matters Europol is involved with are very distinct to the national conditions of some of the EU's nation states, such as the various nationalist terrorist groups that operate in Spain and the United Kingdom. When the Europol headquarters in April 2007 issued a press release to announce the publication of its first "EU Terrorism Situation and Trend Report," it was stated that 498 attacks were carried out "by Islamist, separatist, left-wing and anarchist terrorist groups" in various EU member-states during the year 2006.[21] Of those 498 attacks, however, only 2 involved Islamist terrorism, while the large majority (420 attacks) came from separatist groups active in Spain and in the French territory of Corsica.

Conclusion

Europol is a unique international police organization in having been created by the international governing body of the EU, whereas other international organizations of policing have been formed from the bottom up by police professionals. Europol's dependence on the regulatory oversight capacities of the EU creates a legal framework of police cooperation that can increase the organization's accountability (den Boer 2002) but can also hinder effective cooperation among police, if only because police officials perceive accountability requirements as intrusions on their activities (Alain 2001). Yet, despite being a formally sanctioned institution in the EU, Europol is also dependent on, and a manifestation of, a professional police culture that evolved at the European and broader international level. Broadening its scope beyond the EU, Europol relies on cooperative agreements with professional police agencies inside and outside Europe and with non-governmentally formed international police organizations, such as the CTG and the PCTF. Maintaining relations with such independent police institutions, Europol can rely on police practices in counterterrorism and other areas that have developed on the basis of professional expertise.

Islamic extremist terrorism is conceived by Europol as an international criminal concern that affects security conditions within the EU. Because of the involvement of European al-Qaeda cells in the terrorist attacks of September 11 and in view of the affiliations of the perpetrators of the terrorist attacks in Madrid in 2004 and in London in 2005, these justifications have foundation. Concerns over international and regional terrorist groups can, therefore, be expected to remain important elements in shaping European police efforts.

PART IV
COMPARATIVE CASES

9

UNDERCOVER COUNTERTERRORISM IN ISRAEL

It is not difficult to acknowledge that terrorism issues have special relevance to the state of Israel. Given the country's unique origins and geopolitical development, terrorism and counterterrorism have moved all aspects of Israeli society as in no other place in the world. The policing of terrorism in Israel, therefore, presents a special case in the world of counterterrorism. For it can be expected that the nature and development of the state of Israel have brought about strong political characteristics of counterterrorist police work that stand out among comparable law enforcement organizations in other industrialized democratic states.

This chapter focuses special attention on the organization and operations of one special Israeli counterterrorism force: the Yamas units in the Israeli Border Guard Magav, the combat branch of the Israeli Police. Unlike traditional undercover police tactics aimed at a lengthy probe into a criminal network, the operations of Yamas units typically involve surprise hit-and-run raids targeted at taking out terrorists. The unique characteristics of Yamas undercover counterterrorism are brought out in the context of the development of the state of Israel and the country's long-standing experience with terrorism.[1]

This chapter shows that the development of the Israeli police in general and of the policing of terrorism in the undercover Yamas units in particular is subject to politicization influences related to Israel's centralized government structure and the state's precarious international situation. However, the policing of terrorism in Israel is also shaped by organizational developments that involve an adoption of professional standards of police expertise. Though these organizational developments of counterterrorism always remain framed within a broader security context geared toward the protection of the nation-state, they also indicate the importance of rationalization processes that police institutions are subject to regardless of political conditions.

Bureaucratization and Politicization

It will cause no surprise to posit the Israeli police in close conjunction with the distinctive nature and development of the state of Israel. It can be hypothesized that the police function in Israel is highly rationalized in a purposive sense as the nation is modernized in political and economic respects. In consequence, the Israeli police may be expected to be organized as a professional force. Additionally, however, Israel's specific history can also be expected to have brought about a development of police practices and organizational adaptations that relate to the geopolitical circumstances of Israel as a Jewish state within an Arab-dominated Middle East. Specifically, periods of upheaval, whether sudden and abrupt or of a more enduring nature, will reveal that the autonomy of Israeli policing also depends on the degree to which the police are controlled by government authorities.

The measure of effective political control on the police is determined by the degree of politicization and centralization of society and the continuity of political power (Gamson and Yuchtman 1977). The Israeli police plays a significant political role but is also subject to a professional police subculture. It is, therefore, important to consider that Israeli police institutions (as other state institutions) will be characterized by a relatively high degree of politicization, because the polity in Israel is not only centralized but also dominant. In this sense, the Israeli police is more than usually connected to the state's central government. Besides the political dependency of the Israeli police, however, there will also be organizational developments that shape police work on the basis of professional standards. Yet, because of Israel's geopolitical conditions, the bureaucratization tendencies of the police will remain framed within a broader orientation towards the protection of the state.

Policing Israel

The organization of the Israeli police is historically based on the system of the British Mandate of Palestine that existed from 1922 to 1948.[2] Upon the foundation of the state of Israel, the unitary structure of the British system was maintained in the form of an Israeli National Police with a central police headquarters in Jerusalem and regional districts and subdistricts across the territory. The police function in Israel includes crime control, peacekeeping, service functions, traffic control, and internal security. In the course of its history, the Israeli police adjusted in organizational and functional respects to the changing conditions of Israel's precarious international situation. In 1953, the Border Guard or Magav was set up as a quasi-military gendarmerie force within the Israeli Police to combat infiltrators and patrol Israel's borders. After the Six Day War of 1967, the expanded territory under Israeli control brought about an expansion of police to the eastern part of Jerusalem, Judea and Samaria (the West Bank), Gaza, Northern Sinai, and the Golan Heights. In the West Bank, police sub-districts that were set up were, under military command, staffed by Israeli and local Arab officers.

After the Yom Kippur War of 1973, responsibility for internal security within Israel was handed over to the Israeli National Police. In the late 1980s, the Palestinian uprising now known as the First Intifada led to reinforcements of the Israeli police in Jerusalem and in other main areas of unrest. The Border Guard and the Civil Guard were then enlisted in the execution of regular police tasks. However, when in the early 1990s the Intifada intensified and terrorist bombings increased, the Israeli Police again transferred resources from crime control tasks to internal security functions. The signing of the Oslo Accords in 1993 led to the establishment of a sixth Police District for Judea and Samaria. The Israeli Defense Forces (IDF) redeployment in the West Bank transferred internal security duties in the Lakhish Sub-District to the Israeli Police. Currently, the Israeli Police oversees some 25,000 officers, spread over 6 districts, 10 sub-districts, and about 80 police stations. The Israel Police is commanded by a Commissioner of Police, who reports directly to the Minister of Public Security.

The undercover counterterrorism units of the Yamas (also: Ya'mas; Hebrew: ימ"ס) are organized within the Border Guard Magav. An

Figure 9.1 Qassam rocket destroys home of elderly woman, Sderot, January 4, 2009. The random nature with which terrorist attacks routinely strike Israel is demonstrated most clearly by the Qassam rockets that are regularly fired by Hamas forces from Gaza onto Israeli civilian targets. (Photo by Yehuda Peretz, courtesy of the Israel Project, www.theisraelproject.org.)

acronym for Mishmar Ha-Gvul (Hebrew for "Frontier Guard"), the Magav is in charge of matters of internal security and terrorism (Brewer *et al.* 1988). Magav units are employed in main areas of unrest, mainly in Arab-populated areas, near the Israeli state borders, in Jerusalem, and in the West Bank and the Gaza strip. Since the Israeli disengagement from Gaza in 2005, Border Police and IDF forces have withdrawn from the territory now under Palestinian control, but both military and Magav forces still control the Gaza-Israeli border and have occasionally also undertaken operations in Gaza. The Border Guard consists of professional police officers and soldiers redirected from the IDF, some of them as part of the compulsory military service that all Jewish Israeli citizens beyond the age of 18 are subject to. The service lasts 3 years for males and 18 to 21 months for females.

Since the mid-1970s, both military and civilian forces in Israel have organized counterterrorism units. In 1974, a civilian counterterrorism unit was created in the Magav. Later named Unit Yamam, this force became a specialized counterterror and hostage rescue unit, but it also performs so-called SWAT (special weapons and tactics) duties and engages in undercover police work. After the outbreak of the

Intifada in 1987, several more undercover counterterrorism units were formed in the IDF, in the Magav and, in the mid-1990s, in the Israeli Police as well. Besides Unit Yamam, the Magav presently comprises three additional counterterrorism units: the Matilan, specialized in intelligence gathering and infiltrations interception; the Yamag, a rapid deployment unit for crime and terrorism; and the Yamas, which is in charge of undercover counterterrorism operations.

Israel Undercover: The Organization of the Yamas

The Yamas units in the Magav are among a group of elite Israeli undercover forces that were originally developed in the military.[3] When the First Intifada broke out in 1987, the IDF created two undercover units: the Sayeret Shimshon unit in the Gaza Strip and the Sayeret Duvdevan (Unit 217) in the West Bank. In 1990, the first Yamas units were established for the same two territories: the Gaza Strip Unit Yamas and the Judea and Samaria Unit Yamas. Both units were formed to deal with terrorist activities coming from these predominantly Palestinian regions, whereby the Gaza strip was of special significance because it was also home to some 8,000 Jewish settlers.

The creation of a third Yamas unit for Israel's capital city, the Jerusalem Unit Yamas, dates back to 1992, when the Intifada had begun to extend its reach. The unit was initially established as a so-called Samag or reconnaissance force that is oriented at gathering actionable intelligence, but it became an undercover unit in 1995. The special emphasis in the unit's work is on the eastern (Arab-dominated) side of Jerusalem, which is seen as a particularly dangerous platform for terrorist attacks given the proximity to the western (largely Jewish) parts of the city. The three Yamas units receive the same type of training and equipment, but they lack a unified command. The reason for this decentralized approach is that each relevant region contains Arab populations with their own specific Arabic dialects, customs, and clans, so that each unit has its own unique challenges to effectively infiltrate local culture.

By the very nature of the work undercover counterterrorism units are involved in, details about the establishment and existence of such units are at times carefully guarded. The Yamas units were classified until August 26, 1992, when an undercover operative was accidentally killed by friendly fire.[4] A day after the incident, a Magav commander appeared on Israeli television to confirm the existence of a unit whose members "dressed as Arabs" and operated "routinely, almost every evening" in the administered territories (quoted in Middle East Watch 1993). In the early 1990s, similar undercover units were also exposed in the Israeli media. In 1991, an IDF officer allowed the existence of military undercover units to be disclosed on Israeli television.[5] A few weeks later, a commander in the Border Police in a radio interview confirmed the deployment of Magav undercover units in the territories and in eastern Jerusalem.[6] In 1994, the undercover units of the Border Police were officially disclosed.[7]

Shortly after the creation of the Jerusalem Unit Yamas, the Israeli Police set up its own undercover force, the Unit Gideonim. At that time, then, there were no fewer than six counterterrorist units for three areas: Sayeret Shimshon and Gaza Strip Unit Yamas in Gaza; Sayeret Duvdevan and Judea and Samaria Unit Yamas in the West Bank; and Unit Gideonim and Jerusalem Unit Yamas in Israel's capital city. In 1994, after the establishment of the Palestinian Authority in the Gaza Strip, the IDF Unit Shimshon was disbanded, and the Gaza Strip Unit Yamas was relocated in another Magav force. In that period also, after the Oslo Accords of 1993 had established the contours of a Palestinian right of self-governance in Gaza and the West Bank, Magav forces even cooperated with the Palestinian Police Force to conduct joint patrols of areas that were under Israeli-Palestinian mandate (Geva, Herzog, and Haberfeld 2004:1132). However, as the Oslo Accords gradually collapsed in the wake of continued suicide bombings and the outbreak of the al-Aqsa Intifada in September 2000, all Palestinian-Israeli security collaborations were suspended.

In 2001, the Yamas unit in the Gaza Strip was rebuilt as a separate unit and was reinforced. No public information is available on the Gaza Unit's status since Israel's disengagement from the Gaza region in 2005. The official Web site of the Israeli Police still lists the Gaza territory among the Border Guard's responsibilities.[8] Since the Hamas (an organization whose charter calls for the destruction of the state of Israel) took control of Gaza in June 2007, it is more than likely that the Border Police and the IDF still maintain a level of operational readiness toward the region. This state of preparedness could be operationalized when on December 27, 2008, Israel undertook a military campaign against Hamas that lasted until January 21, 2009, with continued armed hostilities regularly taking place between Hamas and Israeli forces since then.

Yamas units operate as paramilitary forces, and in their overt appearance resemble military special forces rather than a civilian police unit. The Magav Border Police is under the command of the IDF when they operate in the territories. Until 1991, the units were also financed by the IDF. Since then, however, the Yamas is self-sufficient in terms of budget and equipment. Although similar to IDF Unit 217 with respect to tactics, the Yamas is distinct in several respects. Whereas most members of Unit 217 are Jewish, the Yamas units predominantly include Arab minorities who have Arabic as their native language. Also, though most members of Unit 217 are mandatory service soldiers, the Yamas operatives have completed their mandatory service. After a limited number of years in the force, once the operatives' faces may have become too familiar to the people in the communities in which they operate covertly, the officers are either shifted to a different position in the units that involves no undercover work (e.g., snipers) or are moved to another Magav unit.

The recruitment and training programs for the Yamas are very selective.[9] Only about 20 to 30 percent of all applicants to the undercover units are said to eventually become operatives. Based on information provided by Magav command, the initial training involves a very severe 7-day trial period that is particularly oriented at instilling a strong cohesion among the trainees, which is described as *"gibush,"* a Hebrew term that denotes cohesion and that is especially used in education-related settings but also in political parties, informal groups, and military units (Katriel and Nesher 1986). Both physical challenges and mental endurance requirements are central to the training. The complete training period lasts for 1 year and includes half a year of basic and advanced infantry training in the Magav or the IDF, two months additional training in a selected unit, and four months of specialized counterterrorism and undercover training. Training includes instruction in martial arts, Arabic language skills, the use of specialized weaponry (including small Uzis suitable for undercover work), and blending-in exercises in friendly villages and, gradually, in more hostile Arab villages

Figure 9.2 Members of the Magav on duty in Jerusalem, Israel, December 2, 2007. Although agents of the Yamas are part of an undercover police unit, in appearance looking like regular civilians in the target areas, they are in fact part of the Magav Border Guard, which is the quasi-military combat branch of the Israeli Police. (Photo by Jim Greenhill, courtesy of the U.S. Department of Defense.)

in Israel, in addition to special training programs for snipers, drivers, paramedics, and other specialized functions. Self-control and physical and mental stamina are emphasized among the necessary qualities to join the units. In the words of a commander, the candidates need "the correct intuition, courage, and self-confidence. We're not looking for Rambos; we need people with discipline."[10]

Members of the Yamas are at least 24 years of age but typically not much older than 30, and usually unmarried. Since 2003, the units have experimented with integrating a small number of females, but men have always made up the vast majority of operatives. In the world of Yamas undercover operations oriented at gathering intelligence and conducting hit-and-run raids, gender is less relevant as male operatives can dress up as females (aided by the Arab customs of the hijab and burqa).

In terms of its operational objectives, the Yamas is involved in undercover interventions and in intelligence work preparatory to such interventions by Yamas or other undercover forces in the police or military. The units primarily engage in two kinds of interventions. In direct actions, operatives pinpoint terrorists on the basis of intelligence provided by police or military forces. Additionally, undercover operatives infiltrate in crowd control situations and riots, wherein they seek to seize the leaders and take out armed terrorists. In both types of activities, the Yamas operatives operate covertly, dressed in clothing and otherwise acting in a manner that blends with the local culture. Once they have drawn their weapons and revealed their true nature, they typically put on a black ski mask to cover their faces and/or a baseball cap with the Hebrew word for police so that accompanying uniformed forces can recognize them. Once a target is taken out and armed officers have arrived onto the scene, the Yamas operatives (and their targets in the case of a live capture or snatch-and-grab) quickly disappear in a military vehicle or an unmarked white van.

The Dynamics of Yamas Counterterrorism

Modern police organizations are subject to a bureaucratization process that is conditional on societal, especially political, conditions that may lead police agencies to be drawn more closely to the political dictates of their governments. In the case of the Israeli police, and the Yamas in particular, these dual forces are reflected in a number of ways.

Policing National Security

The intimate relation between policing and politics in the Israeli context is most fundamentally revealed in the organization of the police. Organizationally, the political dependency of the Israeli police is reflected in the fact that the Police Commissioner is placed under direct authority of the Minister of Public Security, who represents the government. Israel's police is, thus, not organizationally autonomous but subject to control from a highly centralized government (Gamson and Yuchtman 1977). In consequence, the Israeli police lacks many of the distinctive subcultural traits that police institutions in otherwise comparable nations have obtained. The internal control structure in the Israeli police is very tight, and police unions do not exist. Functionally, Israeli police tasks are not only oriented at criminal and service duties but comprise public security functions directed at protecting the Israeli state. Within the borders of Israel, the security functions of the police are autonomously conducted and, in the territories, they are executed under military command. In the case of the Yamas, the security functions in undercover work are dominant.

In consequence of the political dependence of the Israeli police, its relation with the military is an intimate one. In the Israeli context, police and military institutions and functions are interwoven to a considerable degree, especially in areas of work, such as counterterrorism, that relate more closely to national security concerns. A military style, hierarchical organization, and centralization have been characteristic of the Israeli Police from the start (Herzog 2001). Israel's non-liberal democracy contributed to the use of military force and extreme security measures (Ben-Dor, Pedahzur, and Hasisi 2003). The Palestinian conflict has additionally shaped the militaristic style of the Israeli police and the definition of police functions in terms of national security, even when on strategic grounds alone this approach has not always proven to be efficient (Pedahzur 2009).

The predominance of military security functions over civilian police tasks is further revealed in the very establishment of Israel's undercover counterterrorism units. As mentioned, the first units were set up in the IDF rather than in the National Police or the Border Guard. The major impetus for the formation of the units came from former Israeli Prime Minister and current Minister of Defense Ehud Barak, who at the time was an IDF major general (1987–1991) and chief of staff (1991–1995). Barak had personal experience with undercover operations in April 1973, when he was part of the Sayeret Matkal, a specialized military reconnaissance and counterterrorism team involved in the killings of PLO members in Lebanon. Part of the so-called Operation Wrath of God, the killings took place in retaliation for the 1972 massacre at the Munich Olympic Games. Barak had in the operation masqueraded as a female.[11] Once the military undercover units were established under Barak's leadership, the Border Police and Israeli National Police quickly followed with their own elite units.

In the execution of undercover activities, the Yamas typically cooperate with other police and military agencies. Military forces and specialized intelligence agencies, specifically the Shin Bet, are most often relied upon to gather the necessary intelligence for Yamas interventions. However, Yamas units in turn also gather their own intelligence or disseminate it to other agencies. Unlike the collection of actionable intelligence in routine police work for particular criminal cases, intelligence work conducted by the Yamas is not restricted to a particular case but involves a more routinized information-gathering process, albeit with a view toward action on the part of police or military forces.

The militarization of policing in Israel is not a simple unilinear development. In the 1990s, the Israeli police experienced a trend of demilitarization, involving a shift from a security to a crime control focus (Herzog 2001). Though both crime and security functions have always been part of the Israeli police mandate, the balance shifted owing to a rise in ordinary crimes, such as drug offenses and crime problems related to property and public safety. Local police stations received more autonomy in dealing with such problems, while the image, salary, and working conditions of the civilian police improved, and more women joined the police. Such developments gave the police a more distinct place separate from the military but, ironically, also devalued the role of the police in society. In status and prestige, members of the Israeli police are typically held in much lower standing than IDF soldiers (Brewer *et al.* 1988).

Looking at the implications of the dual police focus on security and crime, not much information is available about the nature and extent of Yamas operations. According to a commander, the units are engaged in "several operations per week." Public sources confirm that Yamas operations take place on an almost daily basis.[12] The undercover operations conducted in a recent year by Border Guard, military, and intelligence forces are said to be "100% successful." However, reliable information on the effects of the interventions is difficult to obtain. On only rare and isolated occasions has the Yamas been identified in media and other sources concerning a specific operation. Among the isolated cases of undercover interventions in which the Yamas has publicly been identified is intelligence work during the late 1990s against Yahya Ayyash, one of the chief bomb makers in Hamas (Katz 2002:186–189). More recently, in the spring of 2007, the Yamas took part in a hit-and-run intervention, killing three members of the Islamic Jihad, including

Figure 9.3 Israeli soldiers evacuate victims of a missile attack on Ashkelon, Israel, December 29, 2008. The counterterrorism functions of the Israeli military are of multiple kinds, involving offensive attacks such as air strikes and rescue missions conducted by IDF Search and Rescue Units. (Photo supplied by the IDF, courtesy of the Israel Project, www.theisraelproject.org.)

the mastermind behind a suicide bombing in February of that year, in the West Bank city of Jenin.[13]

Providing a more general overview, Yamas units had by 1994 reportedly captured some 70 top members of the Hamas and hundreds of low-level operatives.[14] According to a Magav commander speaking in the media, Border Police units had in 1998 carried out some 770 operations in Judea and Samaria, about one-third of which were conducted by undercover units, leading to 180 arrests.[15] By 2007, some 1,500 operations had, according to an unidentified Yamas Unit commander, been conducted by the Yamas since the outbreak of the al-Aqsa Intifada in 2000.[16]

The Professionalism of Undercover Counterterrorism

Despite the politicization processes on Israeli policing, organizational developments are also at work to account for some of the characteristics of Israel's counterterrorism police units. Most noticeable is the strongly expressed sense of commitment to standards of professionalism that is shared among unit operatives and their commanders. As a former intelligence agent explained, security work in the Israeli context always "retains a professional character" because the intelligence community is not subject to the specific changes that take place in the party-political landscape with every election. Among security officials, the expertise of leadership and the professional roles associated with intelligence activities are emphasized to the extent that intelligence information is conceived of as being produced "independently" for the benefit of the political leaders, who are thought of as "customers" or "consumers." Yamas command likewise stresses that "the unit is independent" and that any decision to engage in an intervention is always "based on professional criteria."

Though involving extreme measures, undercover counterterrorism interventions are conceived of by participating police as proactive measures to prevent attacks by terrorists. As a commander explains, the undercover units "deploy to intercept them before they hit us" (quoted in Katz 2005:21). Also emphasized is the ideal of counterterrorism work to take out terrorists without hurting any civilians and to do everything possible to make sure the interventions are as "clean as possible... to catch the bad guy but not hurt civilians."[17] A mission that upon its initiation turns out to be too dangerous will be called off for, in the words of a unit commander, should an operative's true identity be revealed during an investigation, "They would tear him apart. It's very dangerous and very problematic."[18]

The standards of conduct in the Yamas units are reported to be very high, and failure in a mission is said to lead to immediate dismissal from the unit. A commander justifies the high standard by reference to the dangers involved: "A small mistake could result in the death of a comrade... a friend, or someone who is unarmed."[19] Yet, although the seriousness of the job and the potential dangers involved in the operations are readily apparent to the unit members, there is also a sense of excitement involved in choosing a career in undercover counterterrorism. In the words of a Yamas operative, the undercover operatives put on an act as in "reality TV" and is "looking for a challenge... for risk... for self-expression." Another undercover operative speaks of the "exultation" he felt after his first killing in the field.[20] An accomplished mission is seen by unit operatives as "the biggest satisfaction there is."[21] Professional mistakes, in contrast, lead to negative feelings. An undercover officer said he felt "lousy" after he had mistakenly killed a person who, acting eccentrically, turned out to be a psychiatric patient who had escaped from an asylum.[22]

In line with professional standards oriented at efficient policing, a strong emphasis is placed in Yamas activities on knowing the operational targets very intimately and studying and submerging oneself in their culture. This deep-cover role is referred to in Hebrew as "mistaravim" (also: mista'arvim or mista'aravim). The central term appearing in the full name of the Yamas, the expression mistaravim (Hebrew: מסתערבים) is the plural form of a neologism that combines the Hebrew terms for "disguise" and "Arab" (Lockard 2002:61). Most sources translate the full name of the Yamas—Yehida Mishtartit Mistaravim—as "Counter-Terror Undercover Unit," but the Hebrew phrase is more literally to be translated as "Unit Undercover Disguised-as-Arabs."[23] Mistaravim refers to the skill to appear to be Arab in every possible way, including proficiency in the Arabic language and its dialects, knowledge of the Muslim religion and the Koran, specific ways of dressing and behaving, and an understanding of every relevant aspect of local Arab cultures. The term mistaravim is so central to Israeli undercover practices in the police and the military that the units are sometimes referred to more generically as the mistaravim, under which name they are also well known among Israelis and local Arab and Palestinian populations and by critics of Israel's policies in the territories.[24]

Mistaravim practices have a long history. In the late 1990s, it was revealed that the Shin Bet had during the 1950s organized a small group of some 10 to 12 mistaravim operatives to gather intelligence in Arab villages. The experiment was viewed an error and terminated in 1959, when some operatives had married Arab women and had children with them. Under these conditions, as the founder and commander of the unit later explained, problems arose as operatives had to reveal the truth to their wife and children: "Not only are you not the Arab nationalist you pretended to be... but you are a Jew... And what about the children? What is their identity?"[25] Despite such problems, mistaravim units continued to be formed from time to time, especially as part of military operations targeted at suppressing unrest among the Arab populations of Gaza and in Israel's neighboring states. In the late 1980s, with the formation of the undercover units in the military and their expansion in the wake of the First Intifada, mistaravim forces were revived as permanent structures.

As the central goal of the Yamas undercover operations is to effectively blend into a crowd or area of operation, the geographical division of decentralized units enables the undercover operatives to learn to become familiar with the specifics of their respective region. Similarly, the use of certain ethnic Arabs, such as Druze, Circassians, and Bedouins, and Ethiopians, who can pose as Sudanese and North-African immigrants, makes sense from the perspective of deep-cover tactics, as much as does the use of a makeup artist with experience in the Hollywood motion picture industry.[26] Yamas work is very detailed and sophisticated, oriented at completely immersing oneself into the local culture of Arabs to "talk like them, look like them, eat like them, laugh like them, and even smell like them," as a former operative explains.[27] The mistarav has to take "the role of the other" but should also remain mindful of the objectives of the intervention.

The mistaravim practice reinforces a polarization between police and public, between Israeli and Arab, between those who protect the Israeli state and the Jewish people and those who are out to cause harm and destruction. This polarization is not only the result of military pressures on police work and organization but is supported and perpetuated by intra-organizational factors, such as an authoritative leadership style, top-down controls over police discretionary behavior, and strict discipline within the police (Haberfeld and Herzog 2000). Not surprisingly, the combat aspects dominate over the civilian-service functions in the formal training of Israeli Police officers. As a result, the professional police culture is imbedded with notions of crime as warfare, leading police officers to define their position removed from the public and to perceive outside groups, particularly Palestinians, Israeli Arabs, and minorities such as Jews of North-African descent (who are associated with criminal activities) as enemies who pose a "security danger" (Herzog 2000:468; see Ben-Dor *et al.* 2003).

In the case of undercover counterterrorism policing, the militaristic attitude is amplified by the social and ethnic background of many of the operatives, who are predominantly drawn from low-income socioeconomic strata, where an exposure to violence is more common.

Moreover, among the Druze communities, from which Yamas undercover operatives are especially recruited, sentiments against other Arabs, especially Palestinians, are high. Druze, who consider themselves Arabs but who are classified as a distinct ethnic group in Israel, are thought of as traitors among other Arab groups because they participate in many of Israel's institutions, notably the military.[28] More broadly, the unintended consequences of the Yamas interventions and related Israeli police actions toward the Palestinian and Arab population, which human right groups have often addressed, are not dealt with and are instead redefined as unfortunate necessities from the police viewpoint.[29]

The militaristic nature of Israeli policing styles does not mean that the activities of the National Police and the Border Guard are tightly controlled by the IDF and its military leaders or that the military-civilian divide is the predominant dividing line between forces. Instead, organizational dimensions account for the variable degrees of competition and cooperation among units. Most notably, the rivalry that exists among the various Israeli undercover counterterrorism forces does not always harmonize with a separation between police and military. Unit Gideonim, for instance, was initially conceived as an intelligence-gathering force of the Israeli Police. Yet, it gradually developed counterterrorist capabilities and was eventually converted into a full-scale counterterrorism force operating in Israel and in the occupied territories, an area it is officially not assigned to, leading to tensions with Judea and Samaria Unit Yamas. Although the Gideonim is supposed to be an intelligence-oriented unit working only within the Israeli borders, it has actually also engaged in counterterrorism activities in the territories. In terms of jurisdiction, the Gideonim unit also overlaps with the Jerusalem Unit Yamas, has a bigger budget, and is much better staffed than its Yamas counterparts. Therefore, Yamas officers have complained about the relatively small budget and low-quality equipment they have to work with. In matters of undercover work, the Border Police units nonetheless claim a sense of professional superiority, because the operatives are "career service men" whose work is a professional choice, whereas the IDF forces mostly consist of young mandatory-service soldiers.

Despite the inter-agency conflicts that can occur among police and security agencies with overlapping duties, a shared sense of professionalism and expertise can also facilitate cooperation efforts.

Within Israel, intelligence and police agencies at times collaborate despite the fact that intelligence and police activities are functionally differentiated. As Israeli counterterrorism officials themselves recognize, police work in the area of crime control is "evidence-oriented" in view of a specific case involving a criminal violation, whereas in the case of intelligence work, there is "nothing to enforce," as information is broadly collected without a specific actionable purpose. Police work, moreover, is carried out within (and for) the law, whereas intelligence forces operate "outside the law," not necessarily in an illegal but in an extra-legal context (although the very extra-legality of such work may more readily enable illegal actions to take place and prevent their discovery or prosecution).

A special facilitator of cooperation in the Israeli context exists because of the Jewish commonality in the Israeli nation. The special political and social pressures placed on Israel build, in the words of an Israeli intelligence official, a strong internal cohesion and self-identity as "one family of people who belong together." Cooperation is further aided by the compulsory military service and the professional experiences many Israelis enjoy from a relatively young age. Intelligence, military, and police officials often have experience in their respective agencies and, thus, "more likely know one another" and create cooperation "through personal contacts" and can cross, with relative ease, over into political roles as well.

The perceived success of the mistaravim tactics among police professionals has brought about that unit operations have been applied in matters of crime control unrelated to terrorism. The Jerusalem Unit, for example, is involved in controlling major crimes such as smuggling operations between Jerusalem and the West Bank. Yamas units also have been involved in criminal cases involving agricultural theft, such as the smuggling of beehives into the West Bank.[30] The capacity of undercover work to move from security to criminal enforcement duties can be attributed to the technical aspect that is involved in such activities. As an undercover commander in the Magav states: "We knew how to blend into a hostile populace... Why couldn't that knowledge and that level of innovation be used to rid our streets of criminals and drug dealers?"[31]

Undercover Magav units have also engaged in riot control activities within Israeli territory.[32] Mostly these activities are targeted at

Figure 9.4 Site of a rocket strike in Sderot, Israel, December 29, 2008. Israeli security forces typically work in close cooperation in the aftermath of a rocket strike or other terrorist attacks. As shown here, these collaborative security efforts involve military personnel, Magav forces, and police, including a plainclothes officer (in the top right hand corner of the image) identified only by a baseball cap, much like a Yamas undercover operative at the end of a successful mission. (Photo by Marcus Sheff, courtesy of the Israel Project, www.theisraelproject.org.)

Arab populations but, interestingly, undercover strategies have also been adapted to infiltrate demonstrations involving certain Jewish groups. This peculiar undercover practice has been referred to in Hebrew as "מסתחררדים" (phonetic transliteration: "mista-haredim" or "mistharedim"), a neologism that, similar to the term *mistaravim*, contracts the Hebrew for "disguise" and "Haredim" (the plural of Haredi), a term used to refer to ultra-orthodox Jews. The strategy was used by the Israeli Police riot control units of the Yasam (not to be confused with the Yamas) in demonstrations organized in the Haredi community against a gay pride parade in Jerusalem in 2007.[33]

Global Counterterrorism

In the present era of global concerns over terrorism and counterterrorism, it is more than interesting to note that the mutual recognition of professional responsibilities among counterterrorism experts also crosses national borders. In the case of Israel's counterterrorism police, cooperation takes place not only because much of the weaponry used by the Yamas is bought from the United States and Germany[34] but because certain elements of Israel's counterterrorism strategies have found their way into the training of counterterrorist forces across the world. In matters of terrorism, in particular, Israeli officials share their expertise with counterparts abroad through seminars and workshops organized both in Israel and in host countries.[35] Police officials from across the world additionally take part in international police and military exchange programs arranged by private groups, such as the Anti-Defamation League and the Jewish Institute for National Security Affairs.[36]

Crossing the boundaries of the police profession, there are indications that strategies similar to the ones used by mistaravim units have been suggested to the U.S. military in support of its counter-insurgency role in Iraq. An Israeli report obtained by a Pentagon official from a U.S. Army officer comments favorably on the Israeli experience with mistaravim tactics and suggests their use for the U.S. Army and Marines.[37] The award-winning investigative journalist and author Seymour Hersh has reported that U.S. special forces operating in Iraq shortly after the invasion in 2003 were relying on advice from Israeli military intelligence officers who urged the American forces to maintain a network of informants and emulate Israel's mistaravim tactics.[38] Hersh has also written that Israeli operatives have been training Kurds in Iraq in mistaravim tactics to infiltrate Shiite and Sunni insurgent groups and help form a pro-Israeli Kurdish state.[39]

Transfer of police technology across national borders particularly takes place through the private security industry. In the context of this chapter, mention can be made of IMS Security, a Los Angeles-based company that offers "Israeli style security services and anti-terrorist training."[40] An abbreviation of "Israeli Military Specialists," IMS offers bodyguard services for corporate leaders, foreign diplomats, and Hollywood celebrities and also organizes counterterrorism training, including an "Israeli Style Terrorist Warrant Course" that is modeled "after Israel's famed Duvdevan and Yamas Units."[41] In 2005, IMS organized such a 5-day counterterrorist training at an FBI firing range in the state of Washington, attended by representatives of local police, the National Guard, and U.S. Customs.[42] It is obviously difficult to determine whether and to what extent the company can make good on its claims, but it is to be noted that IMS was founded in 2000 by a then-24-year-old former member of the Israeli military with 3 years of experience in an IDF undercover counterterrorism unit.[43] Similarly, the Israeli company Baguera-Israël, which has headquarters in Israel and in the United States, boasts to have "trained, advised, and collaborated with Israel's most elite special forces, both military and police, such as the police covert operational counter terror unit the Yamas."[44] And week-long workshops with Israeli counterterrorism experts, including briefings with the Yamas, have recently been organized by at least two U.S.–based private security companies.[45] It cannot be determined, however, whether the transfer of expertise on counterterrorism from Israel has operational impact.

Conclusion

As I have argued throughout this book, the pacification of society is a necessary condition for the bureaucratization of the police function. The condition of pacification is key to understanding the character of policing in Israel, including undercover counterterrorism activities. Because of the sense of Israel's having been in a permanent state of emergency since the creation of the state in 1948 and, even more intensely, during moments of great international tension and hostility, such as the Six Day and Yom Kippur Wars and the two Intifadas, police institutions in Israel—not least of all in the area of counterterrorism—are inevitably subject to strong politicization pressures. In the case of the Yamas operations, more specifically, the mistaravim practices function as an important tool in the Israeli control of Palestinian-claimed territories. From an organizational viewpoint, however, it is to be noted that within the undercover units a distinct sense of professionalism and efficiency is also observed. In sum, the bureaucratization of the Yamas is constrained within the political context of the Israeli nation-state. The mistaravim practices, especially in the territories, are planned and implemented on the basis of efficiency standards from the police point of view, but they are by some groups, both within and outside Israel, judged as lacking in terms of their civil and human rights implications.

The dual influences of contextual and organizational developments on counterterrorism policing are not unique to the Israeli case. As the analyses of other cases in this book show, police organizations across the world have in the post–9/11 era generally experienced attempts by their respective governments to have policing objectives, especially in matters of counterterrorism, be aligned more closely with political directives of national security. Yet, what is distinct about the Israeli experience is that the bureaucratization of Israel's civilian police forces has historically been hindered by the non-liberal nature of Israeli democracy, the continually strained international situation with the surrounding Arab nations, and the resulting sense of a permanent state of emergency in Israeli society. In this sense, Israel's counterterrorism experience exhibits characteristics that in other societies are observed only during periods of extreme unrest, such as war. In this respect, contemporary Iraq and Afghanistan provide interesting comparative cases of research.

10

TERRORISM AND WAR

Policing Iraq and Afghanistan

Police institutions reach a high degree of autonomy only under conditions of a pacification of society in which the polity is democratized. In autocratic regimes, conversely, police power will remain very closely tied to the quest of governments to maintain power and secure order, often through very violent means and in close conjunction with military forces. These conditions are important to consider in the case of the policing of Afghanistan and Iraq since the invasions of both countries, in 2001 and 2003, respectively. Both states were subject to autocratic rule in the years prior to the invasions. Iraq was under tight control of the Ba'athist regime of Saddam Hussein since 1979, whereas Afghanistan was politically dominated by the Taliban since 1996. The police function in both systems was intimately tied to the political objectives of the state. Since the invasion of both countries and the introduction of democratic systems of government, however, these conditions will have changed to democratize the polities of the two countries and develop accompanying civilian police systems.

The institution of democratic police systems in Iraq and Afghanistan is a very difficult process. This chapter shows that militant and insurgent activities in Iraq and Afghanistan have been purposely aimed at hindering the development of civilian police institutions. As such, the military interventions in Iraq and Afghanistan not only responded, in more and less direct ways, to the terrorism of 9/11; they have brought about a set of entirely new conditions of terrorist violence, part of which is directly targeted at the police in both countries. Given the connections between the development of civilian police and the democratization of society, the terrorist activities from insurgent groups in Iraq and from Taliban forces in Afghanistan are aimed at the police institutions that are being established in those countries because a regularly functioning police would represent an important and highly visible indicator of the pacification and normalization of society. Civilian police forces are ironically a preferred target of terrorist activities in contemporary Iraq and Afghanistan, precisely when these police institutions are needed, even more than under peacetime conditions, to be effectively involved in counterterrorism.

Policing Autocracy

Before examining the current conditions of policing in Iraq and Afghanistan, it is useful to situate the historical development of the organization and function of policing in both countries. Given the variable connection between police and politics, a closer look is in order at the political evolution in both countries.

Ba'athist Rule in Iraq

Originally not a united country but a conglomerate of three vilayets (regions) that belonged to the Ottoman Empire from the sixteenth century onward, the area of the world now known as Iraq was after World War I granted as a mandate by the League of Nations to the United Kingdom.[1] In 1932, Iraq gained independence, after which the Hashemite monarchy ruled the country until 1958, when the Iraqi army established a republic and installed a leftist government that entertained friendly ties with the Soviet Union. In 1963, the Ba'ath Party installed another military government. This regime was soon again overturned but, in 1968, the Ba'ath Party once again seized political power. Within the Party, Saddam Hussein gradually gained power, eventually assuming the Presidency and taking control of the Revolutionary Command Council in July 1979. Largely made up of members of the Sunni community, the Ba'ath Party also controlled all government institutions. Saddam Hussein's rule was as brutal as it was effective, surviving the Iran-Iraq War (1980–1988) and the Gulf War

(1991) and the economic sanctions imposed by the United Nations after Iraq's invasion of Kuwait in August 1990.

Under Saddam Hussein, a sophisticated system of security and intelligence agencies served to uphold the autocratic reign of the Ba'ath Party.[2] Internal security was particularly achieved through a system of overlapping security services, including the Special Security Organization, the General Intelligence Directorate, the General Security Directorate, and the Ba'ath Party Security Agency. Led by Saddam Hussein's youngest son, the Special Security Organization was in charge of the safety of the president, his family, and his palaces. The General Intelligence Directorate, under the command of Saddam Hussein's brother, was in charge of espionage and foreign intelligence gathering. The General Security Directorate was responsible for internal security and public unrest. The Ba'ath Party Security Agency monitored the activities of Iraqi citizens in commerce, factories, unions, and universities.

During the Ba'ath regime, the Iraqi National Police was responsible for all law enforcement duties. Though staffed by officers who were trained in police academies, all Iraqi police institutions were placed under military oversight. Law enforcement functions involving serious criminal violations were delegated to the security services, leaving the police to deal mostly with petty offenses and traffic regulation. Three decades of Saddam Hussein's rule brought about that the police forces at the time of the 2003 invasion were poorly managed and had low standards of education and operation. Corruption among the police was high, as was distrust toward the police among many Iraqi citizens. Police officers would rarely venture outside of their stations and, when they did, they would randomly round up suspects, extort confessions by physical force and torture, or take bribes from family members as a condition to release suspects.

Afghanistan under Taliban Rule

Although Afghan civilization dates back several thousands of years, a modern state of Afghanistan was first founded in the middle of the eighteenth century, when Persian rulers took control of a region that now covers Afghanistan and Pakistan and parts of Iran and India.[3] In the early nineteenth century, the United Kingdom extended its

Figure 10.1 Flames erupt from a building hit by a U.S. air strike in Mosul, Iraq, July 22, 2003. The military forces of the United States and its allies were quick in overturning the regime of Saddam Hussein. In the pictured incident, Saddam Hussein's sons Uday and Qusay, the latter of whom headed the Special Security Organization, were killed as they resisted efforts by coalition forces to apprehend them. (Photo by Robert Woodward, courtesy of the U.S. Department of Defense.)

colonial empire to the Afghan region, until Amanullah Khan was installed as Shah in 1919. The monarchial dynasty was very stable, with Mohammed Zahir Shah ruling from 1933 until 1973, when he was ousted by a relative, Mohammed Daoud Khan, who became the first President of a newly formed Republic of Afghanistan.

In 1978, Daoud Khan was killed after an uprising led by the People's Democratic Party of Afghanistan, after which the country was officially renamed the Democratic Republic of Afghanistan. Backed by the Soviet Union, the new regime was secular and introduced various modernization reforms, leading to opposition from religious conservatives and other factions, including the Islamic warriors of the so-called Mujahideen. As internal unrest mounted, the Soviet Union invaded Afghanistan on December 24, 1979. Faced with international opposition and an increasingly better organized Mujahideen, which could also count on the backing from the United States government, Soviet troops withdrew from Afghanistan in the late 1980s. During the 1990s, secular and Islamic forces in Afghanistan continued fighting over control of the country. In 1996, the Islamic political forces of the Taliban seized the city of Kabul and gradually took control over most of Afghanistan.

Many police functions during the Taliban era were subsumed under military powers, for control over regions and cities continually had to be defended against potential attacks from rivaling militias. Yet, the Taliban also maintained an elaborate internal enforcement regime to impose its strict version of Islamic law (sharia). Partly based on a similar police that exists in Saudi Arabia, this "religious police" was formally overseen by a Ministry for the Propagation of Virtue and the Prevention of Vice (*Amro bil mahroof*) to engage in the enforcement of various Taliban edicts oriented at making Afghan society Islamic in all respects.[4]

Taliban edicts were promulgated to ban all non-religious music, all books not published in Afghanistan, television sets, video cassettes and recorders, satellite dishes, and movies, all of which were judged to be offensive to Islam and, consequently, subject to police action. Behavior forbidden under Taliban law included laughing in public, dancing, keeping pigeons, and smoking. Neckties, fashion catalogues, musical instruments, computer discs, and kite flying were also banned, and police were ordered to seize all such items. Afghan women were particularly targeted by Taliban laws, which forbade women from working or going to school; wearing white shoes or heels that clicked and clothing other than the all-covering burqa; using lipstick; or walking outdoors unaccompanied by a close male relative. In August 2001, a Taliban edict banned all organizations in Afghanistan, except the Taliban militia headquarters in Kandahar, from using the Internet.

The Taliban police publicly beat or imprisoned anyone who broke the rules of Taliban law. Men could be beaten by the religious police for having beards shorter than the length of a fist. Taliban policemen would sometimes stop vehicles on the street and search for music or video tapes, telling people to spend more time praying and going to the mosque. Barbers were arrested for giving men haircuts, known as the "Titanic," which mimicked the style of actor Leonardo DiCaprio in the movie about the famous ship. Thieves could have their arms or legs amputated, anyone caught drinking liquor could get whippings, and adulterers could be stoned to death.

Post-invasion Police Reform

The invasions of Afghanistan and Iraq brought about many immediate and long-term changes in both countries. Although both military interventions were differently motivated in terms of their purported connections to the terrorist attacks of September 11, they each envisioned a political regime change and the installation of a new, democratically elected government. The normalization of primary social institutions, including police and security forces, would have to be part of this process.

Iraqi Police Reform

The invasion of Iraq on March 20, 2003, by an international coalition led by the United States and Great Britain quickly led to the overthrow of Saddam Hussein's reign. On April 9, Baghdad was captured and, on May 1, President Bush declared an end to major combat operations. A Coalition Provisional Authority was installed, followed by an interim government in June 2004, and a transitional government after elections in January 2005. The executive power of the Iraqi government since then resides in a three-person presidential council, consisting of a president and two vice presidents, thus ensuring representation from the country's three major ethnic groups (Shiites, Sunnis, and Kurds). A national referendum in October 2005 led to the adoption of a new constitution, under the provisions of which an Iraqi government was formed (after elections in December 2005) on April 22, 2006, when President Jalal Talabani, a Kurd, named Jawad al-Maliki, a Shiite, as the new prime minister.

After the collapse of the Ba'athist regime, the Iraqi police has undergone important transformations. Immediately after the invasion of Iraq, a situation of general lawlessness erupted, especially in the city of Baghdad.[5] The streets of Iraq's capital could not rely on effective law enforcement because most Iraqi police (and military) had simply gone home. Law enforcement functions were maintained by coalition military forces and law enforcement agencies, some of whom, such as the FBI and the Bureau of Diplomatic Security, now have a permanent presence in Iraq.[6] Although U.S. officials had been informed about the likely breakdown of law and order in the immediate post-war situation, military command did not count on continued unrest after the cessation of major combat operations.

After the invasion, the U.S. military appealed to Iraqi police to return to work, and although they were not allowed to carry weapons, many Iraqi police soon reported back to their stations. By April 2003, joint patrols of Iraqi police and U.S. soldiers were already spotted in the streets of Baghdad. Yet, the initial return of the police produced outrage among Iraqi citizens, as many of the officers were thought to have Ba'athist sympathies. A careful vetting process would have to be conducted to train new officers to adopt principles of democratic police techniques and to weed out corrupt loyalists of Saddam Hussein.

Under the direction of the Coalition Provisional Authority, an Iraqi Police Service (IPS) was established under the authority of the Ministry of the Interior. The new police institution has formal charge of law enforcement duties related to crime control and order maintenance. The Iraqi police can also assist the coalition forces, but the latter remain primarily responsible for investigations involving terrorism and military crimes. Ba'ath party members were initially not allowed to serve in any public sector function. Yet, as the purging of Ba'ath Party members from the Iraqi police implied a loss of leadership positions at the senior and mid-level ranks, the U.S. military has since 2007 attempted to re-integrate Sunnis into the Iraqi police.[7]

Besides the IPS, a new Iraqi National Police has been established out of the merger, in 2006, of the internal security forces of the Public Order Battalion, Mechanized Police Unit, and Emergency Response Unit. Like the IPS, the Iraqi National Police is placed under the Ministry of the Interior. Unlike the IPS, however, officers of the National Police are recruited from the former (Sunni) Ba'athist security forces and elite army units. Expressly involved with counter-insurgency activities, the Iraqi National Police also includes so-called Special Police Commandos who have been recruited by Iraq's Interior Ministry without supervision from U.S. officials.

Many resources have been and still are being devoted to the professionalization of the Iraqi police. To assist with Iraqi police reform, an International Police Training Center was set up by the Coalition Provisional Authority in Amman, Jordan, in December 2003.[8] By October 2005, some 67,500 Iraqi police had been trained in the Jordan training center and in the Baghdad Police College and similar regional academies. The training of Iraqi police is handled by officials from military and justice departments of the United States, Great Britain, and other countries and by a host of private contractors, such as the security company Blackwater USA.[9] Since May 2004, principal responsibility for the training of the Iraqi security forces, including the civilian police, is assigned to the U.S. Department of Defense.[10]

Iraqi police reform has not been a smooth process. In 2006, the U.S. Ambassador to Iraq, Zalmay Khalilzad, announced a "year of the police" as a gesture of goodwill, but right up to the autumn of that year, repeated efforts had to be made to reform and control the Iraqi police forces.[11] As late as June 30, 2009, on the day when U.S. military troops left Iraq's major cities to allow Iraqi security forces to take over, the Iraqi Minister of the Interior admitted that the June 30 date was a beginning rather than an end of Iraq's process to self-governance.[12] Specifically, problems remained in the Iraqi police force because of corruption and a lack of professionalism.

Special difficulties of Iraqi police reform are associated with the experience of the United States with instituting civilian police in other post-war situations (Perito 2002, 2003). Since the Panama invasion (1989–1990), the U.S. Department of Justice oversees an International Criminal Investigative Training Assistance Program (ICITAP) to reform civilian police forces abroad. Yet, ICITAP delegations typically consist of only a few law enforcement officers who organize training courses, and a private contractor is in charge of the staffing of police positions through a Civilian Police Program that is overseen by the Department of State. In Iraq, the program is administered by DynCorp International, which hires personnel from state and local law enforcement across the United States.[13] After the invasion of Iraq, DynCorp oversaw some 1,000 U.S. police officers in Iraq on the basis of a $750 million contract.[14] DynCorp police activities have regularly been the subject of investigations by U.S. authorities for a lack of quality performance and alleged criminal conduct and violations of human rights.[15] Yet, as a private business, DynCorp is not subject to regular oversight and the supervision that applies to public law enforcement agencies. In June 2008, DynCorp received a new contract, worth more than $546 million, to train Iraqi police through 2010.[16]

Figure 10.2 Iraqi police recruits during their first day of training at the Kirkuk Police Academy in Iraq, August 16, 2008. The integration of women is an important development toward the formation of a civilian police. Because of the status traditionally attributed to women in many Muslim societies, integrating female police in Iraq also presents a culturally sensitive issue. (Photo by Margaret C. Nelson, courtesy of the U.S. Department of Defense.)

Afghan Police Reform

Because the al-Qaeda movement was linked to the Taliban regime in Afghanistan, where terrorist training camps were organized and Osama bin Laden was believed to be hiding, the U.S. government, supported by coalition forces of some 50 countries, launched Operation Enduring Freedom on October 7, 2001, in direct response to the September 11 terrorist attacks. After the invasion, local Afghan warlords sided with coalition forces in fighting the Taliban and joined the so-called Northern Alliance, a collection of anti-Taliban Afghan political and religious groups. Once the Taliban forces had been largely defeated, the Alliance helped to install an Afghan Transitional Administration in the summer of 2002, paving the way for a new permanent government after the 2004 Presidential elections, when Hamid Karzai became President of the Islamic Republic of Afghanistan. Congressional elections were held in September 2005 to establish a National Assembly.

In April 2002, an international conference on Afghanistan was held in Geneva to formulate a plan for Afghan security in the post-Taliban era.[17] The initial goal was to install a new Afghan national police that would consist of some 44,300 uniformed police, 12,000 border police, 3,400 highway police, and 2,300 counter-narcotics police. In 2003, a new Afghan National Police (ANP) was established along with an Afghan National Army. The newly formed national police resembles a *gendarmerie* force in having a military character, but it is responsible for regular law enforcement duties, including criminal investigations, drugs enforcement, and border security. The ANP is placed under the supervision of the Afghan Ministry of Interior, which developed a document, the *Tashkil*, that specifies the structure and functions of the new police. The number of police who in 2008 officially belonged to the ANP was 79,000, but no accurate information is available of the number of officers who actually served, as police commanders are known to accept salaries for nonexistent "ghost officers."[18]

The ANP consists of several specialized branches. The Uniformed Police (at 34,000 the largest unit in the ANP) is responsible for general law enforcement, public safety, and internal security. A Civil Order Police is responsible for security involving civil disturbances in large urban areas. Additionally, specialized law enforcement functions are maintained by the Border Police, the Counter Narcotics Police, the Criminal Investigation Division Police, as well as a Counter Terrorism Police.

On the basis of the 2002 Geneva conference, German authorities in 2003 took on the lead role in Afghan police reform in the form of a German Police Project Office aimed at helping the Afghan government to create a national police that is both effective and respectful of the rule of law.[19] Since June of 2007, the German initiative has been expanded to a European effort in the form of the European Union Police Mission to Afghanistan (EUPOL Afghanistan).[20] Largely made up of German as well as other foreign police, EUPOL Afghanistan provides training, advice, and equipment to the Afghan National Police. Presently consisting of some 200 officers, it was decided in May 2008 to bring the size of the mission to a total of 400 personnel on the basis of a budget of more than 35 million Euros (nearly 52 million U.S. dollars).

Besides Germany and the European Union, other coalition forces, especially Canada and the United States, have also assisted in the reorganization of the Afghan police. Members of the Royal Canadian Mounted Police have been deployed to Afghanistan since 2005 to monitor and train the Afghan National Police.[21] The United States policing efforts in Afghanistan are mostly not directly involved with Afghan police reform but are primarily aimed at poppy crop eradication through the U.S. Department of State's Bureau of International Narcotics and Law Enforcement Affairs (and the DEA).[22] Since 2005, the U.S. Department of Defense has taken on efforts to assist the Afghan National Police, using marines and other military units to train police recruits.[23] U.S. military personnel are further involved in setting up Police Mentor Teams that are embedded in Afghan police units.[24] As in Iraq, U.S. efforts to train Afghan police are additionally handled by DynCorp. By June 2006, the private company had 245 police trainers in Afghanistan. Police training is conducted at the Afghan National Police Academy (Central Training Center) in the capital city of Kabul and in several regional training centers across the country. By the spring of 2009, about 82,000 Afghan police officers had received training. Because the government of Afghanistan does not have the necessary funds, the reorganization of the country's police is funded by members of the international community.

Although some former Afghan militia members have been recruited into the army and the police, thousands of militia organizations have continued to exist under the command of local warlords. Additional problems exist because the Afghan criminal justice system has progressed very slowly, and there are not enough attorneys, judges, and others necessary to prosecute criminal activities. Some areas of the country remain unprotected by army or police and are under the control of drugs traffickers and local militia groups. There are plans to increase the size of the national police but, because Afghan police forces have not been able to provide adequate security with respect to civil order, drugs enforcement, and border security, Afghan National Army troops have been deployed in areas that are lacking in law enforcement. Similar to the situation in Iraq, police in Afghanistan have also been accused of being ineffective and unprofessional, using torture to extort confessions and being involved in corruption.[25] As a result, the need for international assistance in Afghan police training remained high as late as the fall of 2008.[26] By the summer of 2009, U.S. officials still had to complain that Afghan security forces, including the civilian police, were not performing well.[27]

Target: Police

The invasions of Iraq and Afghanistan have each brought about continued problems of violence and civil unrest despite the efforts that have been made to introduce democratic rule and set up new institutions. In Iraq, these troubling conditions have at times been described in terms of a civil war, although the official rhetoric of the invading coalition forces has resisted this description. In Afghanistan, likewise, democratic rule has been formally instituted, but ongoing outbursts of violence by Taliban forces have as yet prevented a normalization of Afghan society. In both countries, the newly formed civilian police forces have been especially targeted by the violent unrests.

The Iraqi Insurgency

The insurgency in Iraq refers to the armed campaign by a wide variety of irregular forces, drawn from Iraq and other countries, that are operating against the international coalition forces and the Iraqi government. After the end of major hostilities in the spring of 2003, the insurgency increased in size and became more diverse in composition and objectives. The exact number of insurgent fighters was at some point estimated to be in the tens of thousands, with a reported 19,000 of them having been killed by coalition forces by September 2007.[28] Although the impact and scope of the insurgency diminished after an additional 20,000 U.S. soldiers were deployed to Iraq as part of a so-called troop surge in the spring of 2007, insurgent violence has since remained an important concern in Iraq.

Insurgent fighters include a wide variety of groups and people, including Ba'athist sympathizers of former ruler Saddam Hussein; Sunni extremists; foreign Islamist fighters, including members of al-Qaeda and the group surrounding the now slain militant leader Abu Musab al-Zarqawi; and criminal groups that lack political-ideological motivations. Originally aimed at the coalition military forces, the insurgency gradually spread out across Iraqi society, targeting Iraqi civilians and institutions, including police and security forces. Attacks have also taken place against mosques, political parties, hotels, the United Nations headquarters, foreign embassies, the International Red Cross, and international diplomats. Insurgent tactics include car bombings, suicide bombings, kidnappings, hostage taking, shootings, mortar attacks, and other types of deadly assault.

Insurgent attacks have especially targeted Iraq's new civilian police forces, as media reports have regularly pointed out.[29] Offering a more systematic overview of the police as the target of insurgent violence, the Web site Iraq Body Count provides a database with numerical information, based on a variety of news sources, concerning the incidents and fatalities involving insurgent and other attacks that have taken place since March 2003.[30] By February 2009, when more than 4,252 U.S. soldiers, 179 British soldiers, and an estimated 139 soldiers from other nations had died since the invasion,[31] the Web site estimated the total number of civilian fatalities (based on news reports published until January 2009) to be a minimum of 90,805 and a maximum of 99,151. Because of selective news reporting, findings of the Iraq Body Count Web site have to be treated with care, but they may nonetheless give an indication of the trend in the insurgency's impact on Iraqi society and, in particular, the Iraqi police.

Of the (minimum number of) 90,805 deaths included in the Iraq Body Count database by February 27, 2009 (end-date of last recorded fatality: January 31, 2009), no fewer than 9,490 were police officers killed in 3,291 incidents since May 2003.[32] Although many deaths are reported for which occupational category is not known, police officers are represented in the database more often than any other occupation, including politicians, religious leaders, and legal professionals. A 2005 report from the Iraq Body Count Web site states that of the 2,210 victims on which information about occupation was available for the period from March 2003 to March 2005, no fewer than 977 police officers were counted among the 1,182 deaths recorded among security professionals, followed by 222 Iraqi soldiers, 149 political aids, and 121 government officials, whereas other fatalities encompass a wide cross-section of Iraq's population.[33] Most civilian fatalities have taken place in Baghdad and other large Iraqi cities.

The number of police officials killed in Iraq increased considerably after the end of the invasion, but the number of police fatalities has not been steady from month to month. In 2004, 962 police fatalities were counted in the Iraq Body Count database, a number that rose to 1,454 in 2005, 2,413 in 2006, and 3,107 in 2007. The number of police fatalities was particularly high during the period between the summers of 2006 and 2007, at a time when even the U.S. Director of National Intelligence admitted that the term *civil war* had to be used to describe key elements of the Iraqi conflict.[34] In the 13-month period from July 2006 to July 2007, 3,856 police were killed as a result of 1,401 attacks. In response to the rising violence across Iraqi society at that time, a troop surge brought the total level of U.S. troops in Iraq to 152,000 by March of 2007. Alongside the fact that the extra security provided by U.S. military troops had some positive results,[35] the number of police fatalities caught in Iraq's violent unrests also decreased after July 2007. However, the level of insurgent violence involving police fatalities remained higher after the surge than it was before the summer of 2006. In the 8-month period from November 2005 to June 2006, 1,009 police were killed, and 1,225 police died in the 8-month period from August 2007 to March 2008. In 2008, the total number of police killed was 1,241, considerably fewer than the year before but still more than in 2004. Throughout 2008 and the first half of 2009, deadly attacks on Iraqi police were still regularly reported in the news media.[36]

The Iraq Body Count numbers are very likely considerably lower than the actual death toll among police (and civilians). According to a United States Department of Defense report, no less than 6,100 Iraqi security forces had died between May 1, 2003, and November 8, 2006, with an additional 40,000 reported wounded.[37] Despite the enormous fatality rate among the Iraqi police forces, however, new recruits are readily found. Economic urgency rather than patriotism is a major motivation for many young Iraqis to join the police.[38] One of the new Iraqi police recruits explained the situation well when he argued that joining the police (or the army) is among the few options available for employment in Iraq (where unemployment has been estimated to be as high as 60%),[39] although he fully realized that police officers were "walking dead men".[40]

The Resurgence of the Taliban

Despite the fact that a democratic government is now in place in Afghanistan, Taliban forces have in recent years slowly again taken control over several areas in the country (and in neighboring Pakistan). In

Figure 10.3 Bombing site at a police station in Al-Rashid, Iraq, July 24, 2005. Terrorist attacks by insurgents against Iraqi police personnel and police stations have been very frequent, with devastating consequences. The pictured attack on the Al-Rashid police station killed more than 40 Iraqi civilians and left dozens more wounded. (Photo courtesy of the U.S. Department of Defense.)

2005, coalition forces mounted a new offensive against Taliban positions but, a year later, Taliban resistance again increased, especially by means of attacks involving improvised explosives and suicide bombings. As a result, Afghan society has been destabilized by what is described as a full-fledged Taliban resurgence. The Afghan National Police, moreover, has been judged to be ineffective in dealing with the upsurge in Taliban violence, as the police have remained understaffed, under-trained, and under-equipped.[41] By July 2008, the violence perpetrated by Taliban forces had taken on such proportions that the U.S. government decided to extend the tour of duty of some its troops, additionally asking other NATO nations involved to increase their respective troop levels.[42] In February 2009, President Obama announced that an additional 17,000 troops would be deployed to Afghanistan.[43]

There is no systematic information available on the fatalities of the Taliban resurgence that is comparable to that provided by the Iraq Body Count Web site on the situation in Iraq. In more ways than one, the military intervention in Afghanistan is a "forgotten war." However, on the basis of information provided in published media reports, there are clear indications that the Taliban resurgence has increased in recent years and that its violent tactics have specifically been aimed at Afghanistan's new civilian police forces.[44] Although Afghan police were already targeted by Taliban forces soon after the new National Police was installed,[45] attacks against the police particularly increased during the spring of 2007, when Taliban tactics moved from attacking the military troops of the (foreign) coalition forces to hitting the (domestic) police forces. By early September 2007, at least 379 Afghan police were reported to have been killed in that year alone, compared to a total of 257 police fatalities for all of 2006. On the basis of data provided by Afghanistan's Interior Ministry, more than 900 Afghan police officers were killed as a result of Taliban violence in 2007.[46] Other sources put the numbers even higher, with as many as 1,700 Afghan police officers killed between January and April of 2007.[47]

Throughout 2008 and the first half of 2009, media sources continued to report on Taliban attacks purposely aimed at Afghan police.[48] By the spring of 2009, the U.S. military command estimated that 1,500 Afghan police were killed in 2008.[49] In June of 2008, the first-ever killing of a female Afghan police officer was reported.[50] A few months later, the highest-ranked female police officer in the city of Kandahar was also murdered in an attack claimed by the Taliban as part of the increasing wave of attacks purposely aimed at Afghan women.[51] In February 2009, 25 Afghan police officers were killed when a suicide bomber detonated hidden explosives while joining a police exercise disguised in an Afghan police uniform.[52] Even absent more systematic information on the number of casualties as a result of Taliban violence, it is clear that the total number of fatalities among the Afghan police is considerably lower than the number of insurgency killings of Iraqi police. However, the experiences with systematically organized violence against police in both countries indicate a similar pattern, whereby militants avoid targeting military troops and resort to roadside bombs and suicide attacks directed at civilian police forces. Afghan police officers are additionally vulnerable because many are based in small police stations in regional districts and are attacked at night. More fundamentally, the Taliban forces attack Afghan's new system of policing to bring about a destabilization of society. For the same reason, Taliban terrorist attacks have also targeted schools and mosques.

The Dynamics of Counterterrorism and War

Soon after U.S. Special Operations and other coalition forces invaded Afghanistan in 2001, the Taliban was quickly ousted, and a new democratic regime was installed. After the 2003 invasion in Iraq, likewise, the regime of Saddam Hussein collapsed quickly, much as the U.S. government and the other coalition powers had hoped for. However, the Taliban forces have been able to regain control in some areas of Afghanistan, whereas the democratization of Iraq has also not evolved in the manner that was expected. Among the greatest difficulties in the reconstruction of Afghanistan and Iraq since democratic governments were put in place in both countries have been the resurgence of ethnic and religious factions, the eruption and intensification of militant and insurgent violence, and the very slow and incomplete restoration of primary social institutions. Invading Afghanistan and Iraq, clearly, the coalition forces were prepared for waging war more than for establishing peace.

Continued violence from Taliban militants in Afghanistan and from insurgents in Iraq have hindered the normalization of social life, including the development of civilian police systems, in these countries. Societies that have not reached a degree of pacification are unlikely to develop a regular police force. Pacification is hereby conceived to imply, as a minimal condition, an absence of warfare but additionally also a state of durable peace that allows for a stabilization of the political order and a normalization of social life. As the cases of Afghanistan and Iraq show, conditions of peace and the functioning of social institutions mutually influence one another. For as much as pacification is a condition of civilian police development, so too would the existence of a well-functioning police in Afghanistan and Iraq be a concrete expression of the normalization of both societies. Precisely for these reasons, the Afghan and Iraqi police forces have been among the favored targets of terrorist violence in their societies as a well-established and regularly functioning police would represent an important and highly visible indicator of pacification.

Confirming the importance of the police as a primary social institution, it can be noted that terrorist attacks against police, often specifically targeted at new recruits, have also taken place in many other nations that have gone through periods of instability and turmoil. Especially since the summer of 2008, attacks against police and police stations, organized by a variety of terrorist groups, were reported in countries as diverse as Yemen, Algeria, China, Turkey, Zimbabwe, and the Russian republic of Ingushetia.[53] Although more systematic research would be needed, it can be assumed that at least some of these actions have been undertaken because of the successful implementation of similar attacks against police in other nations, thus indicating a spread of terrorist tactics across national borders. In the case of Pakistan, the systematic attacks against police stations that took place in 2008 and 2009 have been attributed to the same Taliban forces that operate in neighboring Afghanistan.[54]

In view of the difficulties associated with police reform in post-autocratic regimes such as contemporary Afghanistan and Iraq, a pragmatic perspective is in order that acknowledges that "[l]arge-scale breakdowns in public order should be anticipated in the aftermath of international interventions, particularly in societies emerging from brutal oppression" (Perito 2005). Rather than merely claiming that invading powers will be "greeted as liberators," as U.S. Vice President Dick Cheney assumed before the invasion of Iraq, more sobering and realistic estimates are in order about restoration efforts after military interventions.[55] Even under the best of circumstances, police reform in post-autocratic regimes should be expected to take several years.

In the present global era, it is unthinkable that the democratization of any society can occur in isolation from the rest of the world. In the case of civilian police reform in Afghanistan and Iraq, both countries have been able to rely on international assistance that, given their autocratic past and the externally directed overthrow of their former political regimes, can be viewed only as a necessity and a moral obligation. However, these international programs have faced inherent difficulties because they not only depend on support from police in the assistance-providing nations but have to rely on military units and private companies. The police reform capabilities of military and private groups are by definition limited. Members of the military are simply not trained or equipped

Figure 10.4 Afghan National Auxiliary Police officers with U.S. military personnel at a training facility near Asadabad, Afghanistan, June 2008. Both in their training and in the execution of many of their duties, Afghan police officers rely on the assistance of U.S. military personnel. Such reliance on military forces is peculiarly ironic in view of the fact that Afghanistan's new civilian police is attempting to break away from its militaristic traditions during the Taliban era. (Photo, courtesy of the U.S. Department of Defense.)

to deal with matters of law enforcement. Private groups can rely on officers recruited from professional law enforcement agencies, but they lack the accountability that characterizes public police institutions. Such private companies, moreover, also deliver military troops and equipment to assist in foreign missions, thus effectively blurring the boundaries between military and civilian-police powers (Singer 2003). The meshing of police and military is peculiarly ironic in view of the fact that a primary goal of police reform in post-autocratic regimes is precisely to demarcate the civilian police more clearly from the military.

Conclusion

Contemporary Afghanistan and Iraq present two striking real-life experiments on the role of police in newly formed and evolving democratic regimes. The cases of Afghan and Iraqi police reform additionally—and most tragically—reveal the peculiar difficulties involved when factions in society are expressly oriented at destabilizing society, seeking out the police as the preferred targets of their violent operations. At present, indications are that Afghanistan and Iraq do not (yet) have a stable democratic polity and also cannot (yet) count on a police that can truly lay claim to a legitimate and effective monopoly of force.

However, inasmuch as the police institutions of Afghanistan and Iraq are no longer political tools of autocratic regimes, their societies are presently undergoing a slow and difficult process of normalization. It is for this reason precisely that terrorist attacks against the civilian police are meant to thwart the pacification of society. Inasmuch as the Afghan and Iraqi police forces are achieving to no longer function as an arm of an autocratic state and instead strive to become independent and professional law enforcement institutions, they are ironically also more prone to the violent attacks from militant and insurgent groups that continue to be committed to destabilize society by terrorist means.

CONCLUDING REFLECTIONS

Taking the Policing of Terrorism Seriously

Researching the policing of terrorism, this book sought to fulfill two central objectives. First, it aimed to uncover the patterns and dynamics of the policing of terrorism in a variety of socio-historical settings. Approached from an organizational and global perspective, the findings in this book show that the momentous events of September 11 served as an important catalyst in shaping current conditions of counterterrorism policing in a wide range of societies. At the same time, variations are also revealed across nations in terms of locally specific conditions. Second, this work sought to make the case for the criminological study of important developments of counterterrorism. More specifically, this study aimed to show the strength of an approach to the policing of terrorism that is rooted in the sociology of crime and social control to offer a complement to the contributions that are made by other disciplines in the broader field of terrorism studies.

It will be useful to conclude this book by identifying some of the central themes and issues that mark the policing of terrorism in the present era and can be expected to shape security efforts in the coming years. Although research cannot predict the future course of societal developments, it can at least highlight the forces of events and actions that have taken place and in which context ongoing processes and structures must take place. From this approach, also, a more cautious attitude should evolve if the debate on terrorism and counterterrorism is to adopt a more realistic foundation.

The Dynamics of Counterterrorism Policing

This book has shown that police institutions have, both before but especially since September 11, taken on counterterrorism functions. Police agencies thereby place a high emphasis on efficiency, aided by advanced technological means of crime control, whereas the objectives of counterterrorism are likewise defined in terms of professional police expertise. Looking at multiple police experiences across the world, the policing of terrorism is, with variable consequences, also affected by politicization efforts that seek to bring counterterrorism police actions in line with overarching, ideologically framed national security policies.

The world of counterterrorism policing contains variations and trends that are shared across national boundaries. Most critical is the centrality of developments in and radiating from the United States. In matters of U.S. counterterrorism , police agencies at all levels—federal, state, and municipal—are involved in counterterrorism activities. Inter-agency cooperation and a centralization of counterterrorism are thereby revealed to be among the key aspirations, particularly with respect to the organization of U.S. law enforcement at multiple levels of government.

Turning to the global dimensions of counterterrorism policing, variable legal and political contexts are seen to bring about differences and similarities in the policing of terrorism worldwide. In autocratic and highly centralized states, counterterrorism policing is generally subsumed under a national security regime, whereas more autonomy is accorded to police in democratic states. The institutional independence that modern police agencies can acquire across national boundaries also enables international police organizations with multilateral membership to address terrorism issues through enhanced means of communication and information exchange. As is the case with other crimes of a distinctly international nature, international cooperation is a central concern in the policing of terrorism. In the context of the persistent globalization of terrorism and related security concerns, counterterrorism functions transcend the jurisdictional boundaries of single national states and their institutions.

There is a strong preference among police to engage in international counterterrorism missions in a unilateral manner or to engage in cooperation with only a limited number of counterparts from other nations. Larger international partnerships occur in a collaborative form,

Figure 11.1 An Afghan National Police officer and a U.S. Navy Seaman stand guard in the Farah province of Afghanistan, January 24, 2009. The approach to counterterrorism by the military is very different from the strategies developed by police agencies. Yet, military and police nonetheless coexist in the broader constellation of counterterrorism. (Photo by Pete Thibodeau, courtesy of the U.S. Department of Defense.)

thereby affirming the contributions and perceptions of participating police agencies in the individual states. Though affording advantages in terms of the preservation of national sovereignty, this national persistence can also produce rifts in the global order of counterterrorism as the strongest participating agencies are the ones most likely to go about it alone in fulfilling stated counterterrorism objectives. Such unilaterally conceived counterterrorism strategies can produce unintended consequences, inasmuch as the security and police forces of otherwise friendly nations may turn against their more powerful counterparts, such as the law enforcement institutions in the United States, only because a more egalitarian cooperative spirit was missing.

In the post-9/11 era of counterterrorism, the international presence and weight of U.S. law enforcement in the global order intensifies an already existing Americanization of international policing, at least inasmuch as counterterrorism issues of concern to U.S. agencies exert pressures that are stronger in shaping counterterrorism policing than regional terrorism issues elsewhere in the world. Strikingly, these pressures occur even in nations with distinct and often long-standing local terrorism experiences. Yet, resentment and distrust on the part of the world's police agencies against any perceived pressures may bring about difficulties in cooperation and thereby ironically further substantiate the view that unilateral work is all that can be achieved.

Unilateralism need not be and, in view of the terrorism problems in the present world, cannot be the only possible avenue in counterterrorism policing. Instead, counterterrorism police strategies can be developed on the basis of an explicit awareness that the world today is highly interconnected. Rather than trying to build a security order exclusively modeled after the experiences of the United States (or any other nation) in matters of security and law enforcement, a collaborative model of cooperation that can be elaborated takes into account the concerns faced by nations across the world. In this respect, it makes sense to contemplate further strengthening the global security order that has already developed, even among countries that can be very different in political, legal, and cultural respects.

Counterterrorism and the Quest for Policing

The policing of terrorism is only one, albeit important and peculiar, dimension in the broader constellation of counterterrorism. Also framing terrorism as a security issue besides policing are developments in law and policy and related military and intelligence activities. Important is that this study revealed that the legal and policy dimensions of counterterrorism cannot account for the dynamics of counterterrorism at the level of police institutions. Therefore, policing cannot be conceived of as the mere enforcement of law, and police institutions should not be conceived as an instrument of political ordering. Instead, it is important to recognize that the processes and structures of policing are not necessarily in tune with those of other counterterrorism institutions.

In matters of terrorism, there is today arguably no dimension more relevant and more discussed, next to the policing of terrorism, than the military involvement in counterterrorism and the conception of counterterrorism in terms of war. However, the ambitions that are connected to the war on terrorism from the political and legal viewpoint— to coordinate and centralize all aspects of counterterrorism—have not been accomplished at the level of the various institutions involved with counterterrorism. In the case of police, most distinctly, terrorism is not pursued in terms of a war but on the basis of acquired professional standards of crime control.

The confrontation of the policing of terrorism with the war-related dimensions of counterterrorism is of considerable importance as the differences between the policing of terrorism and terrorism-related military actions are profound (McCauley 2007). From the policing point of view, the targets of counterterrorism are treated as suspects who are accorded certain rights of due process on the basis of publicly presented evidence in courts and who, upon a determination of guilt, can receive punishment. Military counterterrorism operations, by contrast, are oriented at enemies who can be killed in combat or who can be temporarily detained to be released when a cessation of hostilities has been declared. The respective logics of criminal justice policy and military counterterrorism operations, then, are very different, although they coexist in the wider constellation of counterterrorism, which is essentially multi-dimensional in nature.

The aims of this book should not be misunderstood to imply a defense of the policing approach to terrorism against the military model. The normative debate on counterterrorism has in this respect again been less than useful in occasionally assuming that a policing response and, more generally, a criminal justice model are better suited in terrorism cases. It is, therefore, typically assumed that a police response would not bring about the problems associated with military counterterrorism operations, such as the enormous loss of innocent lives in large-scale military operations (e.g., those in Iraq and Afghanistan). However, problematic consequences can also be involved in the criminal justice and police approach to terrorism. A large body of criminological research that exists has exposed many potential and real concerns in policing, such as the lack of democratic oversight that marks the actions of highly bureaucratized police agencies and the differential enforcement of criminal justice along the lines of existing disparities in race, gender, age, and class. If a sound normative debate is to take place in the case of counterterrorism, such problems cannot simply be ignored.

Offering realism to the normative counterterrorism debate, this work shows that the many components of counterterrorism are not always

Figure 11.2 President Barack Obama at the FBI headquarters, Washington, DC, April 28, 2009. Just a few months into his presidency, Barack Obama visited the FBI headquarters, indicating his commitment to the work done by America's first-responders and affirming the critical role Obama attributes to police and security forces in counterterrorism. Yet, it remains to be seen whether the Obama administration can abandon the war on terror in favor of a counterterrorism approach that is based primarily on law enforcement. (Photo courtesy of the Federal Bureau of Investigation).

neatly in harmony with one another. Whichever policy models that are suggested at the national and international levels of law and politics to more effectively detect and deter terrorism must also take into account the manner in which counterterrorism operations are undertaken by various institutions. From the viewpoint of the policing of terrorism, counterterrorism does not involve a war on terror but is instead viewed as a permanent function of crime control. Counterterrorism police strategies, therefore, adopt an approach that may very well be realistic in being based on the notion of terrorism as a permanent risk. In contrast, the war on terror is failing, not only because it has not been able to effectively coordinate and centralize all counterterrorism functions but, also because it offers an unwarranted optimistic sense of the possibility of a victory and a lasting peace without terrorism.

Notes

Preview: Why There Is No War on Terror

1 "Transcript: President Bush on 'FOX News Sunday'," Foxnews.com, posted February 11, 2008. Online: http://www.foxnews.com/story/0,2933,330234,00. html.

2 "'There Is No War on Terror': Outspoken DPP Takes on Blair and Reid over Fear-driven Legal Response to Threat," by Clare Dyer, *The Guardian*, January 24, 2007. Online: http://www.guardian.co.uk/politics/2007/jan/24/ uk.terrorism.

3 "Statement for the Record of Louis J. Freeh, Director Federal Bureau of Investigation Before the Senate Select Committee on Intelligence," Washington, DC, January 28, 1998. Online: http://www.yale.edu/lawweb/ avalon/terrorism/t_0011.htm.

4 "Statement for the Record, FBI Director Louis J. Freeh before the Senate Judiciary Committee," September 3, 1998. Online: http://www.fas.org/irp/ congress/1998_hr/98090302_npo.html.

5 "The Threat to the United States Posed by Terrorists." Statement for the Record of Louis J. Freeh, Director Federal Bureau of Investigation, Before the United States Senate Committee on Appropriations Subcommittee for the Departments of Commerce, Justice, and State, the Judiciary, and Related Agencies, February 4, 1999. Online: http://www.fas.org/irp/congress/1999_ hr/990204-freehct2.htm.

6 "Threat of Terrorism to the United States." Testimony of Louis J. Freeh, Director, FBI, Before the United States Senate, Committees on Appropriations, Armed Services, and Select Committee on Intelligence, May 10, 2001. Online: http:// www.fbi.gov/congress/congress01/freeh051001.htm.

7 Among the victims of the 9/11 attacks were an FBI special agent who assisted in the evacuation of the World Trade Center and a former FBI counterterrorism expert who had taken on a new position as director of security at the World Trade Center just days before the buildings were hit (Weiss 2003).

8 "Extraordinary Council Meeting, Justice and Home Affairs," Council of the European Union, Brussels, July 13, 2005. Online: http://ue.eu.int/ueDocs/ cms_Data/docs/ pressdata/en/jha/85703.pdf; "EU's Anti-Terror Response to Madrid Bombings," *Agence France Presse*, March 25, 2004.

9 "EU Ministers Pledge New Terror Fight," *International Herald Tribune*, July 15, 2005. Online: http://www.iht.com/articles/2005/07/14/news/brussels. php.

10 "EU Police Chiefs to Discuss Madrid Attacks," *Agence France Presse*, March 19, 2004.
11 "Police Call in Foreign Terror Experts," by Ian Cobain, *The Guardian*, July 12, 2005. Online: http://www.guardian.co.uk/uk/2005/jul/12/july7.uksecurity3.
12 Unless otherwise noted, the URL addresses of all cited online documents were last retrieved in June of 2009.

1 The Criminology of Terrorism and Counterterrorism

1 This section relies on Jenkins 2006; Sinclair 2003; Townshend 2002.
2 In the professional literature, a distinction is occasionally drawn between antiterrorism as the defensive measures meant to reduce the chance of a terrorist attack or the vulnerability of the possible targets of terrorist tactics, whereas counterterrorism refers to the offensive strategies to prevent, deter, preempt, and respond to terrorism. In this book, counterterrorism is an analytical concept that comprises both defensive and offensive measures.
3 "United Nations Treaty Collection: Conventions on Terrorism." Online: http://untreaty.un.org/English/terrorism.asp.

3 Counterterrorism Policy and Law

1 This and the following sections benefitted from the discussions by Alexander (2006); Alexander and Kraft (2007); Badey (2006); Banks (2005); Donohue (2001); Guiora (2007); Rosenau (2007); Smith (1987); and Wilson (1994).
2 "Antiterrorism and Effective Death Penalty Act of 1996: A Summary," by Charles Doyle, 1996. Online: http://www.fas.org/irp/crs/96-499.htm.
3 "First Annual Report to the President and to the Congress of the Advisory Panel to Assess Domestic Response Capabilities for Terrorism Involving Weapons of Mass Destruction." Online: http://www.rand.org/nsrd/terrpanel/terror.pdf; "Second Annual Report to the President and to the Congress of the Advisory Panel to Assess Domestic Response Capabilities for Terrorism Involving Weapons of Mass Destruction." Online: http://www.rand.org/nsrd/terrpanel/terror2.pdf.
4 "U.S. Commission on National Security/21st Century—Hart-Rudman Commission." Online: http://www.au.af.mil/au/awc/awcgate/nssg/.
5 "Hart-Rudman Calls for Homeland Defense," by Keith J. Costa, *Air Force Magazine*, April 2001, pp. 64–66. Online: http://www.afa.org/magazine/april2001/0401hart.asp.
6 See the official Web site of the Department of Homeland Security, various pages of which have been relied upon throughout this section: http://www.dhs.gov/index.shtm.
7 'Homeland Security Act of 2002.' Public Law 107–296 [116 STAT. 2135]. Online: http://www.whitehouse.gov/deptofhomeland/bill/.
8 See "TSA's New Policelike Badges a Sore Point with Real Cops," by Thomas Frank, *USA Today*, June 15, 2008. Online: http://www.usatoday.com/travel/flights/2008-06-15-tsa-badges_N.htm.

9 "Uniting and Strengthening America by Providing Appropriate Tools Required to Intercept and Obstruct Terrorism (USA PATRIOT ACT) Act of 2001," Public Law 107-56 [115 STAT. 272]. Online: http://news.findlaw.com/cnn/docs/terrorism/hr3162.pdf. See also the "USA Patriot Act" webpages on the website of the White House: http://www.whitehouse.gov/infocus/patriotact/.

10 "Reform the Patriot Act: Community Resolution," ACLU. Online: http://action.aclu.org/reformthepatriotact/resolutions.html.

11 "Address to a Joint Session of Congress and the American People," President George W. Bush, Washington, DC, September 20, 2001. Online: http://www.whitehouse.gov/news/releases/2001/09/20010920-8.html.

12 "Obama Scraps 'Global War on Terror' for 'Overseas Contingency Operation,'" Fox News, March 25, 2009. Online: http://www.foxnews.com/politics/elections/2009/03/25/report-obama-administration-backing-away-global-war-terror/

13 An insightful analysis of the response to 9/11 by the Bush administration and its leading figures is offered in the PBS-produced television documentary "Bush's War." The documentary is available online: http://www.pbs.org/wgbh/pages/frontline/bushswar/.

14 "Authorization for Use of Military Force,' September 18, 2001, Public Law 107-40 [S. J. RES. 23]. Online: http://news.findlaw.com/wp/docs/terrorism/sjres23.es.html.

15 "'Dark Side' Sheds Light on Cheney," by Sam Allis, *The Boston Globe*, June 20, 2006. Online: http://www.boston.com/ae/tv/articles/2006/06/20/dark_side_sheds_light_on_cheney/.

16 "Guantanamo 9/11 Suspects on Trial," *BBC News*, June 6, 2008. Online: http://news.bbc.co.uk/2/hi/americas/7437164.stm.

17 This section is partly revised and updated from Deflem and Dilks (2008).

18 "Bush Lets U.S. Spy on Callers Without Courts," by James Risen and Eric Lichtblau, *New York Times*, December 16, 2005. Online: http://www.nytimes.com/2005/12/16/politics/16program.html.

19 "NSA Domestic Snooping—Resources," Center for Democracy & Technology. Online: http://www.cdt.org/security/nsa/briefingbook.php.

20 "Bush Says He Signed NSA Wiretap Order," CNN.com, December 17, 2005. Online: http://www.cnn.com/2005/POLITICS/12/17/bush.nsa/index.html.

21 "NSA Eavesdropping Program Ruled Unconstitutional," CNN.com, August 17, 2006. Online: http://www.cnn.com/2006/POLITICS/08/17/domesticspying.lawsuit/index.html.

22 "Protect America Act of 2007." Public Law 110-55 [121 STAT. 552]. Online: http://frwebgate.access.gpo.gov/cgi-bin/getdoc.cgi?dbname=110_cong_public_laws&docid=f:publ055.110.pdf.

23 "Responsible Electronic Surveillance That is Overseen, Reviewed, and Effective Act of 2007." Online: http://judiciary.house.gov/Media/PDFS/HR3773FISA.pdf.

24 "FISA Amendments Act of 2008." Online: http://www.opencongress.org/bill/110-h6304/show.

25 "A New Approach to Intelligence?" by Erin Fitzgerald, Foreign Police in Focus, June 25, 2009. Online: http://www.fpif.org/fpiftxt/6214.

26 "CIA & The War on Terrorism." Online: https://www.cia.gov/news-information/cia-the-war-on-terrorism/index.html.

27 Office of the Coordinator for Counterterrorism, Web site. Online: http://www.state.gov/s/ct/.

28 U.S. Treasury—Office of Terrorism and Financial Intelligence (TFI), Web site. Online: http://www.treas.gov/offices/enforcement/.

29 USDOJ: National Security Division, Web site. Online: http://www.usdoj.gov/nsd/.

30 "Intelligence Reform and Terrorism Prevention Act of 2004," Public Law 108-458 [118 STAT. 3638]. Online: http://frwebgate.access.gpo.gov/cgi-bin/getdoc.cgi?dbname=108_cong_public_laws&docid=f:publ458.108.

31 The Office of the Director of National Intelligence, Web site. Online: http://www.dni.gov/.

32 "Homeland Security Council Executive Order," President George W. Bush, The White House, March 19, 2002. Online: http://www.whitehouse.gov/news/releases/2002/03/20020321-9.html.

33 "Secretary Michael Chertoff U.S. Department of Homeland Security Second Stage Review Remarks," Washington, DC, July 13, 2005. Online: http://www.dhs.gov/xnews/speeches/speech_0255.shtm.

4 Homeland Security

1 Besides interviews with FBI officials, various pages on the official Web site of the FBI were helpful for this section: http://www.fbi.gov/. Also relied upon are works by Murphy and Plotkin (2003), Nadelmann (1993), Powers (2004), and Theoharis (2004). For insiders' perspectives before 9/11, see Coulson and Shannon 1999, and after 9/11, see Ashcroft 2006 and Freeh 2006.

2 "PDD-39 U.S. Policy on Counterterrorism," June 21, 1995. Online: http://www.fas.org/irp/offdocs/pdd39.htm.

3 "The Attorney General's Guidelines on General Crimes, Racketeering Enterprise and Terrorism Enterprise Investigations," Attorney General John Ashcroft, May 30, 2002. Online: http://www.ignet.gov/pande/standards/prgexhibitg.pdf.

4 National Counterterrorism Center, Web site. Online: http://www.nctc.gov/.

5 See the official Web site of U.S. Immigration and Customs Enforcement: http://www.ice.gov/.

6 Between November 2003 and October 2005, ICE also oversaw the Federal Air Marshal Service, but it has since been transferred to the Transportation Security Administration (TSA) as that agency's only law enforcement responsibility.

7 "Department of Homeland Security: Office of the ICE Attaché—Brazil and Bolivia," Embassy of the United States, Brazil. Online: http://www.embaixada-americana.org.br/index.php?itemmenu=57&submenu=7&action=ice.php.

8 See the Web site of U.S. Customs and Border Protection: http://www.cbp.gov/.

9 "Secure Fence Act of 2006," Public Law 109-367 [120 STAT. 2638]. Online: http://frwebgate.access.gpo.gov/cgi-bin/getdoc.cgi?dbname=109_cong_public_laws&docid=f:publ367.109.pdf.

10 See Bayer 2005; Griffin 2005; Jones 2005. Additional materials presented in this section are retrieved from the Web site of the Bureau of Diplomatic Security: http://www.state.gov/m/ds/.

11 "Pearl Film Could Help State Bureau," By Matthew Lee, *USA Today*, June 19, 2007. Online: http://www.usatoday.com/news/washington/2007-06-19-1056841891_x.htm.

12 "U.S. Gave Immunity to Blackwater Guards," by Lara Jakes Jordan, *USA Today*, October 30, 2007. Online: http://www.usatoday.com/news/washington/2007-10-29-blackwater-immunity_N.htm.

13 "Grand Jury Probes Blackwater Shootings: Iraqis Testify About Incident," by Karen De Young and Del Quentin Wilber, *The Washington Post*, May 28, 2008. Online: http://www.washingtonpost.com/wp-dyn/content/article/2008/05/27/AR2008052702637.html?hpid=moreheadlines.

14 "FBI Knew Spying Was Illegal in 2004, Did Nothing," by Luke O'Brien, Wired.com, March 19, 2007. Online: http://blog.wired.com/27bstroke6/2007/03/fbi_knew_spying.html#previouspost.

15 "Librarians Speak Out for First Time After Being Gagged by Patriot Act," ACLU, May 30, 2006. Online: http://www.aclu.org/natsec/gen/25702prs20060530.html.

16 "FBI Says Problems with Letters Fixed," MSN.com, April 15, 2008. Online: http://news.moneycentral.msn.com/provider/providerarticle.aspx?feed=AP&date=20080415&id=8490760.

17 Since September 11, militants associated with or inspired by al-Qaeda have been accused of involvement with several recent terrorist incidents, including: the October 2002 nightclub bombing on the Indonesian island of Bali, which killed 200 people; the August 2003 bombing of the Marriott Hotel in Jakarta, Indonesia, which resulted in 15 deaths; the March 2004 bombings of four commuter trains in Madrid, Spain, which killed 191 people; and the four bomb blasts on July 7, 2005, that hit London's public transit system and killed 52.

18 "D.C. Homicides, Violent Crimes Fall: Slayings Jump 65 Percent in Pr. George's, Rise in Many U.S. Cities," by Petula Dvorak and Jamie Stockwell, *The Washington Post*, January 1, 2002, p. A01.

19 "Council Calls Crime Up Since Sept. 11," by Sewell Chan and David A. Fahrenthold, *The Washington Post*, December 5, 2001, p. B08.

20 "United States Crime Rates 1960–2006." Online: http://www.disastercenter.com/crime/uscrime.htm.

21 "FBI Called Slow to Join Terror Fight," by Richard B. Schmitt, *The Los Angeles Times*, May 09, 2008. Online: http://www.policeone.com/police-technology/wire-tap/articles/1693774-FBI-called-slow-to-join-terror-fight.

22 "U.S. Thwarts 19 Terrorist Attacks Against America Since 9/11," by James Jay Carafano, *The Heritage Foundation*, November 13, 2007. Online: http://www.heritage.org/research/HomelandDefense/bg2085.cfm.

23 "Mistrial in Sears Tower Bomb Plot Trial," by Curt Anderson, ABCNews.com, December 13, 2007. Online: http://abcnews.go.com/TheLaw/FedCrimes/wireStory?id=3996409.

24 "Third Trial Pursued in Alleged Sears Tower Plot," *USA Today*, April 23, 2008. Online: http://www.usatoday.com/news/nation/2008-04-23-sears-tower_N.htm.

25 "Miami Jury Convicts Men in Terror Plot," *New York Post*, May 12, 2009. Online: http://www.nypost.com/seven/05122009/news/nationalnews/miami_jury_convicts_five_men_in_terror_p_168893.htm.

26 "JFK Terror Plot Suspect's Alleged Role Draws Disbelief," by Letta Tayler, newsday.com, June 5, 2007. Online: http://www.newsday.com/search/am-guya0605,0,5350432.story; "FBI Thwarts Attacks on NYC Temple, Upstate Airport," cbs2chicago.com, May 20, 2009. Online: http://cbs2chicago.com/national/terror.plot.temple.2.1015397.html.

27 "Terrorism 2002–2005," Federal Bureau of Investigation. Online: http://www.fbi.gov/publications/terror/terrorism2002_2005.htm.

28 "Terrorism 2002–2005." The definition of terrorism in the U.S. Code actually speaks of "violent acts or acts dangerous to human life that are a violation of the criminal laws of the United States or of any State." See United States Code, Title 18: Crimes and Criminal Procedure, Part I: Crimes, Chapter 113b: Terrorism, Section 2331: Definitions. Online: http://caselaw.lp.findlaw.com/casecode/uscodes/18/parts/i/chapters/113b/toc.html.

29 "War on Terrorism." Testimony of Robert S. Mueller, III, Director, FBI Before the Select Committee on Intelligence of the United States Senate, February 11, 2003. Online: http://www.fbi.gov/congress/congress03/mueller021103.htm.

30 "Statement Before the Senate Select Committee on Intelligence," FBI Director Robert S. Mueller, January 11, 2007. Online: http://www.fbi.gov/congress/congress07/mueller011107.htm.

31 "DEA Mission Statement," U.S. Drug Enforcement Administration. Online: http://www.usdoj.gov/dea/agency/mission.htm

32 "FBI Director Robert Mueller on Global Terrorism Today (video)," Chatham House, London, April 7, 2008. Online: http://fora.tv/2008/04/07/FBI_Director_Robert_Mueller_on_Global_Terrorism_Today.

33 "Cuba Deports ICE 'Most Wanted Fugitive' Sought on Sex Tourism Charges," *Imperial Valley News*, June 16, 2008. Online: http://www.imperialvalleynews.com/index.php?option=com_content&task=view&id=1776&Itemid=1.

5 Terrorism and the City

1 In this book, I conceive of local policing as comprising all levels of policing lower than the federal level. In the professional literature, local policing is typically understood in a narrower sense as comprising municipal and county-level policing, differentiated from state policing and federal law enforcement.

2 "Law Enforcement Statistics," Bureau of Justice Statistics. Online: http://www.ojp.usdoj.gov/bjs/lawenf.htm.

3 "Post-9/11 Report Recommends Police, Fire Response Change," *USA Today*, August 19, 2002. Online: http://www.usatoday.com/news/nation/2002-08-19-nypd-nyfd-report_x.htm.

4 On the organization of the NYPD and its terrorism-related functions, see Bornstein 2005; Dickey 2009; Eterno 2003; Nussbaum 2007; Safir and Whitman 2003. See, also, the official Web site of the New York City Police Department: http://www.nyc.gov/nypd/.

5 "Terrorist Plot to Bomb New York Subway System," by Steve Macko, *Daily Intelligence Report*, August 1, 1997. Online: http://www.emergency.com/ternyc97.htm.

6 "Counterterrorism Initiatives," NYPD Shield. Online: http://www.nypdshield.org/public/initiatives.nypd.

7 See the Web site of NYPD Shield: http://www.nypdshield.org/public/.

8 See Davies and Murphy 2004; Davies and Plotkin 2005; Donnermeyer 2002; Edwards 2006; Grossman 2002; Henry 2005; Kelling and Bratton 2006; Loyka, Faggiani, and Karchmer 2005; Murphy and Plotkin 2003; Reuland and Davies 2004; Reynolds, Griset, and Eaglin 2005; Reynolds, Griset, and Scott 2006; Safe Cities Project 2005; Safir and Whitman 2003; Sloan 2002; and Tully and Willoughby 2002.

9 See the research by Clarke and Newman 2007; Davis *et al.* 2004; Erickson *et al.* 2006; Harris 2006; Jones and Newton 2005; Kayyem and Pangi 2003; Kobach 2005; Lyons 2002; Marks and Sun 2007; McArdle 2006; Ortiz, Hendricks and Sugie 2007; Pelfrey 2007; Riley and Hoffman 1995; Riley *et al.* 2005; and Thacher 2005.

10 "Counter Terrorism and Criminal Intelligence Bureau," Los Angeles Police Department. Online: http://www.lapdonline.org/inside_the_lapd/content_basic_view/6502.

11 "Opening of Joint Regional Intelligence Center," Los Angeles Police Department, News Release, July 25, 2006. Online: http://www.lapdonline.org/newsroom/news_view/32984.

12 "Sleek Snoop Center Still Leans on Human Factor," by Joris Evers, *ZDNet*, August 19, 2006. Online: http://news.zdnet.com/2100-1009_22-6107464.html.

13 "Manhattan Institute and LAPD Unveil Counterterrorism Academy for State and Local Cops," Manhattan Institute for Policy Research, Press Release, March 10, 2008. Online: http://www.manhattan-institute.org/pdf/PressReleaseCPT_03-11-08.pdf.

14 "Counter Terrorism," New York State Police. Online: http://www.troopers.state.ny.us/Counter_Terrorism/.

15 "Counter Terrorism," South Carolina Law Enforcement Division. Online: http://www.sled.sc.gov/CounterTerrorHome.aspx?MenuID=CounterTerrorism.

16 "Philadelphia Police Department Counter Terrorism Bureau," Philadelphia Police Department. Online: http://www.ppdonline.org/hq_terrorism.php.

17 "Operation Miami Shield," The City of Miami Police Department. Online: http://www.miami-police.org/dept/overview.asp?page=1&dept=HomelandSecurity.

18 See, e.g., "Terrorism," Tinley Park Police Department. Online: http://www. tinleyparkpolice.org/terror.htm; "Anti-Terrorism and Intelligence Unit," Pembroke Pines Police Department. Online: http://www.ppines.com/police/ anti-terrorism.html; "Terrorism Readiness," Galt Police Department. Online: http://www.galtpd.com/terrorism.htm; "The Long Beach Police Department's Office of Counter Terrorism," City of Long Beach Police Department. Online: http://www.longbeach.gov/police/info/homeland_security.asp.

19 See, for example, "UCSF Police Department Homeland Security and Emergency Management," University of California, San Francisco. Online: http://www.police.ucsf.edu/terrorism.htm; "Terrorism," Pikes Peak Community College. Online: http://www.ppcc.edu/about-ppcc/public-safety/ terrorism/; "Terrorism Response Plan," Baylor University Police Department. Online: http://www.baylor.edu/DPS/index.php?id= 5789; "California Anti-Terrorism Information Center," CSU Bakersfield University Police. Online: http://www.csub.edu/BAS/police/antiterrorism.shtml.

20 "Directives from Attorney General Ashcroft's Speech before EOUSA's Anti-Terrorism Coordinators Conference," November 13, 2001. Online: http:// listserv.buffalo.edu/cgi-bin/wa?A3=ind0111&L=POETICS&E=7bit&P=10 18151&B=--&T=text%2Fplain;%20charset=iso-8859-1.

21 "National Criminal Intelligence Sharing Plan," Institute for Intergovernmental Research. Online: http://www.iir.com/global/ncisp.htm.

22 "Remarks of Attorney General John Ashcroft, National Criminal Intelligence Sharing Plan Event," Department of Justice, May 14, 2004. Online: http:// justice.gov/archive/ag/speeches/2004/51404aginteliacp.htm.

23 "'Portland Seven' Terrorism Investigation," Complete Archive from *The Oregonian*. Online: http://www.oregonlive.com/special/terror/index.ssf?/ special/terror/pdx_archive.html.

24 "In Portland, Ore., a Bid to Pull Out of Terror Task Force," by Sarah Kershaw, *The New York Times*, April 23, 2005. Online: http://www.nytimes.com/2005/04/23/ national/nationalspecial3/23terror.html?_r=1&oref=login&oref=slogin.

6 The Globalizaton of Counterterrorism Policing

1 This section relies on the overviews by Bell (2006), Chalk and Rosenau (2004), Gibbs Van Brunschot and Sherley (2005), Leman-Langlois (2007), Leman-Langlois and Brodeur (2005), Purdy (2007), and Roach (2005).

2 See Public Safety Canada, Web site. Online: http://www.ps-sp.gc.ca/index-en. asp.

3 "The Anti-terrorism Act," Department of Justice, Canada. Online: http:// www.justice.gc.ca/eng/antiter/index.html.

4 Royal Canadian Mounted Police, Web site. Online: http://www.rcmp-grc. gc.ca/.

5 Canadian Security Intelligence Service, Web site. Online: http://www.csis-scrs.gc.ca/.

6 For overviews of counterterrorism in the United Kingdom, see Beckman 2007; Chalk and Rosenau 2004; Donohue 2007; Hewitt 2008; Hindle 2007; Innes 2006; Klein 2006; and Walker 2006.

7 "Counterterrorism Strategy," Home Office, United Kingdom. Online: http://security.homeoffice.gov.uk/counterterrorism-strategy/.

8 Security Service MI5, Web site. Online: http://www.mi5.gov.uk/.

9 Metropolitan Police, Web site. Online: http://www.met.police.uk/.

10 See Chalk and Rosenau 2004; Parmentier 2006.

11 "France: Terrorism," Legislationline, OSCE Office for Democratic Institutions and Human Rights. Online: http://www.legislationline.org/?tid=46&jid=19&less=false.

12 "La Police Nationale," Le site officiel du ministère de l'Interieur. Online: http://www.interieur.gouv.fr/sections/a_l_interieur/la_police_nationale.

13 Gendarmerie, Web site. Online: http://www.defense.gouv.fr/gendarmerie/.

14 "La Direction de la Surveillance du Territoire," Le site officiel du ministère de l'Interieur. Online: http://www.interieur.gouv.fr/sections/a_l_interieur/la_police_nationale/organisation/dst.

15 "French Push Limits in Fight on Terrorism," by Craig Whitlock, The Washington Post, November 2, 2004, p. A01. Online: http://www.washingtonpost.com/ac2/wp-dyn/A17082-2004Nov1.

16 See Das, Huberts, and van Steden 2007; den Boer 2007.

17 See Alonso and Reinares 2005; Beckman 2007.

18 See Jenkins 2008; Ozeren and Yilmaz 2007; Teymur and Sait Yayla 2005.

19 "Turkey: Anti-Terror Law Used Against Peaceful Activists," Human Rights Watch. Online: http://www.hrw.org/english/docs/2006/06/07/turkey13521.htm.

20 See Abdelmattlep 2003; Abou-el-Wafa 2006; Welchman 2005.

21 'The Arab Convention for the Suppression of Terrorism,' League of Arab States, April 1998. Online: http://www.al-bab.com/arab/docs/league/terrorism98.htm.

22 "State Sponsors of Terrorism," U.S. Department of State. Online: http://www.state.gov/s/ct/c14151.htm.

23 Patterns of Global Terrorism 2003, U.S. Department of State. Online: http://www.state.gov/s/ct/rls/crt/2003/c12108.htm.

24 See Grounds et al. 2006; Moore 2007.

25 "On the Fight Against Terrorism," Russian Federation Federal Law No. 130-FZ Signed by Russian Federation President B. Yeltsin, 25 July 1998. Online: http://www.fas.org/irp/world/russia/docs/law_980725.htm.

26 "FBI/KGB 'Counterterrorism' Pact," The New American, January 10, 2005. Online: http://findarticles.com/p/articles/mi_m0JZS/is_1_21/ai_n25103167.

27 United Nations Resolution 1373 (2001), Adopted by the Security Council at its 4385th meeting, on 28 September 2001. Online: http://daccessdds.un.org/doc/UNDOC/GEN/N01/557/43/PDF/N0155743.pdf.

7 Policing World Terrorism

1 On the organization and functions of Interpol, see Anderson 1997; Deflem 2002. Also relied upon throughout this chapter is information presented on Interpol's official Web site: http://www.interpol.int/.

2 "Application of Article 3 of the Constitution," Interpol Resolution No AGN/53/RES/7. Online: http://www.interpol.int/public/ICPO/GeneralAssembly/Agn53/Resolutions/AGN53RES7.asp.

3 "Acts of Violence Committed by Organised Groups," Interpol Resolution No AGN/48/RES/8. Online: http://www.interpol.int/Public/ICPO/GeneralAssembly/AGN48/Resolutions/AGN48RES8.asp.

4 "Terrorism," Interpol Resolution No AGN/52/RES/9. Online: http://www.interpol.int/Public/ICPO/GeneralAssembly/AGN52/Resolutions/AGN52RES9.asp.

5 "Violent Crime Commonly Referred to as Terrorism," Interpol Resolution No AGN/53/RES/6. Online: http://www.interpol.int/Public/ICPO/GeneralAssembly/Agn53/Resolutions/AGN53RES6.asp.

6 "International Terrorism and Unlawful Interference with Civil Aviation," Interpol Resolution No AGN/54/RES/1. Online: http://www.interpol.int/Public/ICPO/GeneralAssembly/AGN54/Resolutions/AGN54RES1.asp.

7 "Cairo Declaration Against Terrorism," Interpol Resolution No AGN/67/RES/12. Online: http://www.interpol.com/Public/ICPO/GeneralAssembly /AGN67/Resolutions/AGN67RES12.asp.

8 "Terrorist Attack of 11 September 2001," Interpol Resolution No AG-2001-RES-05. Online: http://www.interpol.int/Public/ICPO/GeneralAssembly/AGN70/Resolutions/AGN70RES5.asp.

9 "New Guidelines for Co-operation in Combating International Terrorism," Interpol Resolution No AGN/67/RES/6. Online: http://www.interpol.int/Public/ICPO/GeneralAssembly/AGN67/Resolutions/AGN67RES6.asp.

10 "Legal Framework Governing Action by Interpol in Cases of a Political, Military, Religious or Racial Character," Interpol fact sheet. Online: http://www.interpol.int/public/ICPO/LegalMaterials/FactSheets/FS07.asp.

11 "Terrorism," Interpol fact sheet. Online: http://www.interpol.int/Public/ICPO/FactSheets/TE01.pdf.

12 "Addressing Internet Activities Supporting Terrorism," Interpol Resolution No AG-2005-RES-10. Online: http://www.interpol.int/Public/ICPO/GeneralAssembly/AGN74/resolutions/AGN74RES10.asp.

13 "Home-Grown Terrorists—Al-Qaeda linked/ al-Qaeda Inspired Terrorism," Interpol Resolution No AG-2006-RES-09. Online: http://www.interpol.int/Public/ICPO/GeneralAssembly/AGN75/resolutions/AGN75RES09.asp.

14 "70th INTERPOL General Assembly, 24–28 September 2001, Budapest, Hungary," Speech by Ronald K. Noble, Secretary General Interpol. Online: http://www.interpol.int/public/ICPO/speeches/20010924.asp.

15 "Terrorist Attack of 11 September 2001."

16 "Special Session of the Financial Action Task Force (FATF), Washington, DC, 29 October 2001," Remarks by Mr. Ronald K. Noble, Secretary General Interpol, Online: http://www.interpol.int/public/ICPO/speeches/ 20011029.asp.

17 The first Red Notice seeking the arrest of Osama bin Laden was made by police officials from Libya several years before the attacks on September 11 (Brisard and Dasquié 2002:98).

18 "INTERPOL Issues Alert on Embassy Blank Passport Theft," Interpol
    media release, May 1, 2006. Online: http://www.interpol.int/Public/ICPO/
    PressReleases/PR2006/PR200615.asp.
19 "NYPD to Have Access to Interpol Data," by Daryl Khan, *New York Newsday*,
    November 19, 2003. Online: http://cryptome.org/nypd-interpol.htm.
20 "Vatican Adds Anti-Terrorist Units," CathNews, June 11, 2008. Online:
    http://www.cathnews.com/article.aspx?aeid=7565.
21 "The Building of a Network That Is Global and Reliable," by Tim Weiner,
    The *New York Times*, September 23, 2001. Online: http://query.nytimes.com/
    gst/fullpage.html?res=940CE3D7163AF930A1575AC0A9679C8B63.
22 "70th INTERPOL General Assembly."
23 "Interpol: U.K. Not Sharing Terror Information," Associated Press, July 9,
    2007. Online: http://www.msnbc.msn.com/id/19672738/.
24 "Redgrave Posts Bail for Chechen Who Russia Says Is a Terrorist," by Warren
    Hoge, The *New York Times*, December 7, 2002. Online: http://query.nytimes.
    com/gst/fullpage.html?res=9503E3D9103BF934A35751C1A9649C8B63.
25 "Interpol Votes Against Iran in Argentina Terror Case," *International
    Herald Tribune*, November 6, 2007. Online: http://www.iht.com/articles/
    ap/2007/11/07/africa/AF-GEN-Interpol-Iran.php.
26 "Iran Regional Meeting to Champion INTERPOL's Central Asian Anti-
    Terror 'Shield'," Interpol media release, May 20, 2008. Online: http://www.
    interpol.int/Public/ICPO/PressReleases/PR2008/PR200819.asp.
27 "Interpol Needs Thorough Overhaul to Fight Terrorism," Agence France
    Presse, September 26, 2001.
28 "Interpol Assists Cuba in Anti-Terrorist Drive," Agence France Presse,
    January 17, 2002; "Global Plan To Track Terror Funds," by Kurt Eichenwald,
    The *New York Times*, December 19, 2001. Online: http://query.nytimes.com/
    gst/fullpage.html?res=9E00E5DD123EF93AA25751C1A9679C8B63.
29 "France and U.S. Seek to Thwart Passport Forgers," by Paul Betts, *Financial
    Times*, May 6, 2003, p.5.

8 Policing Terrorism in Europe

1 On the origins and development of Europol, see Lavranos 2003 and Occhipinti
  2003. Also relied upon in this chapter are materials available on the official
  Europol Web site: http://www.europol.europa.eu/.
2 "Convention on the Establishment of a European Police Office," Europol
  Convention, Brussels, July 26, 1995. Online: http://www.projuris.org/
  konvencije/organizovani%20kriminal_6.htm.
3 Ibidem.
4 Joint Supervisory Authority Schengen, Web site. Online: http://www.
  schengen-jsa.dataprotection.org/.
5 On counterterrorism policing in Europe and, specifically, at Europol, see
  the sources cited in note 1 and the discussions by Bures 2008; Fijnaut 2004;
  Friedrichs 2008; Lavranos 2003; Monaco 1995; Monar 2005, 2007; and
  Rauchs and Koenig 2001. On EU counterterrorism law, see den Boer 2003
  and Scheppele 2004.

6   "An Overview of the Counter Terrorism Unit Activities January 2006," Europol.   Online: http://www.europol.europa.eu/publications/Serious_ Crime_Overviews/overview_SC5.pdf.

7   "Council Framework Decisions of 13 June 2002 on Joint Investigation Teams; on Combating Terrorism; and on the European Arrest Warrant and the Surrender Procedures Between Member States," *Official Journal of the European Union*, L162/1; L164/3; L190/1. Online: http://europa.eu.int/eur-lex/lex/JOYear.do?year=2002.

8   European Arrest Warrant Project, Web site. Online: http://www.eurowarrant. net/.

9   "EU-U.S. Declaration on Combating Terrorism," Council of the European Union, Dromoland Castle, June 26, 2004. Online: http://www.statewatch. org/news/2004/jun/eu-us-summit-june.pdf; "Declaration on Combating Terrorism," Council of the European Union, Brussels, March 25, 2004. Online: http://www.statewatch.org/news/2004/mar/eu-terr-decl.pdf.

10   "EU Ministers Agree on Bolstering Anti-Terror Laws," *International Herald Tribune*, April 18, 2008. Online: http://www.iht.com/articles/ap/2008/04/18/ europe/EU-Terrorism.php.

11   "EU Counterterrorism Coordinator," Council of the European Union. Online: http://consilium.europa.eu/cms3_fo/showPage.asp?id=1344& lang=en#.

12   See the meetings mentioned in the Preview of this book.

13   Eurojust, official website. Online: http://eurojust.europa.eu/.

14   "European Union—Minutes of Evidence, Examination of Witnesses (Questions 148–159)," House of Lords, November 3, 2004. Online: http://www.parliament.the-stationery-office.co.uk/pa/ld200405/ldselect/ ldeucom/53/4110307.htm.

15   "Future Priorities for Police Cooperation in the European Union," European Confederation of Police, August 2004. Online: http://ec.europa.eu/justice_ home/news/consulting_public/tampere_ii/eurocop.pdf.

16   U.S. National Central Bureau of Interpol, Web site: http://www.usdoj.gov/ usncb/.

17   "Terrorist Activity in the European Union: Situation and Trends Report (TE-SAT), October 2003–17th October 2004," Europol, The Hague, December 2, 2004. Online: http://www.statewatch.org/news/2005/mar/europol-terrorism-rep-2003-4.pdf.

18   Ibidem.

19   "Big Five to Take Lead in Beefing Up EU Security Measures," *Financial Times*, March 20, 2004, p. 7.

20   "As Europe Hunts for Terrorists, the Hunted Press Advantages," by Tim Golden, Desmond Butler, and Don Van Natta Jr., *New York Times*, March 22, 2004. Online: http://query.nytimes.com/gst/fullpage.html?res=9D03EFD91F 31F931A15750C0A9629C8B63.

21   "First Terrorism Situation and Trend Report of Europol Released," Europol press release, The Hague, April 10, 2007. Online: http://www.europol.europa. eu/index.asp?page=news&news=pr070410.htm.

9 Undercover Counterterrorim in Israel

1 Analysis in this chapter relies on archival sources and ethnographic data obtained during a research visit in Israel, which included a stay with a Yamas unit and meetings with officials in the Magav, the Israeli National Police, and other Israeli security agencies. All identifying data, including the identity of counter-terrorism officials and the location and identity of the Yamas unit I visited, are withheld in this study. Ethnographic data are cited in double quotation marks (not followed by a bibliographical reference). I am grateful to Joe Lockard, Gal Soltz, and Amit and Vered Almor for help in translating Hebrew sources.

2 On the history of Israeli police systems, see Brewer *et al.* 1988 and Geva *et al.* 2004. On Israel's counterterrorism experiences, see Merari 2003 and Van Creveld 2007.

3 See Katz 2005; "Yamas Guide," Isayeret.com. Online (pay site): http://www.isayeret.com/content/units/civi/yamas/guide.htm; MAGAV Site officiel France, Web site. Online: http://www.magav.org.

4 "Border Policeman, Two Terrorists Killed in Jenin Shootout," by Michael Rotem, *The Jerusalem Post*, August 27, 1992.

5 "General Staff Decided to Publicize Squads' Existence IDF Undercover Units Operate in Territories," Bradley Burston, *The Jerusalem Post*, June 23, 1991.

6 "Border Police Chief Confirms Existence of Secret Units," by Michael Rotem, *The Jerusalem Post*, June 30, 1991.

7 "Border Police Undercover Unit Revealed," by Bill Hutman and Batsheva Tsur, *The Jerusalem Post*, November 4, 1994, p. 16A.

8 Israel Police, official Web site. Online: http://www.police.gov.il/.

9 "Hunting for Suicide Bombers," by Samuel M. Katz, *Moment Magazine* 26(1), February 1, 2001. Online: http://www.freerepublic.com/focus/news/725362/posts.

10 "Undercover Police in Jerusalem," by Amir Ben-David, *Judea Electronic Magazine* 8(6):6–7, 2000. Online: http://www.womeningreen.org/judea/jm86.htm.

11 "Hunting for Suicide Bombers."

12 "Yamas Guide."

13 "IDF's 'Contractors' Pay a Visit to Jenin," by Yaakov Katz, *The Jerusalem Post*, March 1, 2007, p. 2; "Uprooting Islamic Jihad," by Rebecca A. Stoil, *The Jerusalem Post*, April 23, 2007, p. 7.

14 "Israeli Agents Live with the Enemy," by Samuel M. Katz, The *Washington Times*, October 7, 2001. Online: http://www.militaryphotos.net/forums/archive/index.php/t-12828.html.

15 "Search Continues for Terrorist," by Margot Dudkevitch and Ben Lynfield, *The Jerusalem Post*, January 15, 1999, p. 2.

16 "IDF's 'Contractors' Pay a Visit to Jenin."

17 "Border Police Go Undercover in Umm Al Fahm during Unrest," by Sharon Gal, *Ha'aretz*, October 25, 2000.

18 "Undercover Police in Jerusalem."

19 "Hunting for Suicide Bombers."

20 "מסתערבים מספרים על שירות מספרי מסתערבים שירותם (Mistaravim Tell About Their Service)," *Anashim* magazine, January 14, 1997. Online: http://www.soldiertestimony. org/Israel/1987–1999/Document.2004-07-25.2716.

21 "רבכעו לותח קחשמב ונחנא:ב":'גמ יברעתסמ דקפמ (Commander of Magav Mistaravim: We Are in a Cat-and-Mouse Game)," March 23, 2007. Online: http://www.ynet.co.il/articles/0,7340,L-3379453,00.html.

22 Ibidem.

23 Mistaravim units are also referred to as "Arabists," "marauders," "masqueraders," and "Arab-masquerader units" (Cohen 1993; Rodman 2003).

24 "Call for the Charges Against Two Peaceful Demonstrators to be Dropped!" Amnesty International, May 31, 2005. Online: http://web.amnesty.org/pages/ isr-action-POCs; "Bil'in: A Lesson in Creative Resistance," by Bex Tyler, *News From Within* 21(4):6–11, 2005. Online: http://www.alternativenews.org/ downloads/task,doc_download/gid,20.

25 "I'm Not Your Husband Ahmed. I'm Yossi from the Shin Bet," by Yossi Melman, *Ha'aretz*, September 29, 1998. Online: http://www.lebanon.net/ newdiscussion.nsf/8178b1c14b1e9b6b8525624f0062fe9f/2c7b33721faddbd4 852566910023f77b?OpenDocument.

26 "Farewell to Arms," by Jonathan Cook, *Al-Ahram Weekly Online*, December 6–12, 2001. Online: http://weekly.ahram.org.eg/2001/563/re4.htm.

27 "Hunting for Suicide Bombers."

28 See Amara and Schnell 2004; "Brutality with a Badge," by Larry Derfner, *The Jerusalem Post*, December 4, 1998, p. 8.

29 "Israel's Military Conundrum," by Matt Rees, *Time*, October 27, 2001. Online: http://www.time.com/time/world/article/0,8599,181538,00.html.

30 "Yamas Guide"; "Outgoing Border Police Chief Proud of His Force's Improved Image," by Rebecca A. Stoil, *The Jerusalem Post*, April 23, 2007, p. 7.

31 "Hunting for Suicide Bombers."

32 "Border Police Go Undercover..."

33 "םידרחתסמ (Mistharedim)," YouTube.com (video), posted by theshomer (Israel), June 18, 2007. Online: http://www.youtube.com/watch? v=fScKH7UokzA.

34 "Deutsche Gewehre für Israels Scharfschützen," by Gerhard Piper, *Neues Deutschland*, August 21, 2001. Online: http://www.uni-kassel.de/fb5/frieden/ regionen/Israel/gewehre.html.

35 "Israeli Experts Teach Police On Terrorism Training Programs Prompt Policy Shifts," by Sari Horwitz. The *Washington Post*, June 12, 2005. Online: http://www.washingtonpost.com/wp-dyn/content/article/2005/06/11/ AR2005061100648.html; Morgenstern and Dempsey 2005.

36 "US Cops Tour Airport," Ynetnews, June 27, 2007. Online: http://www. ynetnews.com/articles/0,7340,L-3418119,00.html; Jewish Institute for National Security Affairs, Web site. Online: http://www.jinsa.org. Accessed July 20, 2007.

37 "Lesson From Israel: Drones and Urban Warfare," by Vernon Loeb, Washingtonpost.com, September 23, 2002. Online: http://findarticles.com/p/ articles/mi_m0NTQ/is_2002_Sept_20/ai_111276015.

38 "Moving Targets: Will the Counter-Insurgency Plan in Iraq Repeat the Mistakes of Vietnam?," by Seymour M. Hersh, *The New Yorker*, December 15, 2003. Online: http://www.newyorker.com/archive/2003/12/15/031215fa_fact.

39 "Plan B: As June 30th Approaches, Israel Looks to the Kurds," by Seymour M. Hersh, *The New Yorker*, June 28, 2004. Online: http://www.newyorker.com/archive/2004/06/28/040628fa_fact.

40 IMS Security, Web site. Online: http://www.ims-security.com.

41 Ibidem.

42 "DefRev Attends Advanced Israeli Anti-Terrorist SWAT School at Camp Bonneville," by David Crane, DefenseReview.com, December 25, 2005. Online: http://www.defensereview.com/article821.html.

43 "Security—Israeli Style," by Phil Shuman, JewishJournal.com, October 11, 2002. Online: http://www.jewishjournal.com/home/preview.php?id=9405.

44 Baguera-Israël, Web site. Online: http://www.baguera-israel.org.

45 "Counter Terrorism Workshop," Falcon International Services, Inc. Online: http://www.ctwisrael.com; The Ultimate Counter-Terrorism Mission, Web site. Online: http://ultimatectmission.com.

10 Terrorism and War

1 On the political history of Iraq and the military invasion of 2003, see Keegan 2004 and Marr 2004.

2 See Jones *et al.* 2005 and Perito 2003, 2005.

3 On the political history of Afghanistan and the invasion of 2001, see Ewans 2002; Rogers 2004; and Runion 2007.

4 On policing under the Taliban, see Mohammad and Conway 2003; "Afghanistan Bans TV Sets, VCRs," by Zaheeruddin Abdullah, Associated Press, July 12, 1998. Online: http://www.afghanistannewscenter.com/news/1998/july/july12e1998.htm; "Taliban Demands Rigid Conformity," by Timothy W. Maier, Insight on the News, October 22, 2001. Online: http://findarticles.com/p/articles/mi_m1571/is_39_17/ai_79167198; "'Ministry of Vice' Fills Afghan Women with Fear," by Christina Lamb, *The Sunday Times*, July 23, 2006. Online: http://www.timesonline.co.uk/tol/news/world/article691340.ece; "The Taliban," by Anna Shoup, Online Newshour, PBS, October 3, 2006. Online: http://www.pbs.org/newshour/indepth_coverage/asia/afghanistan/keyplayers/taliban.html.

5 On the Iraqi police situation after the 2003 invasion, see Ashraf 2007; Jones *et al.* 2005; and Perito 2004, 2005, 2006, 2007; "Pentagon Was Warned over Policing Iraq," by Julian Borger, *The Guardian*, May 28, 2003. Online: http://www.guardian.co.uk/Iraq/Story/0,2763,965096,00.html; "The New Iraq," Transcript of Newshour with Jim Lehrer, PBS, April 21, 2003. Online: http://www.pbs.org/newshour/bb/military/jan-june03/recon_4-21.html; "Frontline, Interview: Robert M. Perito," PBS, September 5, 2003. Online: http://www.pbs.org/wgbh/pages/frontline/shows/truth/interviews/perito.html; "Misjudgments Marred U.S. Plans for Iraqi Police," by Michael Moss and

David Rohde, *New York Times*, May 21, 2006. Online: http://www.nytimes.com/2006/05/21/world/middleeast/21security.html.

6 "The FBI in Iraq: The Work of Our Legal Attaché," Federal Bureau of Investigation, June 29, 2007. Online: http://www.fbi.gov/page2/june07/iraq062907.htm; "ICE in Iraq," U.S. Immigration and Customs Enforcement, July 27, 2006. Online: http://www.ice.gov/pi/news/factsheets/ice_in_iraq.htm.

7 "Iraq Hampers U.S. Bid to Widen Sunni Police Role," by Michael R. Gordon. *New York Times*, October 28, 2007. Online: http://www.nytimes.com/2007/10/28/world/middleeast/28sunnis.html.

8 "Crash Course in Law Enforcement Lifts Hopes for Stability in Iraq: Academy Set to Train A New Generation of The Country's Police," Ariana E. Cha, *Washington Post*, December 9, 2003, p. A22.

9 "Blackwater Iraq Contract to be Renewed," by Elise Labott, CNN.com, April 4, 2008. Online: http://www.cnn.com/2008/US/04/04/blackwater/index.html.

10 "United States Participation in International Police (CIVPOL) Missions," Factsheet, Bureau for International Narcotics and Law Enforcement Affairs, U.S. Department of State, May 18, 2005. Online: http://www.state.gov/p/inl/rls/fs/47759.htm.

11 "In Iraq, 2006 is the 'Year of the Police,' says U.S. General," by David I. McKeeby, *The Washington File*, March 24, 2006. Online: http://www.globalsecurity.org/wmd/library/news/iraq/2006/03/iraq-060324-usia01.htm; "U.S. Offers Plan to Curb Rogue Iraqi Police Forces," by Solomon Moore, *Los Angeles Times*, August 15, 2006. Online: http://articles.latimes.com/2006/aug/15/world/fg-iraq15.

12 "Iraq: Mission Not Yet Accomplished," by Jawad Al Bolani, *Washington Post*, June 30, 2009. Online: http://www.washingtonpost.com/wp-dyn/content/article/2009/06/29/AR2009062903458.html.

13 The policing activities of DynCorp are not to be confused with those of Blackwater and other private security companies that also operate in Iraq (and Afghanistan). DynCorp acts on behalf of, not merely alongside, the U.S. government.

14 "DynCorp Took Part in Chalabi Raid," by Renae Merle, *Washington Post*, June 4, 2004. Online: http://www.washingtonpost.com/wp-dyn/articles/A13904-2004Jun3.html.

15 "State Department Use of Contractors Leaps in 4 Years," by John M. Broder and David Rhode, *New York Times*, October 24, 2007. Online: http://www.nytimes.com/2007/10/24/washington/24contractor.html.

16 "DynCorp Wins $546M Police Training Contract in Iraq," *Washington Business Journal*, June 23, 2008. Online: http://www.bizjournals.com/washington/stories/2008/06/23/daily17.html.

17 On the police situation in Afghanistan, see Murray 2007; Sedra 2003; and Wardick 2004; "Cops or Robbers? The Struggle to Reform the Afghan National Police," by Andrew Wilder, Afghanistan Research and Evaluation Unit, 2007. Online: https://www30.a2hosting.com/~areuorg/index.php?option=com_docman&Itemid=26&task=doc_download&gid=523; "Fact Sheet Afghan

National Police," Combined Security Transition Command, Afghanistan, April 20, 2008. Online: http://www.cstc-a.com/mission/AfghanistanPoliceFacts. html; "Situation in Afghanistan," Nancy J. Powell, Acting Assistant Secretary for International Narcotics and Law Enforcement Affairs, Testimony Before the House Armed Services Committee, Washington, DC, June 22, 2005. Online: http://www.state.gov/p/inl/rls/rm/51067.htm; "Country Profile: Afghanistan," Library of Congress, May 2006. Online: http://lcweb2.loc. gov/frd/cs/profiles/Afghanistan.pdf; "Interagency Assessment of Afghanistan Police Training and Readiness," U.S. Department of State, November 2006. Online: http://oig.state.gov/documents/organization/76103.pdf; "Afghan National Police Gain More Than 1,600 New NCOs," by Beth Del Vecchio, American Forces Press Service, May 22, 2008. Online: http://www.defenselink. mil/news/newsarticle.aspx?id=49967.

18 "Corruption Eats Away at Afghan Government," by Doug Saunders, *The Globe and Mail*, May 3, 2008. Online: http://www.theglobeandmail.com/ servlet/story/RTGAM.20080502.afghan03/BNStory/International/home.

19 "Germany's Support for Rebuilding the Afghan Police Force," Auswärtiges Amt (German Ministry of the Exterior). Online: http://www.auswaertiges-amt.de/ diplo/en/Aussenpolitik/RegionaleSchwerpunkte/AfghanistanZentralasien/ Polizeiaufbau.html.

20 "EU Police Mission in Afghanistan (EUPOL AFGHANISTAN)." Online: http://consilium.europa.eu/cms3_fo/showPage.asp?id=1268&lang=EN.

21 "Canadian Civilian Policing Efforts in Afghanistan," RCMP, International Peace Operations Branch. Online: http://www.rcmp-grc.gc.ca/peace_ operations/afghanistan_e.htm.

22 "Public-Private Partnership for Justice Reform in Afghanistan," Bureau of International Narcotics and Law Enforcement Affairs, U.S. Department of State. Online: http://www.state.gov/p/inl/partnership/.

23 "Overhaul of Afghan Police is Expensive New Priority," by David Rhode, *New York Times*, October 18, 2007. Online: http://www.nytimes.com/2007/10/18/ world/asia/18afghan.html.

24 "Afghan Police Play Critical Role in Country's Future," by Jim Garamone, U.S. Department of Defense Web site, April 28, 2009. Online: http://www. defenselink.mil/news/newsarticle.aspx?id=54104.

25 "Police Face Huge Training Challenges in Afghanistan," *Aftenposten* (Norway), September 30, 2008. Online: http://www.aftenposten.no/english/ local/article2681857.ece; "Afghan Stability is a Tall Order," by Tom Vanden Brook. *USA Today*, January 12, 2009. Online: http://www.tennessean.com/ article/20090112/NEWS08/901120342/1025.

26 "Afghan President Calls for More Help Training Troops, Police," by Steven Edwards, Canwest News Service, September 24, 2008. Online: http://www. canada.com/topics/news/world/story.html?id=a5ee8e2e-b9e2-4d3a-a45b-15600d9b0661; "Germany Boosts Number of Police Trainers in Afghanistan," Deutsche Welle, September 24, 2008. Online: http://www.dw-world.de/dw/ article/0,2144,3668723,00.html.

27 "Erratic Afghan Forces Pose Challenge to U.S. Goals," by C. J. Chivers, *New York Times*, June 7, 2009. Online: http://www.nytimes.com/2009/06/08/world/asia/08afghan.html.

28 "19,000 Insurgents Killed in Iraq since '03," by Jim Michaels, *USA Today*, September 27, 2007. Online: http://www.usatoday.com/news/world/iraq/2007-09-26-insurgents_N.htm.

29 See, for example, "Bomb Kills Six Iraqi Police Officers," *The International Herald Tribune*, June 29, 2008. Online: http://www.iht.com/articles/2008/06/29/mideast/iraq.php; "Roadside Bombs Target Iraqi Police, Officials Say," CNN.com, March 3, 2007. Online: http://www.cnn.com/2007/WORLD/meast/03/03/iraq.main/; "Iraqi Police Fear Danger in Ranks," by Jeremy Redmon, *The Atlanta Journal-Constitution*, February 23, 2006. Online: http://www.ajc.com/blogs/content/shared-blogs/ajc/guard/entries/2006/02/23/iraqi_police_fe.html.

30 Iraq Body Count, Web site: http://www.iraqbodycount.org/.

31 Iraq Coalition Casualty Count, Web site: http://icasualties.org/.

32 The statistics discussed in this section are based on the numbers reported in Deflem and Sutphin (2006), supplemented by additional research of the database on the Iraq Body Count Web site for the period from July 2006 until January 2009.

33 "A Dossier of Civilian Fatalities in Iraq 2003–2005," Iraq Body Count. Online: http://www.iraqbodycount.org/analysis/reference/press-releases/12/.

34 "Spy Chief Uses 'Civil War' to Describe Iraq," by Jim Michaels, *USA Today*, February 27, 2007. Online: http://www.usatoday.com/news/washington/2007-02-27-mcconnell_x.htm.

35 "'War Czar': Iraq Surge Has Mixed Results" (audio file), All Things Considered, NPR, June 7, 2007. Online: http://www.npr.org/templates/story/story.php?storyId=10819104.

36 See, for example, "15 Iraqi Police Killed by Explosion," CBS News, February 19, 2008. Online: http://www.cbsnews.com/stories/2008/02/19/iraq/main3848542.shtml; "Blasts Kill 13 in Iraq," CNN, May 31, 2008. Online: http://cnnwire.blogs.cnn.com/2008/05/31/blasts-kill-13-in-iraq/; "Roadside Bomb Kills Five Policemen in Iraq," Reuters, June 25, 2009. Online: http://www.reuters.com/article/latestCrisis/idUSLP075814s.

37 "Iraqi Police and Security Forces Casualty Estimates," by Hannah Fischer, Knowledge Services Group, CRS Report for Congress, November 17, 2006. Online: http://fpc.state.gov/documents/organization/77707.pdf.

38 "Police Recruits Targeted In Iraq," by Rajiv Chandrasekaran, *Washington Post*, September 15, 2004, p. A1.

39 "Iraq: Unemployment and Violence Increase Poverty," Reuters, October 17, 2006. Online: http://www.alertnet.org/thenews/newsdesk/IRIN/c14c2cc0f6c99e87f284df922a039cad.htm.

40 "For Police Recruits, Risk Is Constant Companion," by Steve Fainaru, *Washington Post*, September 27, 2004. Online: http://www.washingtonpost.com/wp-dyn/articles/A52561-2004Sep26.html.

41 "Lacking Sufficient Support, Afghan Police Struggle to Work a Beat in a War," by C.J. Chivers, *New York Times*, January 13, 2008. Online: http://

query.nytimes.com/gst/fullpage.html?res=9401E5DF153AF930A25752C0A
96E9C8B63&partner=rssnyt&emc=rss; "Afghanistan's Police Force a Weak
Link: General," CTV.ca, May 14, 2008. Online: http://www.ctv.ca/servlet/
ArticleNews/story/CTVNews/20080514/Afghanistan_army_080514/20080
514?hub=Canada.

42 "APNewsBreak: US Military Extends Afghanistan Tour of 2,200 Marines
After Saying It Would Not," *International Herald Tribune*, July 3, 2008.
Online: http://www.iht.com/articles/ap/2008/07/03/america/NA-US-
Afghanistan-Marines.php.

43 "Obama Orders 17,000 More U.S. Troops into Afghanistan," by Sheldon
Alberts, *National Post*, February 17, 2009. Online: http://www.nationalpost.
com/story.html?id=1299426.

44 "Afghan Police Suffer Setbacks as Taliban Adapt," by David Rhode, *New York
Times*, September 2, 2007. Online: http://www.nytimes.com/2007/09/02/
world/asia/02taliban.html; "Taliban Turn Gunsights to Afghan Police," by
Jason Motlagh, *The Christian Science Monitor*, June 25, 2007. Online: http://
www.csmonitor.com/2007/0625/p06s02-wosc.html; "A Day in Kabul: Police
Remain a Target in Southeast," *The Toronto Times*, June 2, 2006. Online:
http://thetorontotimes.com/content/view/451/69/.

45 See, e.g., "22 Die in Taliban Attack on Police Station," by Rory McCarthy, *The
Guardian*, August 18, 2003. Online: http://www.guardian.co.uk/world/2003/
aug/18/afghanistan.rorymccarthy.

46 "Taliban Attack Kills 11 Officers at a Police Post in Afghanistan," by Taimoor
Shah and Carlotta Gall, *New York Times*, April 15, 2008. Online: http://www.
nytimes.com/2008/04/15/world/asia/15afghan.html.

47 "Erratic Afghan Forces."

48 "Taliban Targets Afghan Police, Civilians," by Ayaz Gul, VOA News,
April 23, 2008. Online: http://www.voanews.com/english/archive/2008-
04/2008-04-23-voa20.cfm?CFID=7358292&CFTOKEN=37996088; "Five
Afghan Police Killed in Bombing and Attack," The Canadian Press, June 9,
2008. Online: http://canadianpress.google.com/article/ALeqM5jLE7S-
umRBXZHoKfsxYr6SiGxn3Q; "Taliban Kill 20 Afghan Police," by Taimoor
Shah, *New York Times*, January 1, 2009. Online: http://www.nytimes.
com/2009/01/02/world/asia/02afghan.html?ref=todayspaper; "Taliban Kill
Three Afghan Police, Abduct Eight," *The News International*, January 20,
2009. Online: http://www.thenews.com.pk/updates.asp?id=65723; "Double
Suicide Bombing Kills Afghan Police Officer," *New York Times*, February 23,
2009. Online: http://www.nytimes.com/aponline/2009/02/23/world/AP-AS-
Afghanistan.html.

49 "Afghan Police Play Critical Role."

50 "First Female Police Officer Killed in Afghanistan," Aljazeera.com, June 24,
2008. Online: http://aljazeera.com/news/newsfull.php?newid=133507.

51 "Taliban Kill Afghan Police Official," by John F. Burns, *The International
Herald Tribune*, September 29, 2008. Online: http://www.iht.com/
articles/2008/09/29/asia/29afghan.php.

52 "Suicide Bomber Kills 25 Afghan Policemen," by Ben Farmer, *The Daily
Telegraph*, February 2, 2009. Online: http://www.telegraph.co.uk/news/

worldnews/asia/afghanistan/4436576/Suicide-bomber-kills-25-Afghan-policemen.html.

53 "Yemen: Car Bombing Hits Police Headquarters," Al Bawaba, July 25, 2008. Online: http://www.albawaba.com/en/countries/Yemen/232822; "2 Police Killed in South Russia Blast," *Moscow News Weekly*, July 31, 2008. Online: http://mnweekly.ru/news/20080731/55339970.html; "Explosion Rocks Main Police Station in Harare," Reuters, August 2, 2008. Online: http://www.alertnet.org/thenews/newsdesk/L2121243.htm; "16 Chinese Police Killed in Suspected Uighur Attack," by Simon Montlake, *Christian Science Monitor*, August 4, 2008. Online: http://www.csmonitor.com/2008/0804/p99s01-duts.html; "Bombing Wounds 9 Turkish Police," *USA Today*, August 19, 2008. Online: http://www.usatoday.com/news/world/2008-08-19-Turkey-bombs_N.htm; "At Least 43 Killed as Suicide Bomber Attacks Police Academy in Algeria," *The Guardian*, August 20, 2008. Online: http://www.guardian.co.uk/world/2008/aug/20/terrorism.algeria; "Five Killed in Attack on Police Bus in Turkey," Reuters, October 8, 2008. Online: http://www.reuters.com/article/worldNews/idUSTRE4977NZ20081008.

54 See, for example, "Bomb Hits Police Center in Islamabad," by Salman Masood, *New York Times*, October 9, 2008. Online: http://www.nytimes.com/2008/10/10/world/asia/10pstan.html; "Attack on Pakistan Police Station Kills 4," by Ismail Khan, *New York Times*, October 16, 2008. Online: http://www.nytimes.com/2008/10/17/world/asia/17pstan.html; "Seven Police Killed in Pakistan," BBC News, February 7, 2009. Online: http://news.bbc.co.uk/2/hi/south_asia/7876188.stm; "Bomb Kills 1 at Police Station in Pakistani Capital," Reuters, June 6, 2009. Online: http://www.reuters.com/article/featuredCrisis/idUSSP454725.

55 "Upbeat Tone Ended With War," by Dana Milbank, *Washington Post*, March 29, 2003. Online: http://www.washingtonpost.com/ac2/wp-dyn/A44801-2003Mar28.

Bibliography

Abdelmattlep, Mamdooh Abdelhameed. 2003. "Antiterrorism Strategy in the Arab Gulf States." Pp. 205–224 in *Meeting the Challenges of Global Terrorism: Prevention, Control, and Recovery*, edited by D. K. Das and P. C. Kratcoski. Lanham, MD: Lexington Books.

Abou-el-Wafa, Ahmed. 2006. "Egypt." Pp. 152–189 in *Counterterrorism Strategies: Successes and Failures of Six Nations*, edited by Y. Alexander. Washington, DC: Potomac Books.

Abrams, Norman. 2006. "Developments in US Anti-Terrorism Law: Checks and Balances Undermined." *Journal of International Criminal Justice* 4(3):1117–1136.

Ackleson, Jason. 2005. "Border Security Technologies: Local and Regional Implications." *Review of Policy Research* 22(2):137–155.

Alain, Marc. 2001. "Transnational Police Cooperation in Europe and in North America: Revisiting the Traditional Border Between Internal and External Security Matters." *European Journal of Crime Criminal Law and Criminal Justice* 9(2):113–129.

Alexander, Yonah. 2006. "United States." Pp. 9–43 in *Counterterrorism Strategies: Successes and Failures of Six Nations*, edited by Y. Alexander. Washington, DC: Potomac Books.

Alexander, Yonah and Michael B. Kraft, editors. 2007. *Evolution of U.S. Counterterrorism Policy*. 3 volumes. Westport, CT: Praeger Security International.

Alonso, Rogelio and Fernando Reinares. 2005. "Terrorism, Human Rights and Law Enforcement in Spain." *Terrorism and Political Violence* 17(1-2):265–278.

Altheide, David L. 2006. *Terrorism and the Politics of Fear*. Lanham, MD: AltaMira.

Amara, Muhammad and Izhak Schnell. 2004. "Identity Repertoires among Arabs in Israel." *Journal of Ethnic and Migration Studies* 30(1):175–193.

Anderson, Malcolm. 1997. "Interpol and the Developing System of International Police Cooperation." Pp. 89–102 in *Crime and Law Enforcement in the Global Village*, edited by W. F. McDonald. Cincinnati, OH: Anderson.

Andreas, Peter and Ethan Nadelmann. 2006. *Policing the Globe*. New York: Oxford University Press.

Arena, Michael P. and Bruce A. Arrigo. 2006. *The Terrorist Identity: Explaining the Terrorist Threat*. New York: New York University Press.

Ashcroft, John. 2006. *Never Again: Securing America and Restoring Justice*. New York: Center Street.

Ashraf, M. A. 2007. "The Lessons of Policing in Iraq—A Personal Perspective." *Policing* 1(1):102–110.

Badey, Thomas. 2006. "US Counter-terrorism: Change in Approach, Continuity in Policy." *Contemporary Security Policy* 27(2):308–324.

Banks, William C. 2005. "United States and Responses to September 11." Pp. 490–510 in *Global Anti-Terrorism Law and Policy*, edited by V. V. Ramraj, M. Hor, and K. Roach. Cambridge, UK: Cambridge University Press.

Bassiouni, M. Cherif. 2002. "Legal Control of International Terrorism: A Policy-Oriented Assessment." *Harvard International Law Journal* 43(1):83–103.

Bayer, Michael. 2005. "Operation Global Pursuit: In Pursuit of the World's Most Dangerous Fugitives and Terrorists." *The Police Chief* 72(8):32–37.

Beckman, James. 2007. *Comparative Legal Approaches to Homeland Security and Anti-Terrorism*. Aldershot, UK: Ashgate.

Bell, Colleen. 2006. "Subject to Exception: Security Certificates, National Security and Canada's Role in the 'War on Terror'." *Canadian Journal of Law and Society* 21(1):63–83.

Ben-Dor, Gabriel, Ami Pedahzur, and Badi Hasisi. 2003. "Anti-Liberalism and the Use of Force in Israeli Democracy." *Journal of Political and Military Sociology* 31:119–142.

Bittner, Egon. 1990. *Aspects of Police Work*. Boston, MA: Northeastern University Press.

Black, Donald. 2004. "Terrorism as Social Control." Pp. 9–18 in *Terrorism and Counter-Terrorism: Criminological Perspectives*, edited by M. Deflem. Amsterdam, The Netherlands: Elsevier/JAI Press.

Bornstein, Avram. 2005. "Antiterrorist Policing in New York City after 9/11: Comparing Perspectives on a Complex Process." *Human Organization* 64(1):52–61.

Brandl, Steven G. 2003. "Back to the Future: The Implications of September 11, 2001 on Law Enforcement Practice and Policy." *Ohio State Journal of Criminal Law* 1:133–154.

Brewer, John D., Adrian Guelke, Ian Hume, Edward Moxon-Browne, and Rick Wilford. 1988. *The Police, Public Order and the State*. New York: St. Martin's Press.

Brisard, Jean-Charles and Guillaume Dasquié. 2002. *Forbidden Truth: U.S.-Taliban Secret Oil Diplomacy and the Failed Hunt for Bin Laden*. New York: Thunder's Mouth Press.

Bures, Oldrich. 2008. "Europol's Fledgling Counterterrorism Role." *Terrorism and Political Violence* 20(4):498–517.

Carberry, Jacqueline A. 1999. "Terrorism: A Global Phenomenon Mandating a Unified International Response." *Indiana Journal of Global Legal Studies* 6:685–719.

Chalk, Peter and William Rosenau. 2004. *Confronting "the Enemy Within": Security Intelligence, the Police, and Counterterrorism in Four Democracies*. Santa Monica, CA: RAND Corporation.

Clarke, Ronald V. and Graeme R. Newman. 2006. *Outsmarting the Terrorists*. Westport, CT: Praeger Security International.

Clarke, Ronald V. and Graeme R. Newman. 2007. "Police and the Prevention of Terrorism." *Policing* 1(1):9–20.

Cohen, Stuart A. 1993. "'Masqueraders' in the Israel Defense Forces, 1991–1992: The Military Unit and the Public Debate." *Low Intensity Conflict and Law Enforcement* 2(2):282–300.

Costanza, Steven E., John C. Kilburn Jr., and Ronald Helms. 2009. "Counterterrorism." Pp. 91–115 in *Terrorism in America*, edited by K. Borgeson and R. Valeri. Sudbury, MA: Jones and Bartlett Publishers.

Coulson, Danny O. and Elaine Shannon. 1999. *No Heroes: Inside the FBI's Secret Counter-Terror Force*. New York: Pocket Books.

Das, Dilip K. and Peter C. Kratcoski, editors. 2003. *Meeting the Challenges of Global Terrorism: Prevention, Control, and Recovery*. Lanham, MD: Lexington Books.

Das, Dilip, Leo Huberts, and Ronald van Steden. 2007. "The Changing 'Soul' of Dutch Policing: Responses to New Security Demands and the Relationship with Dutch Tradition." *Policing: An International Journal of Police Strategies and Management* 30(3):518–532.

Davies, Heather J. and Gerard R. Murphy. 2004. *Protecting Your Community from Terrorism. Improving Local-Federal Partnerships. Vol. 2: Working with Diverse Communities*. Washington, DC: Police Executive Research Forum.

Davies, Heather J. and Martha R. Plotkin. 2005. *Protecting Your Community from Terrorism. Improving Local-Federal Partnerships. Vol. 5: Partnerships to Promote Homeland Security*. Washington, DC: Police Executive Research Forum.

Davis, Lois M., Jack K. Riley, Greg Ridgeway, Jennifer Pace, Sarah K. Cotton, Paul S. Steinberg, Kelly Damphousse, and Brent L. Smith. 2004. *When Terrorism Hits Home: How Prepared are State and Local Law Enforcement?* Santa Monica, CA: RAND. Online: http://rand.org/pubs/monographs/2004/RAND_MG104.pdf.

Deflem, Mathieu. 2000. "Bureaucratization and Social Control: Historical Foundations of International Policing." *Law & Society Review* 34(3):601–640.

Deflem, Mathieu. 2002. *Policing World Society: Historical Foundations of International Police Cooperation*. Oxford, UK: Oxford University Press.

Deflem, Mathieu. 2004a. "Social Control and the Policing of Terrorism: Foundations for a Sociology of Counter-Terrorism." *The American Sociologist* 35(2):75–92.

Deflem, Mathieu, editor. 2004b. *Terrorism and Counter-Terrorism: Criminological Perspectives*. Sociology of Crime, Law and Deviance, Volume 5. Amsterdam, The Netherlands: Elsevier/JAI Press.

Deflem, Mathieu. 2004c. "The Boundaries of International Cooperation: Problems and Prospects of U.S.-Mexican Police Relations." Pp. 93–122 in *Police Corruption: Challenges for Developed Countries - Comparative Issues and Commissions of Inquiry*, edited by Menachem Amir and Stanley Einstein. Huntsville, TX: Office of International Criminal Justice.

Deflem, Mathieu. 2006a. "Global Rule of Law or Global Rule of Law Enforcement? International Police Cooperation and Counter-Terrorism." *The Annals of the American Academy of Political and Social Science* 603:240–251.

Deflem, Mathieu. 2006b. "Europol and the Policing of International Terrorism: Counter-Terrorism in a Global Perspective." *Justice Quarterly* 23(3):336–359.

Deflem, Mathieu. 2008. "Terrorism Counter-Terrorism Approaches." Pp. 929–931 in *Encyclopedia of Social Problems*, edited by Vincent N. Parrillo. Thousand Oaks, CA: Sage Publications.

Deflem, Mathieu. 2009. "Terrorism." In *21st Century Criminology: A Reference Handbook*, edited by J. Mitchell Miller. Thousand Oaks, CA: Sage Publications.

Deflem, Mathieu and Lisa Dilks. 2008. "Terrorism Domestic Spying." Pp. 931–933 in *Encyclopedia of Social Problems*, edited by Vincent N. Parrillo. Thousand Oaks, CA: Sage Publications.

Deflem, Mathieu and Suzanne Sutphin. 2006. "Policing Post-War Iraq: Insurgency, Civilian Police, and the Reconstruction of Society." *Sociological Focus* 39(4):265–283.

den Boer, Monica. 2002. "Towards an Accountability Regime for an Emerging European Policing Governance." *Policing & Society* 12(4):275–289.

den Boer, Monica. 2003. "9/11 and the Europeanisation of Anti-terrorism Policy: A Critical Assessment." *Notre Europe*, Policy Papers No. 6. Online: http://www.notre-europe.eu/fileadmin/IMG/pdf/Policypaper6.pdf.

den Boer, Monica. 2007. "Wake-up Call for the Lowlands: Dutch Counterterrorism from a Comparative Perspective." *Cambridge Review of International Affairs* 20(2):285–302.

Dickey, Christopher. 2009. *Securing the City: Inside America's Best Counterterror Force, the NYPD*. New York: Simon & Schuster.

Donnermeyer, Joseph F. 2002. "Local Preparedness for Terrorism: A View from Law Enforcement." *Police Practice and Research* 3(4):347–360.

Donohue, Laura K. 2001. "In the Name of National Security: US Counterterrorist Measures, 1960–2000." *Terrorism and Political Violence* 13(3):15–60.

Donohue, Laura K. 2007. "Britain's Counterterrorism Policy." Pp. 17–58 in *How States Fight Terrorism: Policy Dynamics in the West*. Boulder, CO: Lynne Rienner.

Dow, Mark. 2007. "Designed to Punish: Immigrant Detention and Deportation." *Social Research* 74(2):533–546.

Edwards, Frances L. 2006. "Law Enforcement Responses to Biological Terrorism: Lessons Learned from New Orleans After Hurricane Katrina." *Law Enforcement Executive Forum* 6(1):139–143.

Erickson, Kris, John Carr, and Steve Herbert. 2006. "The Scales of Justice: Federal-Local Tensions in the War on Terror." Pp. 231–253 in *Uniform Behavior: Police Localism and National Politics*, edited by S. K. McGoldrick and A. McArdle. New York: Palgrave-Macmillan.

Eterno, John. 2003. *Policing Within the Law: A Case Study of the New York City Police Department*. Westport, CT: Praeger Security International.

Ewans, Martin. 2002. *Afghanistan: A New History*, 2nd edition. London, UK: Routledge.

Fijnaut, Cyrille. 2004. "The Attacks on 11 September 2001, and the Immediate Response of the European Union and the United States." Pp. 15–36 in *Legal Instruments in the Fight Against International Terrorism: A Transatlantic Dialogue*, edited by C. Fijnaut, J. Wouters, and F. Naert. Leiden, The Netherlands: Martinus Nijhoff Publishers.

Fogelson, Robert. 1977. *Big-City Police*. Cambridge, MA: Harvard University Press.

Freeh, Louis J. 2006. *My FBI: Bringing Down the Mafia, Investigating Bill Clinton, and Fighting the War on Terror*. New York: St. Martin's Griffin.

Friedrichs, Jörg. 2008. *Fighting Terrorism and Drugs: Europe and International Police Cooperation*. New York: Routledge.

Fussey, Pete. 2007. "Observing Potentiality in the Global City: Surveillance and Counterterrorism in London." *International Criminal Justice Review* 17(3):171–192.

Gamson, William A. and Ephraim Yuchtman. 1977. "Police and Society in Israel." Pp. 195–218 in *Police and Society*, edited by D. H. Bayley. Beverly Hills, CA: Sage Publications.

Geva, Ruth, Sergio Herzog, and Maki Haberfeld. 2004. "The Israel Police." Pp. 1130–1134 in *Encyclopedia of Law Enforcement*, edited by L. Sullivan, M. Rosen, D. Schulz, and M. Haberfeld. Thousand Oaks, CA: Sage Publications.

Gibbs Van Brunschot, Erin E. and Alison J. Sherley. 2005. "Communicating Threat: The Canadian State and Terrorism." *Sociological Quarterly* 46(4):645–669.

Graham, Bob and Jeff Nussbaum. 2004. *Intelligence Matters: The CIA, the FBI, Saudi Arabia, and the Failure of America's War on Terror*. New York: Random House.

Griffin, Richard J. 2005. "State's Global Security and Law Enforcement Team." *Foreign Service Journal* 82(9):33–37.

Grossman, Dave. 2002. "Terrorism and Local Police." *The Ohio Police Chief* (Summer 2002):39.

Grounds, Randy, Thomas J. Jurkanin, Ted Street, Gregory Sullivant, and Vladimir A. Sergevnin. 2006. "Russian Law Enforcement Response to Terrorist Incidents: Implications for Illinois Anti-Terrorism Preparedness." *Law Enforcement Executive Forum* 6(1):157–181.

Guiora, Amos N. 2007. *Global Perspectives on Counterterrorism*. New York: Aspen Publishers.

Haberfeld, Maria and Sergio Herzog. 2000. "The Criminal Justice System in Israel." Pp. 55–78 in *Comparative and International Criminal Justice Systems: Policing, Judiciary and Corrections*, edited by O. Ebbe. New York: Butterworth/ Heineman.

Harris, David A. 2006. "The War on Terror, Local Police, and Immigration Enforcement: A Curious Tale of Police Power in Post-9/11 America." *Rutgers Law Journal* 38:1–60.

Henderson, Nicole J., Christopher W. Ortiz, Naomi F. Sugie, and Joel Miller. 2006. "Law Enforcement & Arab American Community Relations After September 11, 2001: Engagement in a Time of Uncertainty." New York: Vera Institute of Justice. Online: http://www.vera.org/policerelations.

Henry, Vincent E. 2005. "Developing Local Law Enforcement's Strategic Capacity to Combat Terrorism in the United States." Pp. 148–165 in *Public Order: A Global Perspective*, edited by D. K. Das and A. Y. Jiao. Upper Saddle River, NJ: Prentice Hall.

Herzog, Sergio. 2000. "Is There a Distinct Profile of Police Officers Accused of Violence? The Israeli Case." *Journal of Criminal Justice* 28(6):457–471.

Herzog, Sergio. 2001. "Militarization and Demilitarization Processes in the Israeli and American Police Forces: Organizational and Social Aspects." *Policing and Society* 11:181–208.

Hewitt, Steve. 2008. *British War on Terror: Terrorism and Counter-terrorism on the Home Front Since 9-11.* London, UK; New York: Continuum.

Hindle, Garry. 2007. "Policing Terrorism in the UK." *Policing* 1(1):38–42.

Hogg, Russell. 2007. "Criminology, Crime and Politics before and after 9/11." *Australian and New Zealand Journal of Criminology* 40(1):83–105.

Innes, Martin. 2006. "Policing Uncertainty: Countering Terror through Community Intelligence and Democratic Policing." *The Annals of the American Academy of Political and Social Science* 605:222–241.

Jenkins, Brian M. 2006. "The New Age of Terrorism." Pp. 117–130 in *The McGraw-Hill Homeland Security Handbook*, edited by D. G. Kamien. New York: McGraw-Hill.

Jenkins, Gareth. 2008. "Capabilities and Restraints in Turkey's Counter-Terrorism Policy." *Terrorism Monitor* 6(8):7–10.

Jiao, Allan Y. and Harry M. Rhea. 2007. "Integration of Police in the United States: Changes and Development after 9/11." *Policing & Society* 17(4):388–408.

Jones, David T. 2005. "A Thankless Job: The Bureau of Diplomatic Security." *Foreign Service Journal* 82(9):23–32.

Jones, Mark and John M. Newton. 2005. "Localized Terrorism: Local Law Enforcement Anti-Terrorism Programs in North Carolina." *Law Enforcement Executive Forum* 5(6):29–48.

Jones, Seth G., Jeremy M. Wilson, Andrew Rathmell, and K. Jack Riley. 2005. *Establishing Law and Order After Conflict.* Santa Monica, VA: RAND Corporation.

Kappeler, Victor E. and Karen S. Miller-Potter. 2004. "Policing in the Age of Terrorism." Pp. 27–40 in *Controversies in Policing*, edited by Q. C. Thurman and A Giacomazzi. Cincinnati, OH: Anderson.

Katriel, Tamar, and Pearla Nesher. 1986. "Gibush: The Rhetoric of Cohesion in Israeli School Culture." *Comparative Education Review* 30(2):216–231.

Katz, Samuel M. 2002. *The Hunt for the Engineer: The Inside Story of How Israel's Counterterrorist Forces Tracked and Killed the Hamas Master Bomber.* Guilford, CT: The Lyons Press.

Katz, Samuel M. 2005. "Task Force Gaza: Under Fire with the Israeli Border Guard's Ya'mas Counterterrorist Unit." *Special Operations Report* 3:14–23.

Kayyem, Juliette N. and Robyn L. Pangi, editors. 2003. *First to Arrive: State and Local Responses to Terrorism.* Cambridge, MA: The MIT Press.

Keegan, John. 2004. *The Iraq War.* New York: Alfred A. Knopf.

Keller, William W. 1989. *The Liberals and J. Edgar Hoover: Rise and Fall of a Domestic Intelligence State.* Princeton, NJ: Princeton University Press.

Kelling, George L., and William J. Bratton. 2006. "Policing Terrorism." *Civic Bulletin* No. 43, September 2006. Online: http://www.manhattan-institute.org/html/cb_43.htm.

Klein, Joanne. 2006. "The Failure of Force: Policing Terrorism in Northern Ireland." Pp. in *Uniform Behavior: Police Localism and National Politics*, edited by S. K. McGoldrick and A. McArdle. New York: Palgrave-Macmillan.

Kobach, Kris W. 2005. "The Quintessential Force Multiplier: The Inherent Authority of Local Police to Make Immigration Arrests." *Albany Law Review* 69:179–235.

Lavranos, Nikolaos. 2003. "Europol and the Fight Against Terrorism." *European Foreign Affairs Review* 8(2):259–275.

Leman-Langlois, Stéphane. 2007. "Le Terrorisme et l'Antiterrorisme." Pp. 199–222 in *Traité de Sécurité Intérieure*, edited by M. Cusson, B. Dupont, and F. Lemieux. Montréal, Canada: Hurtubise HMH.

Leman-Langlois, Stéphane and Jean-Paul Brodeur. 2005. "Terrorism Old and New: Counterterrorism in Canada." *Police Practice and Research* 6(2):121–140.

Lockard, Joe. 2002. "Somewhere Between Arab and Jew: Ethnic Re-Identification in Modern Hebrew Literature." *Middle Eastern Literatures* 5(1):49–62.

Loyka, Stephan A., Donald A. Faggiani, and Clifford Karchmer. 2005. *Protecting Your Community from Terrorism. Improving Local-Federal Partnerships. Volume 4: The Production and Sharing of Intelligence*. Washington, DC: Police Executive Research Forum.

Lyons, William. 2002. "Partnerships, Information and Public Safety: Community Policing in a Time of Terror." *Policing: An International Journal of Police Strategies & Management* 25(3):530–542.

Manning, Peter K. 2005. "The Study of Policing." *Police Quarterly* 8(1):23–43.

Marenin, Otwin. 2005. "Policing Terrorism: Rhetoric and Implementation." Pp. 168–181 in *Combating Terrorism and Its Implications for the Security Sector*, edited by T. H. Winkler, A. H. Ebnöther, and M. B. Hanson. Stockholm, Sweden: Swedish National Defence College and Geneva Centre for the Democratic Control of Armed Forces.

Marks, Daniel E. and Ivan Y. Sun. 2007. "The Impact of 9/11 on Organizational Development among State and Local Law Enforcement Agencies." *Journal of Contemporary Criminal Justice* 23(2):159–173.

Marr, Phebe. 2004. *The Modern History of Iraq*. Boulder, CO: Westview Press.

McArdle, Andrea. 2006. "Policing after September 11: Federal-Local Collaboration and the Implications for Police-Community Relations." Pp. 177–202 in *Uniform Behavior: Police Localism and National Politics*, edited by S. K. McGoldrick and A. McArdle. New York: Palgrave-Macmillan.

McCauley, Clark. 2007. "War Versus Justice in Response to Terrorist Attacks: Competing Frames and Their Implications." Pp. 56–65 in *Psychology of Terrorism*, edited by B. Bongar, L. M. Brown, L. E. Beutler, J. N. Breckenridge, and P. G. Zimbardo. Oxford, UK: Oxford University Press.

McDonough, Shannon and Mathieu Deflem. 2008. "Civil Liberties and Surveillance in the Post-9/11 World: The Fear of Counter-Terrorism." Paper presented at the Society for the Study of Social Problems annual meeting, Boston, MA, August 2008.

Merari, Ariel. 2003. "Israel's Preparedness for High Consequence Terrorism." Pp. 345–370 in *Countering Terrorism: Dimensions of Preparedness*, edited by A. M. Howitt and R. L. Pangi. Cambridge, MA: MIT Press.

Middle East Watch. 1993. *A License to Kill: Israeli Undercover Operations Against "Wanted" and Masked Palestinians*. New York: Human Rights Watch.

Miller, John and Michael Stone. 2002. *The Cell: Inside the 9/11 Plot, and Why the FBI and CIA Failed to Stop It*. New York: Hyperion.

Mohammad, Fida and Paul Conway. 2003. "Justice and Law Enforcement in Afghanistan Under the Taliban: How Much is Likely to Change?" *Policing: An International Journal of Police Strategies & Management* 26(1):162–167.

Monaco, Francis R. 1995. "Europol: The Culmination of the European Union's International Police Cooperation Efforts." *Fordham International Law Journal* 19(1):247–307.

Monar, Jörg. 2005. "Anti-terrorism Law and Policy: The Case of the European Union." Pp. 425–452 in *Global Anti-Terrorism Law and Policy*, edited by V. V. Ramraj, M. Hor, and K. Roach. Cambridge, UK: Cambridge University Press.

Monar, Jörg. 2007. "The EU's Approach post-September 11: Global Terrorism as a Multidimensional Law Enforcement Challenge." *Cambridge Review of International Affairs* 20(2):267–283.

Moore, Cerwyn. 2007. "Combating Terrorism in Russia and Uzbekistan." *Cambridge Review of International Affairs* 20(2):303–323.

Morgan, Richard E. 1980. *Domestic Intelligence: Monitoring Dissent in America*. Austin, TX: University of Texas Press.

Morgenstern, Henry and Tom Dempsey. 2005. "Homeland Security Training in Israel: A Trip Report." *Law Enforcement Executive Forum* 5(6):165–172.

Müller-Wille, Björn. 2008. "The Effect of International Terrorism on EU Intelligence Co-operation." *Journal of Common Market Studies* 46(1):49–73.

Murphy, Gerard R. and Martha R. Plotkin. 2003. *Protecting Your Community from Terrorism. Improving Local-Federal Partnerships. Volume 1: Improving Local-Federal Partnerships*. Washington, DC: Police Executive Research Forum.

Murray, Tonita. 2007. "Police-Building in Afghanistan: A Case Study of Civil Security Reform." *International Peacekeeping* 14(1):108–126.

Nadelmann, Ethan A. 1993. *Cops Across Borders: The Internationalization of U.S. Criminal Law Enforcement*. University Park, PA: The Pennsylvania State University Press.

National Commission on Terrorist Attacks upon the United States. 2004. *The 9/11 Commission Report: Final Report of the National Commission on Terrorist Attacks Upon the United States*. Available online: http://www.9-11commission.gov/report/911Report.pdf.

Nussbaum, Brian. 2007. "Protecting Global Cities: New York, London and the Internationalization of Municipal Policing for Counter Terrorism." *Global Crime* 8(3):213–232.

Occhipinti, John D. 2003. *The Politics of EU Police Cooperation: Toward a European FBI?* Boulder, CO: Lynne Rienner.

Oliver, Willard M. 2007. *Homeland Security for Policing*. Upper Saddle River, NJ: Pearson/Prentice Hall.

Ortiz, Christopher W., Nicole J. Hendricks, and Naomi F. Sugie. 2007. "Policing Terrorism: The Response of Local Police Agencies to Homeland Security Concerns." *Criminal Justice Studies* 20(2):91–109.

Ozeren, Suleyman and Ismail Yilmaz. 2007. "Counterterrorism in Turkey: Organizational and Operational Structure and Training." Pp. 371–385 in *Police Education and Training in a Global Society*, edited by P. C. Kratcoski and D. K. Das. New York: Lexington Books.

Parmentier, Guillaume. 2006. "France." Pp. 44–71 in *Counterterrorism Strategies: Successes and Failures of Six Nations*, edited by Y. Alexander. Washington, DC: Potomac Books.

Pedahzur, Ami. 2009. *The Israeli Secret Services and the Struggle Against Terrorism*. New York: Columbia University Press.

Pelfrey, William V., Jr. 2007. "Local Law Enforcement Terrorism Prevention Efforts: A State Level Case Study." *Journal of Criminal Justice* 35(3):313–321.

Perito, Robert M. 2002. *The American Experience with Police in Peace Operations*. Clementsport, Canada: The Canadian Peacekeeping Press.

Perito, Robert M. 2003. "Establishing the Rule of Law in Iraq." United States Institute of Peace, Special Report 104. Online: http://www.usip.org/pubs/specialreports/sr104.html.

Perito, Robert M. 2005. "The Coalition Provisional Authority's Experience with Public Security in Iraq." United States Institute of Peace, Special Report 137. Online: http://www.usip.org/pubs/specialreports/sr137.html.

Perito, Robert M. 2006. "Policing Iraq: Protecting Iraqis from Criminal Violence." United States Institute of Peace, USIPeace Briefing. Online: http://www.usip.org/pubs/usipeace_briefings/2006/0629_policing_iraq.html.

Perito, Robert M. 2007. "Reforming the Iraqi Interior Ministry, Police, and Facilities Protection Service." United States Institute of Peace, USIPeace Briefing. Online: http://www.usip.org/pubs/usipeace_briefings/2007/0207_iraqi_interior_ministry.html.

Pickering, Sharon, Jude McCulloch, and David Wright-Neville. 2008. *Counter-Terrorism Policing: Community, Cohesion and Security*. New York: Springer.

Powers, Richard Gid. 2004. *Broken: The Troubled Past and Uncertain Future of the FBI*. New York: Free Press.

Purdy, Margaret. 2007. "Canada's Counterterrorism Policy." Pp. 105–131 in *How States Fight Terrorism: Policy Dynamics in the West*. Boulder, CO: Lynne Rienner.

Rauchs, Georges and Daniel J. Koenig. 2001. "Europol." Pp. 43–62 in *International Police Cooperation: A World Perspective*, edited by D. J. Koenig and D. K. Das. New York: Lexington Books.

Reeve, Simon. 1999. *The New Jackals: Ramzi Yousef, Osama bin Laden and the Future of Terrorism*. Boston, MA: Northeastern University Press.

Reuland, Melissa and Heather J. Davies. 2004. *Protecting Your Community from Terrorism. Improving Local-Federal Partnerships. Volume 3: Preparing for and Responding to Bioterrorism*. Washington, DC: Police Executive Research Forum.

Reynolds, K. Michael, Pamala L. Griset, and Ron Eaglin. 2005. "Controlling Terrorism Through Automated Sharing of Low-Level Law-Enforcement Data." *Law Enforcement Executive Forum* 5(6):127–136.

Reynolds, K. Michael, Pamala L. Griset, and Ernest Scott. 2006. "Law Enforcement Information Sharing: A Florida Case Study." *American Journal of Criminal Justice* 31(1):1–17.

Riley, Kevin J. and Bruce Hoffman. 1995. *Domestic Terrorism: A National Assessment of State and Local Preparedness*. Santa Monica, CA: RAND Corporation.

Riley, K. Jack, Gregory F. Treverton, Jeremy M. Wilson, and Lois M. Davis. 2005. *State and Local Intelligence in the War on Terrorism*. Santa Monica, CA: RAND Corporation.

Roach, Kent. 2005. "Canada's Response to Terrorism." Pp. 511–533 in *Global Anti-Terrorism Law and Policy*, edited by V. V. Ramraj, M. Hor, and K. Roach. Cambridge, UK: Cambridge University Press.

Rodman, David. 2003. "Israel's National Security Doctrine: An Appraisal of the Past and a Vision of the Future." Review essay. *Israel Affairs* 9(4):115–140.

Rogers, Paul. 2004. *A War on Terror: Afghanistan and After*. London, UK: Pluto Press.

Romaniuk, Peter, 2009. *Global Counterterrorism: How Multilateral Co-operation Works*. London, UK: Routledge.

Rosenau, William. 2007. "US Counterterrorism Policy." Pp. 133–156 in *How States Fight Terrorism: Policy Dynamics in the West*, edited by D. Zimmermann and A. Wenger. Boulder, CO: Lynne Rienner.

Rosenfeld, Richard. 2004. "Terrorism and Criminology." Pp. 19–32 in *Terrorism and Counter-terrorism: Criminological Perspectives*, edited by M. Deflem. Amsterdam, The Netherlands: Elsevier/JAI Press.

Runion, Meredith L. 2007. *The History of Afghanistan*. Westport, CT: Greenwood Press.

Safe Cities Project. 2004. *Hard Won Lessons: How Police Fight Terrorism in the United Kingdom*. New York: Manhattan Institute of Policy Research. Online: http://www.manhattan-institute.org/pdf/scr_01.pdf.

Safe Cities Project. 2005. *Hard Won lessons: Policing Terrorism in the United States*. New York: Manhattan Institute of Policy Research. Online: http://www.manhattan-institute.org/pdf/scr_03.pdf.

Safir, Howard and Ellis Whitman. 2003. *Security: Policing Your Homeland, Your State, Your City*. New York: Thomas Dunne.

Salter, Mark B. 2004. "Passports, Mobility, and Security: How Smart Can the Border Be?" *International Studies Perspectives* 5(1):71–91.

Scheppele, Kim L. 2004. "Other People's PATRIOT Acts: Europe's Response to September 11." *Loyola Law Review* 50:89–148.

Sedra, Mark. 2003. "Police Reform in Afghanistan: An Overview." Pp. 33–39 in *Confronting Afghanistan's Security Dilemma*, edited by M. Sedra. Bonn, Germany: International Center for Conversion.

Shulman, Rita. 2003. "USA Patriot Act: Granting the US Government the Unprecedented Power to Circumvent American Civil Liberties in the Name of National Security." *University of Detroit Mercy Law Review* 80:427–444.

Shutt, J. Eagle and Mathieu Deflem. 2005. "Whose Face at the Border? Homeland Security and Border Policing Since 9/11." *Journal of Social and Ecological Boundaries* 1(2):81–105.

Sinclair, Andrew. 2003. *An Anatomy of Terror: A History of Terrorism.* London, UK: Macmillan.

Singer, P. W. 2003. *Corporate Warriors: The Rise of the Privatized Military Industry.* Ithaca, NY: Cornell University Press.

Sloan, Stephen. 2002. "Meeting the Terrorist Threat: The Localization of Counter Terrorism Intelligence." *Police Practice and Research: An International Journal* 3(4):337–245.

Smith, Brent L. 1987. "Anti-Terrorism Legislation in the United States." Pp. 107–118 in *International Terrorism: The Domestic Response*, edited by R. H. Ward and H. E. Smith. Chicago: Office of International Criminal Justice.

Storbeck, Jürgen. 2003. "The European Union and Enlargement: Challenge and Opportunity for Europol in the Fight Against International Crime." *European Foreign Affairs Review* 8:283–288.

Swan, Ronald D. 2006. "Profiling and Terrorism." *Law Enforcement Executive Forum* 5(7):69–74.

Tak, Peter J.P. 2000. "Bottlenecks in International Police and Judicial Cooperation in the EU." *European Journal of Crime Criminal Law and Criminal Justice* 8(4):343–360.

Teymur, Samih and Ahmet Sait Yayla. 2005. "How Did Change Help the Country of Turkey to Deal with Terrorism More Effectively?" Pp. 341–352 in *Istanbul Conference on Democracy & Global Security 2005*, edited by R. Gultekin *et al.* Ankara, Turkey: ONCU Press.

Thacher, David. 2005. "The Local Role in Homeland Security." *Law & Society Review* 39(3):635–676.

Theoharis, Athan G. 2004. *The FBI & American Democracy: A Brief Critical History.* Lawrence, KS: University Press of Kansas.

Townshend, Charles. 2002. *Terrorism: A Very Short Introduction.* New York: Oxford University Press.

Tully, Edward J. and E. L. Willoughby. 2002. "Terrorism: The Role of Local and State Police Agencies." *National Executive Institute Associates.* Online: http://www.neiassociates.org/state-local.htm.

Van Creveld, Martin. 2007. "Israel's Counterterrorism." Pp. 157–173 in *How States Fight Terrorism: Policy Dynamics in the West.* Boulder, CO: Lynne Rienner.

Ventura, Holly, J. Mitchell Miller, and Mathieu Deflem. 2005. "Governmentality and the War on Terror: FBI Project Carnivore and the Diffusion of Disciplinary Power." *Critical Criminology* 13(1):55–70.

Walker, Clive. 2006. "Clamping Down on Terrorism in the United Kingdom." *Journal of International Criminal Justice* 4(5):1137–1151.

Wardick, Ali. 2004. "Building a Post-War Justice System in Afghanistan." *Crime, Law, and Social Change* 41:319–341.

Weber, Max. (1922) 1980. *Wirtschaft und Gesellschaft: Grundriss der verstehenden Soziologie.* Tübingen, Germany: J.C.B. Mohr (Paul Siebeck).

Weiss, Murray. 2003. *The Man Who Warned America: The Life and Death of John O'Neill, The FBI's Embattled Counterterror Warrior.* New York: Regan Books.

Welch, Michael. 2003. "Ironies of Social Control and the Criminalization of Immigrants." *Crime, Law and Social Change* 39(4):319–337.

Welch, Michael. 2004. "Quiet Constructions in the War on Terror: Subjecting Asylum Seekers to Unnecessary Detention." *Social Justice* 31:113–129.

Welch, Michael. 2006. *Scapegoats of September 11th: Hate Crimes and State Crimes in the War on Terror.* New Brunswick, NJ: Rutgers University Press.

Welchman, Lynn. 2005. "Rocks, Hard Places, and Human Rights: Anti-terrorism Law and Policy in Arab States." Pp. 581–608 in *Global Anti-Terrorism Law and Policy*, edited by V. V. Ramraj, M. Hor, and K. Roach. Cambridge, UK: Cambridge University Press.

Wilson, Brent J. 1994. "The United States' Response to International Terrorism." Pp. 173–210 in *The Deadly Sin of Terrorism: Its Effect on Democracy and Civil Liberty in Six Countries,* edited by D. A. Charters. Westport, CT: Greenwood Press.

Wong, Kam C. 2006. "The USA PATRIOT Act: Some Unanswered Questions." *International Journal of the Sociology of Law* 34(1):1–41.

Index

deviance 11, 16, *see also* crime
Director of Homeland Security 32, *see also* Office of Homeland Security
Director of National Intelligence 41, 42, 178
discipline 150, 157
domestic spying 39, 40
domestic terrorism 25, 46, 58, 66, 71, 109
drug enforcement 48, 67, 127
Drug Enforcement Administration *see* DEA
drugs 59, 66, 67, 128, 175
Druze 157, 158
dynamite 12
DynCorp International 172, 175

Egypt 100, 101, 104, 113, 117
El Salvador 112
Electronic Frontier Foundation 40
electronic surveillance 35, 40
enemy alien 31
Estonia 129, 136
ETA 97, 137
Eurojust 133
European Arrest Warrant 131
European Chiefs of Police Task Force 3
European Parliament 129
European Police Office *see* Europol
European Union (EU) 3, 97, 99, 127, 130, 132, 133, 135, 174
Europeanization (of counterterrorism) 132, 139
Europol 3, 8, 20, 112, 118, 120, 127–40
Europol Convention 128, 129

Fahrenheit 9/11 (movie) 36, 56
FBI (Federal Bureau of Investigation) 21, 26, 35, 41, 44, 170, 190; and counterterrorism 2, 45–8, 61, 62, 63, 66–7, 76, 84, 91, 103, 138; criticisms of 55, 56, 57–60, 64, 68, 69, 119
fear 11, 57, 67, 76
Federal Air Marshal Service 33, 52
Federal Bureau of Investigation *see* FBI

Federal Office of Justice 80
financing of terrorism 31, 35, 115, 122, 123, 134
FISA (Foreign Intelligence Surveillance Act) 35, 40
Foreign Terrorist Organizations list 41
Fortuyn, Pim 96
France 3, 92, 93–6, 105, 112, 113, 124
Freeh, Louis 2
French National Assembly 12
French Revolution 12, 94

Gaza 8, 145, 146, 147, 148
Geneva Convention 39, 174
Germany 3, 22, 115, 137, 138, 161, 174
Gilmore, James 31
Glasgow International Airport 22, 92
Global Counterterrorism Strategy 15
global war on terror *see* war on terror
Great Britain 170, 172, *see also* United Kingdom
Griffin, Richard 54
Group of Eight 107
Guantanamo Bay 39, 76
Gulf War 37, 166
GWOT *see* war on terror

Hamburg, Germany 138
Hart, Gary 31
Hague, The, Netherlands 128, 129, 132, 133, 136
Hersh, Seymour 161
hijab 139, 150
hijackings 14, 24, 30, 46, 66
Homeland Security Act 32
Homeland Security Advisory System 42
homicide 123
hostage-taking 102, 177
Houston 59
human rights 99, 111, 113, 121, 129, 158, 162, 172
Hungary 114
Hurricane Katrina 43
Hussein, Saddam 38, 55, 165, 166, 167, 168, 170, 171, 176, 181